Durable Goods

STUDIES IN THEORETICAL AND APPLIED ETHICS

Sherwin Klein
General Editor

Vol. 10

PETER LANG
New York · Washington, D.C./Baltimore · Bern
Frankfurt · Berlin · Brussels · Vienna · Oxford

Gerol Petruzella

Durable Goods

Pleasure, Wealth and Power in the Virtuous Life

PETER LANG
New York · Washington, D.C./Baltimore · Bern
Frankfurt · Berlin · Brussels · Vienna · Oxford

Library of Congress Cataloging-in-Publication Data

Petruzella, Gerol.
Durable goods: pleasure, wealth and power in the virtuous life / Gerol Petruzella.
pages cm — (Studies in theoretical and applied ethics; vol. 10)
Includes bibliographical references and index.
1. Philosophy, Ancient. I. Title.
B178.P48   170.938—dc23   2012049105
ISBN 978-1-4331-1699-5 (hardcover)
ISBN 978-1-4539-1073-3 (e-book)
ISSN 1086-6809

Bibliographic information published by **Die Deutsche Nationalbibliothek**.
Die Deutsche Nationalbibliothek lists this publication in the "Deutsche
Nationalbibliografie"; detailed bibliographic data is available
on the Internet at http://dnb.d-nb.de/.

The paper in this book meets the guidelines for permanence and durability
of the Committee on Production Guidelines for Book Longevity
of the Council of Library Resources.

Printed in Germany

Dedication

For Michael, who reminds me that

οἱ δὲ βουλόμενοι τἀγαθὰ τοῖς φίλοις ἐκείνων ἔνεκα μάλιστα φίλοι

and

जाड्यं धियो हरति सिञ्चति वाचि सत्यं
मानोन्नतिं दिशति पापमपाकरोति।
चेतः प्रसादयति दिक्षु तनोति कीर्तिं
सत्संगतिः कथय किं न करोति पुंसाम्।।

For Julie, my Praxilla:

κάλλιστον μὲν ἐγὼ λείπω φάος ἠελίοιο,
δεύτερον ἄστρα φαεινὰ σεληναίης τε πρόσωπον
ἠδὲ καὶ ὡραίους σικύους καὶ μῆλα καὶ ὄγχνας·

but I must hasten to add—

οὐ ἐλάσσον πυρρὴν κόμην ἀγλαήν.

Table of Contents

Acknowledgments   ix

Introduction   1

Chapter 1: The Humanist: Socrates in the Real World   17

Chapter 2: The Idealist: Plato in the Realm of Forms   51

Chapter 3: The Philosopher: Aristotle in Two Worlds   87

Chapter 4: The Hard-Liners: The Stoics Bite the Bullet   117

Chapter 5: Applied Intellectualism: Eudaimonist Synthesis   153

Bibliography   163

Index   175

Acknowledgments

I am profoundly grateful indeed to a large number of individuals who have been critically supportive in the birth of this work. I owe a great weight of thanks to the editorial and production teams at Peter Lang, particularly for their forebearance and flexibility. Sherwin Klein, the series editor and a fellow scholar of ancient philosophy, has been a true colleague, challenging me with both rigor and generous intellectual support to develop the manuscript to its fullest. Whatever errors and lacunae remain are fully my own responsibility.

My home institution, the Massachusetts College of Liberal Arts, has been a wonderful environment in which to pursue my research in the robust and enriching milieu of a pedagogically active community.

Finally, I acknowledge my colleagues and collaborators in various online communities, too many to list here without being tedious: our ongoing and vital conversations in the digital humanities have broadened the scope of my scholarship in unexpected ways. Thank you.

Introduction

Social science now finds itself in almost total darkness about the qualities that make life most worth living.

Martin Seligman, 1998

At least as early as Herodotus' account of the encounter between Solon and Croesus,[1] the connection between having external goods and leading a happy human life is a live and important issue within Greek thought. Two distinct theses vie for our assent. On one hand, health, wealth, political advantage, and prosperity—all circumstances contingent upon chance—are generally accepted as inextricable parts of a fully human life. Indeed, the very terms we have come to use to translate the Greek εὐδαιμονία,[2] 'flourishing' or 'well-being,' carry with them definitive overtones of completeness. The person who flourishes does so not merely in virtue of a narrowly applied set of behaviors or states, but rather precisely insofar as, in a wide range of areas of living and conduct—the intellectual, the moral, the physical, the social, the technical, the spiritual—he exhibits an overarching, all-encompassing state of excellence that transcends any one of these individually. This is the ideal most explicitly expressed in Aristotle's concept of the unity of the virtues, and it is certainly compatible with, if not an explicit doctrine within, other philosophers' systems of thought.

On the other hand, beginning with Socrates' investigations linking, and even identifying, happiness and virtue with knowledge throughout Plato's 'Socratic' dialogues, a central tenet of the ethical tradition is the premise that achieving happiness is within the control of the individual human agent. It would be incomprehensible for the world to be ordered in such a way that the best kind of life for us should be inaccessible to our human efforts, or that we should be held morally responsible for accomplishments or failings which result from circumstances beyond our control. Aristotle expresses this insight when he says that 'all who are not maimed with respect to excellence may win it by a certain kind of study and care' (*EN* I.9, 1099b18–19).

The way in which a philosopher attempts to resolve the tension between these two deeply held, yet opposing intuitive ethical insights has a major impact on the direction of his ethics as a whole. Many contemporary and current issues in the study of ancient Greek ethics, epistemology, and philosophy of mind are squarely grounded in interpreting the connection between prosperity, virtuous character, knowledge, and the 'good life,' εὐδαιμονία, generally. Examples, for instance, include the debate between intellectualism and inclusivism in Aristotle's ethics, and investigating the Stoic 'revival' of Socrates' identity of virtue and knowledge.

Despite the critical significance of this issue for the development of eudaimonistic ethics, scholarship on the topic of external goods has been piecemeal, parceled out and investigated according to individual figure or philosophic tradition; there has been no comprehensive analysis. As a result, the contemporary discourse in virtue ethics lacks a coherent treatment of the connections—developments, refinements, rejections, responses—between successive philosophers' thoughts on external goods and εὐδαιμονία. The first task of this work will be to present and develop such an historical analysis of the treatment of external goods in the thought of four central figures and traditions of ancient Greek philosophy: Socrates, Plato, Aristotle, and the Stoics. Each of these traditions addresses the question of external goods, and their role in giving an account of the good life, in a manner uniquely its own, yet is also responsive to the broader *milieu* of the philosophic community and history it inherits. Following upon this exegetical task, I will present and explore analyses of external goods and their role in the constitution of εὐδαιμονία within each school of thought, and considered overall. In what follows I present synopses of each chapter individually.

Chapter 1: The Humanist: Socrates in the Real World

The Socrates we know is, of course, primarily a literary construction, almost a fictional character, so little do we know of Socrates the historical man. Since our account of his philosophy is at best second-hand, preserved primarily in the Platonic dialogues, in which it is used by Plato for his own purposes, we cannot make such bold claims about his thought as we can about other philosophers whose work has survived through a more direct manuscript tradition. Nevertheless, it may be less important philosophically (though certainly of interest historically) to reconstruct the positions of the historical Socrates—whatever those positions might have been—than to analyze and respond to the received understanding and interpretation of what we might call the 'Socratic tradition.' This philosophical tradition had a formative influence on Western ethics starting from Socrates' immediate successors, through late antique and mediaeval philosophy and even up to the scholarship of the modern period.

One thing that we can derive with reasonable confidence about Socratic ethics is the claim that wisdom, virtue, and happiness share an essential focal meaning, if not a strict identity. Arguments for this claim are found in several of Plato's dialogues (*Philebus, Theaetetus, Republic*), and particularly in the *Euthydemus* and *Meno*. Here Socrates maintains both that people take good fortune (εὐτυχία) to be 'the greatest of the goods,' and that wisdom (σοφία) can be identified with good fortune because it makes people more fortunate (*Euthydemus* 279c7–8; 279d6). The reason for this is because wisdom never makes a mistake 'but must necessarily do right and be lucky—otherwise she would no longer be wisdom' (280a7–8). Inasmuch as knowledge rules and rightly conducts action, it provides people with good fortune and well-doing (εὐπραγία) (281b). The commonly-held thesis that we do well through having many goods might, then, be true, on one important condition: what people usually call 'goods'—including moral virtues, such as justice, temperance, and courage—are not goods in themselves, but count as goods if and only if practical wisdom (φρόνησις) and wisdom (σοφία) rule over them (*Euthydemus* 281a8–e1). We are not happy by the mere presence of things such as wealth or beauty (*Meno* 87e–88a), because such things can harm us if not guided by σοφία. Similarly, if one takes away knowledge from crafts, such as medicine or shoemaking, no craft can be performed rightly: medicine cannot produce health, nor can shoemaking produce shoes, nor can the pilot's craft prevent loss of life at sea (*Charmides* 174c–d).[3] The right use of these goods (wealth, beauty) and crafts (medicine, shoemaking, piloting) benefits us, and their wrong use harms us (*Meno* 88a–b); knowledge is what guarantees their right use. This distinction can be applied to the moral virtues as well. If we suppose that a moral good, such as courage, is a certain kind of recklessness or boldness, and that, accordingly, it is not accompanied by wisdom, it can indeed harm us. If we want to defend the thesis that moral virtues are necessarily beneficial components of the happy life, they must somehow be forms of wisdom, since 'all the qualities of the soul are in themselves neither beneficial nor harmful', but when directed by wisdom or folly they become beneficial or harmful (*Meno* 88c–d).

The Socratic thesis outlined above not only makes positive claims about wisdom and happiness, however; it equally clearly argues that the standard complement of 'goods' shares in the happy life only derivatively, if at all. The premise that wealth, health, beauty, strength, courage, generosity, and the rest of the ἀρεταί are completely neutral with respect to value for our lives is of course appropriated and developed by the Stoics as their central doctrine of 'indifferents.' Our investigation into Socrates' conception of happiness will need to explore the origin and development of this claim, as well as the criteria of harm and benefit to which he appeals in order to justify it. Once we have done this, we will have the basis for evaluating the Socratic position in relation to later traditions, both concurring with and dissenting from his own.

Xenophon tells us that Socrates αὐτὸς δὲ περὶ τῶν ἀνθρωπίνων ἀεὶ διελέγετο σκοπῶν, 'himself always spoke looking toward human affairs' (*Mem.* I.i.16), and that he chastised other thinkers by questioning them thus:

καὶ πρῶτον μὲν αὐτῶν ἐσκόπει πότερά ποτε νομίσαντες ἱκανῶς ἤδη τἀνθρώπινα εἰδέναι ἔρχονται ἐπὶ τὸ περὶ τῶν τοιούτων φροντίζειν ἢ τὰ μὲν ἀνθρώπεια αρέντες, τὰ δαιμόνια δὲ σκοποῦντες ἡγοῦνται τὰ προσήκοντα πράττειν.

In the first place, he would inquire of them, did these thinkers suppose that they knew enough about human affairs already that they must think on such [new issues], or that it was their duty to neglect human affairs and consider only things divine? (*Mem.* I.i.12)

In his *Protagoras*, and indeed throughout the early dialogues, Plato presents a portrait of Socrates consistent with this account. Little as we know about the historical Socrates, and as much difficulty as we have in constructing Socrates' philosophy in many cases from the conflicting testimony of his successors, a broad point of agreement is that Socrates cares intensely about investigating the sort of questions central to the human condition, rather than the abstract subject matter traditionally the stuff of natural philosophy. What is justice? What is piety? What is goodness? What is beauty? And, underlying all these, What is the good life? These are the matters that engage and constitute Socratic inquiry—specifically ἀνθρώπινα, not δαιμόνια, matters.

At first glance, this preoccupation with human affairs would seem quite compatible with a view that Socrates considered external goods to be viable components of living a happy human life. However, the role played by the 'goods of chance' in this human inquiry is subject to serious challenge. Socrates famously held that virtue is knowledge, and that even someone who suffers the greatest misfortunes can truly be called happy, so long as he does not flag in exercising his ἀρεταί, that is, by the Socratic equivalence, his knowledge. In addition to this doctrinal commitment, attributed to him by Plato, the extant accounts of Socrates' life all show that he demonstrated a singular unconcern for acquiring, enjoying, or retaining the sorts of external goods commonly held to be important: money, property, civic or military honors, or political influence. As he tells Antiphon,

> Ἔοικας, ὦ Ἀντιφῶν, τὴν εὐδαιμονίαν οἰομένῳ τρυφὴν καὶ πολυτέλειαν εἶναι· ἐγὼ δὲ νομίζω τὸ μὲν μηδενὸς δεῖσθαι θεῖον εἶναι, τὸ δ' ὡς ἐλαχίστων ἐγγυτάτω τοῦ θείου, καὶ τὸ μὲν θεῖον κράτιστον, τὸ δ' ἐγγυτάτω τοῦ θείου ἐγγυτάτω τοῦ κρατίστου.
>
> You seem, Antiphon, to imagine that happiness is luxury and extravagance. But I believe that to have no wants is divine; to have as few as possible comes next to the divine; and as that which is divine is best, so that which approaches nearest to its nature is nearest to the best. (Xen. *Mem.* I.vi.10)

Yet we should not judge too hastily, nor leap to the conclusion that an extreme of asceticism represents the pinnacle of virtue. After all, moderation, not deprivation, is the keyword we find so often in his discussions, and Socrates himself never endorses (nor practices) detachment from, but rather throwing oneself into, the enjoyment of the goods of fortune when they are appropriate. Indeed, enjoyment [ὄψος] is a crucial part of practicing moderation: οὐκ οἶσθ', ὅτι ὁ μὲν ἥδιστα ἐσθίων ἥκιστα ὄψου δεῖται, ὁ δὲ ἥδιστα πίνων ἥκιστα τοῦ μὴ παρόντος ἐπιθυμεῖ ποτοῦ; 'Do you not know that the greater the enjoyment of eating the less the need of sauce; the greater the enjoyment of drinking, the less the desire for drinks that are not available?' (Xen. *Mem.* I.vi.5)

Given that Socrates' aim is to search out the sorts of things that truly count in living a human life, we have much evidence to support the idea that Socrates recognized a suitable place for the goods of chance in his conception of the flourishing life, rather than attempting to exclude them.

Chapter 2: The Idealist: Plato in the Realm of Forms

Any conscientious commentator on Plato will have to deal with the issue of organizing his works: whether the Platonic corpus can convincingly be interpreted chronologically, illustrating a development of Plato's thought from a derivative disciple of Socrates' doctrines to a fully mature philosopher presenting his own theories;[4] or whether we must, as John Cooper convincingly argues, suspend definitive judgments about the relative composition of the various works and, as he puts it,

> relegate thoughts about chronology to the secondary position they deserve and ...concentrate on the literary and philosophical content of the works, taken on their own and in relation to the others....chronological hypotheses must not preclude the independent interpretation and evaluation of the philosophical arguments the dialogues contain; so far as possible, the individual texts must be allowed to speak for themselves.[5]

Such eminent Plato scholars as Gregory Vlastos, Charles Kahn, and Gail Fine have weighed in on the debate concerning the appropriate ordering of the dialogues. For our purposes, however, we can afford to set this issue aside as secondary. No matter how one approaches the Platonic corpus, it is accepted that the *Philebus* is certainly one of Plato's last works, and is also generally agreed to be the work that represents Plato's most mature positions on the question of identifying the good human life overall. Unlike the earlier 'Socratic' dialogues, the *Philebus* portrays the character of Socrates not in a state of perpetual inquiry and ἀπορία, but rather propounding a definite set of views through the development of the conversation: Protarchus tells him 'we should not take it that the aim of our meeting is universal confusion; if we cannot solve the problem, you must do it, for you promised' (*Philebus* 20a3–4), and Socrates proves more than willing to oblige him.

Philebus, Socrates' first interlocutor, represents the position that pleasure constitutes the good for humans (though through most of the dialogue it is Protarchus who converses on behalf of this position, with Philebus contributing occasional supporting comments). 'Philebus holds that what is good for all creatures is to enjoy themselves, to be pleased and delighted, and whatever else goes together with that kind of thing' (*Philebus* 11b3–4). On the other hand, Socrates is committed to defending the thesis that 'not these, but knowing, understanding, and remembering, and what belongs with them, right opinion and true calculations, are better than pleasure and more agreeable to all who can attain them; those who can, get the maximum benefit possible from having them' (*Philebus* 11b6–c3). Given these initial competing positions, Socrates gives the guiding structure of the inquiry: 'each of us will be trying to prove some possession or state of the soul to be the one that can render life happy for all human beings' (*Philebus* 11d3–4).

The first section of the dialogue (11a–20) sets up and takes us through several difficulties faced by both the proponents of pleasure and of reason before we can legitimately endorse one as being truly the good for humans. But before the reader (or the discussants) can get too comfortable with a rehashing of the well-established conflict between pleasure and reason, however, Socrates introduces a novel course for the discussion to take. At 20b3, when the discussion has hit a seemingly insoluble knot, after an involved discussion of unity and plurality, limit and unlimitedness, Socrates interjects, as a divinely-inspired memory, 'a doctrine that once upon a time I heard in a dream—or perhaps I was awake—that I remember now, concerning pleasure and knowledge, that neither of the two is the good, but that there is some third thing which is different from and superior to both of them.' Since, if we can identify some third item other than reason or pleasure as being identical with the good, it makes moot the project of pinning down the precise characteristics of pleasure (which had led to the previous difficulties), since it would be thereby disqualified from its candidacy for the good.

With the tangle of metaphysics safely bypassed, the main discussion of the identity of the human good is free to continue. Socrates and Protarchus first come to agree on some characteristics of whatever turns out to be the good: it 'is necessarily bound to be perfect (τελείος)' (*Philebus* 20d1)—and in fact 'the most perfect thing of all' according the the enthusiastic Protarchus!—and is *sufficient* (ἵκανος): in setting up a fair comparison between the life of pleasure and the life of reason, Socrates reminds us that 'if either of the two is the good, then it must have no need of anything in addition. But if one or the other should turn out to be lacking anything, then this can definitely no longer be the real good we are looking for' (*Philebus* 20e5–6).

8

The centrally relevant feature of this dialogue is precisely Plato's characterization of the best human life as a 'mixture' or 'combination' of reason and pleasure. Just as one living the life of pure, unadulterated pleasure 'would thus not live a human life but the life of a mollusk' (21c), neither does the life of pure reason qualify as the good life, 'since otherwise it would be sufficient, perfect, and worthy of choice for any of the plants and animals that can sustain [it], throughout their lifetime' (22b). The exact character of this 'mixture' is investigated in some depth as the dialogue progresses; however, the salient point to note initially here is the definite non-intellectualist consequences of Plato's position. It is frequently emphasized that Plato, following Socrates, identifies virtue and the good with knowledge; it is not so frequently noted that he does not thereby mean to devalue applied knowledge or science. When discussing the method of mixing knowledge and pleasure together in the well-balanced life, Socrates asks Protarchus which sciences should be included in the mix—the purest and truest only, or some of the others as well:

> **Soc.** [O]ne kind [of science] deals with a subject matter that comes to be and perishes (τὰ γιγνόμενα καὶ ἀπολλύμενα), the other is concerned with what is free of that, the eternal and self-same (ὡσαύτως ὄντα ἀεί). Since we made truth our criterion, the latter kind appeared to be the truer one....If we took from each sort the segments that possess most truth and mixed them together, would this mixture provide us with the most desirable life (τὸν ἀγαπητότατον βίον), or would we also need less-true ones? **Prot.** We should do it this way, it seems. **Soc.** Suppose, then, there is a person who understands what justice itself is and...all the rest of what there is....Will he be sufficiently versed in science if he knows the definition of the circle and of the divine sphere itself but cannot recognize the human sphere? **Prot.** We would find ourselves in a rather ridiculous (γελοίαν) position if we were confined entirely to those divine kinds of knowledge (ἐν ταῖς θείαις...ἐπιστήμαις), Socrates! **Soc.** But how about music: Ought we also to mix in the kind of which we said a little earlier that it is full of lucky hits and imitation (στοχάσεώς τε καὶ μιμήσεως) but lacks purity (καθαρότητος ἐνδεῖν)? **Prot.** It seems necessary to me, if in fact our life is supposed to be at least some sort of *life* (εἴπερ γε ἡμῶν ὁ βίος ἔσται καὶ ὁπωσοῦν ποτε βίος) (*Philebus* 62ba4–5)

The answer agreed upon by Socrates and Protarchus is the broader alternative: the best human life needs even the applied sciences, those fields of knowledge whose objects are the imperfect, impermanent products of generation, and even the sorts of pursuits that involve chance, if our life is to be a meaningful lived experience.

Chapter 3: The Philosopher: Aristotle in Two Worlds

Although Aristotle never presents a unified account of external goods in the *Nichomachean Ethics*, there is evidence that he understood the need for such an account. In some passages, Aristotle explicitly argues that the exercise of at least certain virtuous actions requires external goods (*Magna Moralia* ii.8, 1207b16); while elsewhere, he equally clearly maintains that it would be 'too defective' for the highest human good to be left to τύχη, 'chance' (*EN* i.9, 1099b24).

In Book i of the *Nicomachean Ethics*, Aristotle identifies certain essential features of flourishing. εὐδαιμονία is 'an activity of soul...in accordance with... the best and most *teleios* excellence' (*EN* i.7, 1098a16); it is 'living well and doing well' in general (*EN* i.8, 1098b21). It is τέλειον [καὶ] αὐταρκές (*EN* i.7, 1097b20), and τέλος καὶ τέλειον...παντῇ παντῶς (*EN* i.10, 1101a18); it must be ἔτι δ' ἐν βίῳ τελείῳ (*EN* i.7, 1098a18); we consider it 'thoroughly established and not at all changeable' (*EN* i.10, 1100b3); changes after one's death, even though they can affect one's εὐδαιμονία to a degree, are never enough to reverse it (*EN* i.11, 1101b6). The permanence of εὐδαιμονία ensures that 'that which is sought will belong to the εὐδαίμων, and he will be such [i.e., εὐδαίμων] throughout his life' (*EN* i.10, 1100b18). All of these descriptions, which emphasize the nature of εὐδαιμονία as τέλειον, or complete, create a picture of εὐδαιμονία as free of the influence of chance circumstances. The individual who is properly brought up, has the appropriate disposition, and thereby chooses to act in accordance with virtue, actually acts so, and desires and enjoys acting so—this person will enjoy the best and most excellent sort of life. He will not be subject to conflicts of desires, as are those who pursue various external goods (*EN* i.8, 1099a12), but will instead aim at and achieve those goods which are not only pleasant to himself, but pleasant by nature: 'the life of these [those who are lovers of excellence] does not need pleasure as a sort of ornament, but has pleasure within itself' (*EN* i.8, 1099a15).

This conception of εὐδαιμονία as self-sufficient seems to be compatible with another account Aristotle gives in *EN* i chapters 8 and 12. Here, Aristotle emphasizes that the potentiality or state (δύναμις), the simple possession (κτῆσις) of virtue, is not sufficient to constitute εὐδαιμονία (1098b32–1099a5, 1101b10–1102a4). Rather, εὐδαιμονία is the *activity* of soul according to complete excellence. Someone who possesses the potentialities of certain virtues but does not actively express them, such as, in Aristotle's own examples, someone asleep, or a spectator at the Olympic games, cannot truly be said to be εὐδαίμων. However, a consequence of this stipulation is that at least some minimal external goods become necessary for the exercise of some virtues: for example, the virtue of generosity requires one to have property with which to be generous, friendship requires worthy friends, and courage requires circumstances conducive to the expression of bravery (*EN* i.8, 1099a32 et seq.). In addition, there are certain minimal external goods with which everyone must be supplied in order even to have a life at all—dependable food, shelter, and so on: without these being adequately provided, it will not be possible to achieve εὐδαιμονία. And finally, as noted both here (1097b11 et al.) and in the *Politics* (*Pol.* i.7, 1253a2), man is a ζῷον πολιτικόν by nature; and as such, a complete human life cannot be limited to the individual, but must include his own immediate circumstances: 'parents and children and wife and altogether friends and fellow-citizens' (*EN* i.7, 1097b10). This necessary connection of the individual's good with his family and peers directly informs the discussion in chapter 10, where it is examined whether and to what extent one's εὐδαιμονία is affected by the character and deeds of one's ancestors and descendants. All of these considerations suggest—indeed, require—an understanding of εὐδαιμονία that extends beyond one's own character or virtues. What makes this understanding problematic is that it seems incompatible with Aristotle's initial characterization of εὐδαιμονία as stable, permanent, or somehow insulated from changeable circumstance. As Heinaman notes, self-sufficiency is a formal requirement of εὐδαιμονία for Aristotle, both in Book i and in Book x (1097b7 ff., 1176b5). At 1097b14–15, the self-sufficient (τὸ αὐταρκές) is defined as 'that which alone makes life desirable and lacking nothing.' If εὐδαιμονία is truly self-sufficient, it is unclear how it can be lacking in any respect, according to the above definition. Yet it is apparent that εὐδαιμονία by itself, when we understand it as Aristotle defines it, 'activity of soul in conformity with virtue,' leaves out many items which make our life desirable.

Chapter 4: The Hard-Liners: The Stoics Bite the Bullet

Commentators have made much of the apparent similarities between the way the Stoics account for and describe the good human life and the description offered by Plato's Socrates. And indeed, there is a great deal of support one can adduce to a thesis identifying strong ties between the two traditions. Compare Socrates' decision exclusively to study ethics, leaving off his initial forays into metaphysics and other philosophical fields, with Chrysippus' observation, relayed by Plutarch: 'For the theory of good and bad things must be attached to these, since there is no other starting-point or reference for them that is better, and physical speculation is to be adopted for no other purpose than for the differentiation of good and bad things' (*On Stoic self-contradictions* 1035d). Again, compare the central Socratic thesis—that knowledge, full and complete, is sufficient for right action—with the basically identical, if much more finely developed, tenet of Stoicism that virtue is 'a certain character and power of the soul's commanding-faculty, engendered by reason, or rather, a character which is itself consistent, firm, and unchangeable reason' (Plutarch, *On moral virtue* 441d).

The Stoics begin with a definition of the good as that whose peculiar property is that it is always beneficial. After explaining their notion of benefit in terms of perfect proper functions, they address the question: what sorts of things meet the criterion of being good, that is, being always and only beneficial? In perhaps the *locus classicus* of Stoic doctrine on the topic of the good, Diogenes Laertius writes the following to explain why certain items commonly held to be goods, such as wealth or bodily health, do not in fact qualify as good:

> ὡς γὰρ ἴδιον θερμοῦ τὸ θερμαίνειν, οὐ τὸ ψύχειν, οὕτω καὶ ἀγαθοῦ τὸ ὠφελεῖν, οὐ τὸ βλάπτειν...ἔτι τέ φασιν, ᾧ ἔστιν εὖ καὶ κακῶς χρῆσθαι, τοῦτ' οὐκ ἔστιν ἀγαθόν.

> For just as heating, not chilling, is the peculiar characteristic [ἴδιον] of what is hot, so too benefiting, not harming, is the peculiar characteristic of what is good....Furthermore they say: that which can be used well and badly is not something good. (Diogenes Laertius 7.103)

It is the fact that health, wealth, and such things are capable of both benefiting *and* harming, as the Stoics argue, that disqualifies them from the class of goods. I wish to bring attention to Diogenes' description of that which is essentially and peculiarly characteristic of any good thing, namely, what is elsewhere in Stoic literature called 'firmness' or 'fixity': it is not simply that one can be or is occasionally benefited by some state of affairs—if it were, the class of goods would be enormous, and would indeed include such external contingencies as health, property, social standing, and the like; but rather, the good is always and only beneficial, and nothing that is not always and only beneficial is good.

This account must be supplemented with some further explanation of exactly what 'benefiting' entails. On this point, we find very little significant disputation or doctrinal variation among the Stoics; the core explanation of benefit is always given in terms of harmony or accordance with nature and right reason: '[S]ome proper functions are perfect, and...these are also called right actions' (Stobaeus 2.86,4); 'since reason, by way of a more perfect management, has been bestowed on rational beings, to live correctly in accordance with reason comes to be natural for them' (Diogenes Laertius 7.86). A complete understanding of the Stoics' conception of the connection between nature and reason must include a familiarity with their naturalistic presuppositions about the origin of ethical value. By observing the natural processes and behaviors of plants, non-human animals and infants, Stoics perceived that living things seem intrinsically to possess the impulse to preserve themselves and their particular constitution. From this basis, they conclude that nature, since it is responsible for the impulses of living things, must itself be operating according to the principles of rationality which we recognize as characterizing the natural development of organisms. This picture of a rationally active nature or universe is what lies behind the Stoic association of nature, reason, and the foundation of ethical action.

Once we have gotten clear what the Stoics mean by the good (that which always and only benefits) and by benefit (that which is in accordance with nature and reason), it still remains to be determined what sorts of things meet their criteria to be considered good. A clear understanding of what goods there are is necessary for answering the question: how can we live a happy life? Aristotle notes that there is universal agreement that the happy life is that in which one does well (εὖ πράττειν) (*EN* i.4 1095a16–18). And yet there is just as much conflict over the specific content of the notion of happiness or what constitutes it as there is agreement over it in general terms. The Stoics took it as a central concern of their ethics to offer an account of what things count as good or goods, and in what ways these things constitute the final end of action, that is, achieving happiness.

The Stoic criteria for the good have been made clear. Let us see what things meet them. We can already see that many items which are commonly believed to be goods are, on these criteria, not really goods at all: 'life, health, pleasure, beauty, strength, wealth, reputation, noble birth...are not good but indifferents of the species "preferred"' (Diogenes Laertius 7.102). These things that appear to (and sometimes do in fact) benefit us, and thereby seem worthy to be considered goods, fail to qualify as truly good precisely because each of them is capable of producing *both* benefit *and* harm—thus falling short of the 'οὐδὲν ἄλλο' standard which essentially characterizes the good. Even though possessing great wealth, for example, does sometimes benefit one, it is easy to conceive of—or even point to historical examples of—wealth resulting in harm to its possessor. This variability is characteristic of all these so-called external goods, and in fact can be extended to any condition or state of affairs subject to definite description. Let me attempt to make clearer what I mean by this. Suppose we decide that some item on the list of external goods is, in fact, truly a good, whose possession results always and only in benefit to ourselves and, in general, the state of the world is better when we possess it. Even further, suppose that, all things being equal, we are correct, and anyone who possesses this external good is indeed always and only benefited by it, and the world at large is also so benefited. But imagine now that we fall into the power of a corrupt monarch; and that this monarch decides to effect great evils upon the world by conscripting into his army all persons with this external good. (We are assuming that he does in fact have the power to do as he intends.) Surely in such a case, it would be better overall if there were no, or at least few, people capable of conscription into the tyrant's army, i.e., people who possess this external good. Precisely this sort of thought experiment is given by Aristo of Chios, as reported by Sextus Empiricus in *Against the professors* 11.64–7. The Stoics, then, were particularly sensitive to the impact contingent circumstance has upon ethical action; in fact, this forms the basis of the well-known Stoic distinction between value and indifference.

Chapter 5: Applied Intellectualism: The Eudaimonist Synthesis

Through evaluating and connecting the strengths and weaknesses of each major school's treatment of the question, I address the issue of whether a satisfactory account of the relation of external goods to happiness must accommodate both the insight that there is an essential connection between prosperity and the flourishing life, and that there is a real sense in which happiness is independent of any particular state of such prosperity. This apparent discrepancy may be explicable through recognizing elements common among these four traditions. I advance and evaluate an interpretation of eudaimonism that accommodates important insights of each tradition, including: a) Aristotle's account of human nature, specifically the role of external goods as necessary preconditions for leading a human life; b) the consequence of Socratic and Stoic thought that external goods ('preferred indifferents') are necessary constituents of moral action; c) Plato's and Aristotle's recognition that there must be a criterion for judging the degree of external prosperity compatible with a happy life.

A second goal of this project is to demonstrate the relevance of this topic to central concerns of contemporary ethics. I draw connections between the issues that form the basis for ancient discussions of happiness and those relevant to modern-day conceptions of flourishing, pointing toward some areas wherein an inclusive understanding of εὐδαιμονία appears to be germane and useful, not only to resolving the historical puzzle of ancient eudaimonism, but also for supporting contemporary efforts to provide firmer footing for virtue-based ethics.

In general, the relation between ethics and what the ancients called τεχνή χρηματιστική—the money-making craft, or what we might more commonly call economics—is, I argue, often misunderstood, to the detriment of ethical responses to real-world concerns. Typically, τεχνή χρηματιστική is understood to operate according to its own standards and goals, as is typical of the ancient conception of τέχναι: the good money-maker is unrelated to (and often at odds with) the good moral person. When this typical way of doing business fails (as it does cyclically, with large, noticeable crashes that cause much harm to many people), the typical ethical response is to offer some variation of the claim that money-makers ought to structure their activities so as not to care so much about the goals of mere money-making, but rather so as to assimilate the end of ethics. In other words: an adequate τεχνή χρηματιστική must include an ethical τέλος. Contemporary economic studies devote much time to measuring and evaluating economics both in its own right and as either actually or prospectively modeled upon ethical goals (e.g. socially responsible investing, green industry, etc.). Likewise, ethical studies devote time and effort to defending and explaining the necessity of ethical considerations for business relations, practices, and systems.[6] However, it seems to be an unexplored area to evaluate ethical systems on the basis of how well they recognize, acknowledge, or explain observable facts about human economic nature; in particular, what gives rise to economic man, such that his nature seems to have a part which enjoys well-being precisely through economic interaction with his fellows?

Furthermore, the connection between ethics and harm is centrally relevant for any consideration of external goods. If harm entails a physicality, such that the sufferer of the harm be enmattered, ethics rather deeply rests on the significance of embodiment, which in turn rests fundamentally on matter and the material circumstances of existence, such as external goods and chance. The work concludes, then, with a few prospective, though necessarily tentative, thoughts on future developments of issues in applied eudaimonism.

Notes

[1] Herodotus, *Histories* I.30–32.
[2] I refrain from using systematically one English translation of the term εὐδαιμονία because of the great danger of inadequate or incomplete translation. For the most part, I will use 'flourishing,' 'well-being' and 'happiness' relatively interchangeably for ease of reading when the context allows. In cases wherein fine distinctions of meaning are of foremost concern for the discussion at hand, I will leave the term and its related forms untranslated.
[3] Plato's Socrates here argues, of course, that it is s specific type of knowledge, i.e., knowledge of the good, that is essential.
[4] See C.M. Young's 'Plato and Computer Dating' in C.C.W. Taylor (ed.) (1994), *Oxford Studies in Ancient Philosophy* XII (Oxford: Clarendon Press) for a survey of various stylometric investigations into the relative dating of Plato's works.
[5] Cooper (ed.) (1997), pp. xiv–xv.
[6] In his "Platonic Reflections on Business Ethics," Sherwin Klein provides a thoughtful and challenging view of the role of the τεχνή χρηματιστική for εὐδαιμονία within Plato's ideal city. My brief summation here, being ancillary to a different project, fails to engage his positions in any substantive way; nevertheless I hope eventually to develop this point further, as it is rather a centrally relevant component of any complete discussion of εὐδαιμονία within a community.

Chapter 1
The Humanist: Socrates in the
Real World

Sōcratēs autem prīmus philosophiam dēvocāvit ē caelō et in urbibus conlocāvit et in domūs etiam introduxit et coēgit dē vitā et moribus rebusque bonīs et malīs quaerere.

But Socrates was the first who called philosophy down from heaven and placed it in cities, introduced it into families, and obliged it to examine into life and customs and matters good and evil.

Cicero, *Tusculanae Disputationes*

Introduction

The received tradition in the history of Western philosophy is that, as Brickhouse and Smith have aptly put it, 'Socrates was the first thinker to offer an explanation of why and how being moral always makes one better off' (Brickhouse and Smith 2000, 127–8). The Socrates we know is, of course, primarily a literary construction, almost a fictional character, so few reliable details do we know of Socrates the historical man.[1] Our account of his philosophy is at best second-hand, preserved primarily in the Platonic dialogues, in which it is often used by Plato for his own purposes, and in Xenophon's works, the non-philosophical character of whose writing presents its own set of challenges. As a result, we cannot make such bold claims about his thought as we can about other philosophers whose work survives through a more direct manuscript tradition. Nevertheless, it is important both philosophically and historically to reconstruct the positions of the historical Socrates[2] and to analyze and respond to the received understanding and interpretation of what we might call, following Vander Waerdt and others, the 'Socratic tradition' or 'Socratic movement.' This Socratic tradition has had a formative influence on Western ethics starting from Socrates' immediate successors, the authors of the various Σωκρατικοὶ λόγοι, the Academic, Stoic, Cynic, Skeptic, and Cyrenaic schools, through late antique and mediaeval philosophy and even up to the scholarship of the modern period. The general tenor of Socrates' philosophic approach, method, goals, and underlying values has left clear footprints in the various accounts recorded by his successors. We can use these traces to discover some important features of Socrates' mission—a mission characterized by a specifically human-centered eudaimonism.

More than anything else, Socrates conceives of his mission as fundamentally human—inquiring into precisely those issues which most influence the daily experience of life. This focus is a large part of what distinguishes him from the tradition of natural philosophy which preceded him, and from which he early disengages himself. The purpose of philosophy, Socratically conceived, is to benefit the individual: to benefit him *qua* rational being, certainly, in one's critical and collaborative pursuit of truth; but, just as surely, to benefit him *qua* citizen, in one's civic practices of justice or courage, and *qua* social being, in one's relations of piety or magnanimity. This distinctly human focus is a crucially important lens through which to properly investigate and interpret Socrates' conception of what part external goods play within εὐδαιμονία. In fact, the balance of textual evidence indicates that Socrates envisions external goods as fundamental to a coherent account of the sort of happiness human beings can and should properly achieve.

A Background to Socrates: The Sources

Of the three[3] primary sources of our knowledge about Socrates—Plato's and Xenophon's Socratic dialogues and Aristophanes' *Clouds*—each is less than fully satisfactory, for various reasons, as definitive source material. A brief survey of these sources will provide a background for understanding the approach to the textual evidence presupposed by the present project.

Aristophanes. Aristophanes' account of Socrates in the *Clouds* has been given the least evidentiary weight historically, largely due to its discrepancies and contradictions with the testimony of Plato and Xenophon, as well as to the problems of interpretation associated with such a complex genre as the comic or satiric play.[4] While it is true that Socratic scholarship of the past century has come to repudiate the wholesale disdain toward Aristophanes' picture of Socrates characteristic of earlier commentators,[5] still the *Clouds* is accepted as, at best, ancillary to Plato and Xenophon,[6] rather than offering substantive contributions to our understanding of the man Socrates, or of his thought, on its own merits. Even among commentators who are sympathetic to the project of 'rehabilitating' or re-evaluating the Socratic evidence of Aristophanes and other non-Platonic sources (Brickhouse and Smith, Vander Waerdt, Diskin Clay and Burnet, for example), there is a justifiably cautious approach common to the entire project: 'the hazards of relying upon a comic parody for information on which to reconstruct Socrates' philosophical biography should not be underestimated.'[7] Inasmuch as resolving the question of how to interpret the Aristophanic evidence for the historical Socrates constitutes a substantive scholarly project in its own right, the present work, its arguments and conclusions, will not rely in any substantive way on evidence from the Aristophanic testimony.

Xenophon. Xenophon's Socratic writings (the *Memorabilia, Oeconomicus, Symposium,* and *Apology*) constitute a significant corpus of testimony from one of Socrates' close contemporaries. Yet this source has experienced uneven acceptance, to put it charitably, throughout the history of Socratic studies; a less charitable, though possibly more bluntly accurate, gloss would characterize the scholarly attitude toward Xenophon as fickle. We have, of course, only limited access to the antique reception of Xenophon; but there is a conspicuous lack of any credible indications that his Socratic writings were in any way suspect. On the contrary, we do have several strong indications that he was accepted among the primary sources for understanding the philosophy and personality of the historical Socrates,[8] along with the lost works of other contemporaries. Yet modern commentary has seen public opinion of Xenophon's testimony swing from supremacy—

> Xenophon has come to be regarded as the only perfectly trustworthy authority for the philosophy of Socrates: to all the others, Plato himself included, at most a supplementary value is allowed.[9]

to worthlessness—

> After constituting the supreme court of appeal on matters Socratic in some past generations, [Xenophon] has...not only been removed from the bench, but even at times quite thrown out of court and denied the right to appear either as advocate or witness.[10]

back to sort of guarded acceptance, as in the work of A.A. Long, D.R. Morrison (1987, 9–22), P.A. Vander Waerdt, Leo Strauss, and other recent scholars (though notably Vlastos, among others, remains unsympathetic). Nevertheless, if our intent is to understand as much of Socrates as we can, we can certainly not ignore this evidence, though it will of course behoove us to retain our critical faculties when evaluating it. Regardless of what the current scholarly climate in philosophy happens to be, it is of importance to remember that Socrates' successors took into account not only the Platonic 'canon,' but sources such as Xenophon—remember that Zeno began his philosophical career, according to Diogenes Laertius, after reading about Socrates in Xenophon's *Memorabilia*, not Plato's *Apology*! Our interpretation is obliged to make a good faith attempt to understand this connection. The importance of Xenophon for a complete portrait of Socrates is not to be overlooked.

Among the most prominent charges leveled against the usefulness of Xenophon's Socratic works is that, as a non-philosophic writer, Xenophon's understanding, and hence presentation, of Socrates' philosophy is of questionable adequacy. This limitation, it is frequently claimed, manifests itself in numerous contradictions with the positions ascribed to Socrates in the works of Plato, who, as a student and *bona fide* philosophical successor of Socrates, is expected to be a more reliable transmitter of the intricacies of philosophical dialogue. As Lacey writes, 'Plato is a philosopher and Xenophon is not, and it is easier to extract philosophy from a source that contains too much of it than from one that contains too little.'[11] The relationship between the laws of the πόλις and justice generally, and one's obligations to each; Socrates' justification for accepting his death; the role of his δαιμόνιον; the episode of the oracle at Delphi; whether Socrates ever proposed and defended positive doctrines, or limited himself to elenctic midwifery: all of these issues highlight often serious differences between the Socrates of Xenophon and that of Plato.

Still, in general, we can accept that '[t]he object of Xenophon throughout [the *Memorabilia*] is to prove that the system of education inculcated by Socrates was the best possible; that Socrates was himself the embodiment of that system, and was therefore the pattern of a good and happy man.'[12] This stated goal is by no means antithetical to the Socrates of Plato. Indeed it is rather the same in spirit as well as in many particulars, if admittedly incompatible in many others; and it is in the points of convergence, rather than divergence, that the present project looks to find testimony useful for understanding Socrates' thoughts about εὐδαιμονία in relation to external goods.[13]

Plato. In many ways, the work of Plato promises to be our best evidence for reconstructing, indeed knowing anything about, the philosophy of Socrates. Unlike Aristophanes' portrait in the *Clouds*, it is serious work, thus *prima facie* less susceptible to charges of inaccuracy or exaggeration, which our historical distance and dearth of textual corroboration would make it difficult, if not impossible, for us to recognize or refute; unlike Xenophon's Socratic writings, it is philosophical, thus capable of explicating (accurately, we presume) the subtleties of Socrates' thought. It is the work of a sympathetic disciple, close to the source in time, having firsthand personal knowledge of the man and his teaching, as well as in inclination, undertaking as his life's work the pursuit of philosophical inquiry and teaching. It has survived as an intact, coherent corpus of significant size and continuity, providing over twenty books in which Socrates formulates theses and argues at length on topics of central concern and philosophic merit, and which also provide details about Socrates' habits, associates, civic activity, and life in general.

Yet we know that a naïve acceptance of the Platonic evidence at face value is no more possible than of Xenophon's or Aristophanes' account. The question of distinguishing between Socrates, the historical philosopher, and 'Socrates,' the character in the Platonic dialogues who is the vehicle for expressing Plato's own philosophies, is long recognized, and well entrenched, in both the philosophical and historical literatures—in Vlastos' memorable phrase, 'that bugbear of Platonic studies, the so-called "Socratic Problem".'[14] Cicero, in his *Republic*, opines that Plato appropriates Socrates' reputation and attaches to it Plato's own subsequent projects and interests, which are not at all characteristic of Socrates himself:

> dein Tubero: 'nesciō, Africāne, cur ita memoriae proditum sit, Socratem omnem istam disputationem reiecisse, et tantum dē vītā et dē moribus solitum esse quaerere. quem enim auctorem dē illō locupletiōrem Platōne laudāre possumus? cuius in librīs multīs locīs ita loquitur Socrates, ut etiam cum dē moribus dē virtutibus denique dē rē publicā disputet, numerōs tamen et geometriam et harmoniam studeat Pythagorae more coniungere.' tum Scipiō: 'sunt ista ut dicis; sed audisse tē credō, Tubero, Platonem Socrate mortuō primum in Aegyptum discendī causā, post in Italiam et in Siciliam contendisse,

ut Pythagorae inventa perdisceret, eumque et cum Archytā Tarentinō et cum Timaeō Locrō multum fuisse et Philolāī commentariōs esse nanctum, cumque eō tempore in hīs locīs Pythagorae nomen vigeret, illum sē et hominibus Pythagoreīs et studiīs illīs dedisse. itaque cum Socratem unice dilexisset, eīque omnia tribuere voluisset, leporem Socraticum subtilitātemque sermōnis cum obscuritāte Pythagorae et cum illa plurimārum artium gravitāte contexuit.'

Then Tubero [said]: 'Africanus, I don't know why it's been traditionally passed down that Socrates rejected all that sort of arguing, and was accustomed to inquire entirely about life and customs. For what author can we praise [as being] a more credible witness about him than Plato? And in his books in many places he says about Socrates that although he also would dispute about customs and virtues and about public affairs, nevertheless he would, after the Pythagorean custom, join to them numbers and geometry and proportion.' Then Scipio replied: 'These things are as you say; but I believe that you've heard, Tubero, that Plato, after Socrates died, first betook himself to Egypt for the sake of study, and afterward to Italy and to Sicily, so that he might learn what Pythagoras had discovered, and he was much with Archytas of Tarentium and with Timaeus of Locris, and collected the commentaries of Philolaus, and since at that time in these places the name of Pythagoras was gaining in fame, he gave himself both to the students of Pythagoras and to these studies. And so while he had cherished Socrates alone, and had wished to attribute everything to him, he wove together the Socratic eloquence, and the subtlety of his speech, with the obscurity of Pythagoras, and with the latter's seriousness of so many different pursuits.' (Cicero, *Rep.* i.10)

The contemporary literature concerning this issue is substantial. Any conscientious commentator on Socrates or Plato is obliged to deal with it, if not to stake out a new position, then at least to state for the record his or her starting point of interpretation. Vlastos, Kahn, Santas, Fine, among others, have weighed in on the debate over the appropriate ordering of the dialogues, and the degree to which the views put in the mouth of Socrates in a given work can safely be taken as representative of the man himself. Whether the Platonic corpus can convincingly be interpreted as illustrating Plato's development from scribe and faithful recollector of Socrates' teachings to mature philosopher presenting his own theories using the prestige of his mentor to the advantage of his own doctrines; or whether we should suspend definitive judgments about the relative composition of the various works and 'relegate thoughts about chronology to the secondary position they deserve and to concentrate on the literary and philosophical content of the works,'[15] or whether it is best to take some other position, demands a response, a commitment. For my part, I find Vlastos' analysis, that the earlier period

Socrates is 'Plato's re-creation of the historical figure,'[16] especially convincing, and am inclined generally to accept his grouping of the dialogues into Early, Middle, Late, and Transitional groups.

With this having been said for the record, however, it is worth noting that there seems to be a core of agreement about the Socratic character of certain dialogues. Even Vlastos and Irwin, for example, as much as they differ in their interpretation of many issues, nevertheless agree on the Socratic character of no fewer than eight dialogues: the *Apology, Charmides, Crito, Euthyphro, Hippias Minor, Ion, Laches,* and *Protagoras.* It is to these dialogues that I shall turn, in the main, for the core textual support from Plato of my analyses.[17] I will occasionally cite other dialogues; such passages will not constitute the main textual support for my point, but will be included for the purpose of providing ancillary support. In these cases I will use dialogues that are accepted as representative of the historical Socrates in at least one plausible interpretation, though not necessarily unanimously.

The Socratic Nexus: Happiness, Virtue, and the Good

The central thesis we can derive with reasonable confidence about the Socratic ethics, one which is characteristic of eudaimonism generally, is the claim that happiness, virtue, and the good form a closely woven nexus. This fact alone, however, tells us very little. In an ideal world, we would have a comprehensive and exhaustive lexicon of the philosophically relevant terms, their definitions, relations, and taxonomy; starting with this, we could precisely reconstruct and deductively analyze Socrates' positions and claims free of the imprecision of the common-language discourse in which they are presented. Socrates, unfortunately, does not provide us with exegetical footnotes for his philosophic vocabulary. Further complicating the issue is the uncertainty whether Socrates himself consistently maintained linguistic precision in his free-ranging dialogues, so often full of Plato's literary word play, or simply the relaxed cadences of natural conversation. Still, we need to understand the precise relationships in which Socrates' concepts stand with one another in order to discover important features of his philosophy. Are happiness and virtue identical? When Socrates talks about τὸ ἀγαθόν, is this something composed of individual goods—and how are these defined? What does Socrates mean when, as he frequently does, he calls εὐδαιμονία and τὸ ἀγαθόν, or some other two concepts, ταὐτόν, 'the same'? Once these questions are answered, how do these answers contribute to a coherent overall account of Socrates' eudaimonism?

This section will address these several issues within a framework meant ultimately to clarify the relation between εὐδαιμονία and external goods. The first step will be to discuss the Socratic use and meaning of the term ταὐτόν, used frequently both in Plato and in Xenophon to link concepts crucial to understanding the core of Socrates' eudaimonism: εὐδαιμονία, ἀρετή, ὠφέλεια, τὸ ἀγαθόν, and τὰ ἀγαθά in their several relations. Once we have a workable understanding of this term, we will use it to examine first the relation of εὐδαιμονία and ἀρετή, which constitutes one of the two so-called 'Socratic paradoxes,' the central positive doctrines attributed to Socrates. There are competing interpretations about the nature of this relationship in the contemporary literature, each of which must be evaluated. I will argue that each of the primary interpretations allows theoretical space for external goods to be considered components of εὐδαιμονία. The next step will be to examine Socrates' thoughts on the connection between εὐδαιμονία and τὸ ἀγαθόν and τὰ ἀγαθά; specifically, why τὸ ἀγαθόν is considered identical to εὐδαιμονία; how Socrates understands the relation of τὸ ἀγαθόν and τὰ ἀγαθά; how Socrates defines τὸ ἀγαθόν—and how he does not; and how this definition relates to his conception of human beings and their nature. Next, I will examine the evidence for the Socratic conception of human nature, the divine nature, and how each relates to the good. On the basis of the preceding evidence, I will argue ultimately that Socrates fully intends to identify external goods as goods, and thus that they properly play a role in his account of the good life for human beings.

ταὐτόν: *What It Means to be 'The Same'*. At *Crito* 48b6, Socrates asks Crito whether '[living] well and nobly and justly are the same,' τὸ [ζῆν] δὲ εὖ καὶ καλῶς καὶ δικαίως ὅτι ταὐτόν ἐστιν, with Crito responding affirmatively. Elsewhere Socrates claims that ἀρετή and ἐπιστημή are the same (Xenophon *Memorabilia* III.ix.5, IV.vi.7, Plato *Protagoras* 319a, 360d, *Laches* 194e–195a, *Meno* 70a, 79c, 87d, 89a); still elsewhere that εὐδαιμονία and τὸ ἀγαθόν are the same (*Gorgias* 494e, *Euthydemus* 278e). A key point on which proper interpretation hinges is the precise meaning of this ταὐτόν, that is, in what sense these various concepts are 'the same.' Vlastos' analysis of this term in the context of Socrates' discussion of εὐδαιμονία and ἀρετή stands as a closely-reasoned and relevant piece of philological analysis in support of his philosophical interpretation.[18] Vlastos begins by examining Aristotle's discussion of the three possible meanings of the term in the *Topics* 103a23–31 and b10–12.[19] Aristotle identifies three distinct possible meanings of the term. First, A and B are ταὐτόν if they are 'the same in definition,' that is, synonyms. Second, ταὐτόν can mean that B is an ἴδιον, or *proprium*, of A; that A and B are necessarily interentailing, even though not related essentially. Vlastos uses the term 'interentailment' to express Aristotle's ἀντικατηγορεῖται: for all x, x has A if, and only if, x has B.[20] Third, ταὐτόν can express 'accidental sameness.' Upon comparing these three options to Socrates' statement about εὐδαιμονία and ἀρετή, Vlastos concludes that, since happiness and virtue are surely not accidentally ταὐτόν, nor are they ταὐτόν in definition, the only relevant sense of ταὐτόν applicable here is being ἴδιον, that is, as he puts it, interentailing, a conclusion he lauds as the '*pièce de résistance* of the whole dialogue [i.e., the *Crito*].'[21]

This premise becomes important as we encounter other Socratic statements of the form 'X is Y' or 'X and Y are ταὐτόν.' Why is this important for our investigation? We must be careful not to assume casually that Socrates' use of the term ταὐτόν is meant as a relation of identity, precisely because the different ways in which we can interpret this relation lead to equivalences that have significantly different consequences for Socrates' eudaimonism. We saw above that Socrates relates εὐδαιμονία with ἀρετή,[22] and ἀρετή with ἐπιστήμη; if this relation were read as identity, Socrates would have a straightforward logical argument for a strictly intellectualist form of εὐδαιμονία (compare *Meno* 89a, where he relies on exactly the same form of argument in constructing the conclusion that virtue is wisdom). On the other hand, if, as I will argue, there is compelling evidence that Socrates' eudaimonism is more comprehensive than an intellectualist reading allows, it will be important to recognize something like Vlastos' conclusions about the meaning of 'being ταὐτόν.'

εὐδαιμονία *and* ἀρετή. The relation between εὐδαιμονία and ἀρετή is among the better-addressed topics in the literature of Socratic philosophy, meriting book-length treatments from most scholars of note in the field. It goes without saying that the present work, focused more broadly, can of necessity do no more than sketch the outlines of this substantive and detailed debate. Nevertheless it is relevant to our topic at least to review the major positions,[23] after which we can attempt to trace the implications this issue will have for the overall direction of Socratic eudaimonism, and in particular any consequences that may obtain for our central topic of interest, external goods in their relation to the flourishing life.

We have already seen, in the previous section, Vlastos' argument for the claim that εὐδαιμονία and ἀρετή are ταὐτόν in the sense of being interentailing, the conclusion he calls the '*pièce de résistance*' of the *Crito*. This claim makes up a part of a larger view proposed in Vlastos 1991, called the 'Sovereignty of Virtue' thesis, as a way of understanding the supreme emphasis Socrates places on virtue for happiness, while, at the same time, acknowledging and making sense of the seeming relevance of non-moral factors as well. Starting with three passages (*Apology* 28b5–9 and 28d6–10, *Crito* 48c6–d5), Vlastos lays out the *prima facie* position that Socrates completely identifies εὐδαιμονία with ἀρετή:

> [T]he form of life we call 'happiness' when viewing it under desirability criteria...is *the same form of life* we call 'virtue' when viewing it as meeting moral criteria...[I]f this is what Socrates holds, it commits him unavoidably to the third of the positions laid out above: he is holding that virtue *is* happiness— virtue its sole component, the only thing that makes life good and satisfying.[24]

Vlastos calls this principle, entailed by *Crito* 48b4–10, 'the Identity Thesis'; but he proceeds to argue that this *prima facie* plausible thesis fails to account for some very important features of εὐδαιμονία, inasmuch as it falsely concludes that certain non-moral considerations have no bearing at all on happiness. It produces the implausible consequence that a '[virtuous] inmate of Gulag should be as happy as an equally virtuous inmate of a Cambridge college,' if happiness and virtue are identical as per the Identity Thesis.[25] In place of the 'unicomponent' model of happiness based on the Identity Thesis, Vlastos sets forth a 'multicomponent' model based on what he calls the Sufficiency Thesis: that virtue is 'the sovereign good,' both necessary and sufficient for happiness, but that there are other components to happiness as well. These other components, such as health, wealth, and so on, though themselves neither necessary nor sufficient for happiness, still enhance happiness if present and used or enjoyed in conjunction with virtue. *In toto*, Vlastos' view of the relation of virtue to happiness is that it is partially, but essentially, *constitutive*.

Irwin, by contrast, advocates a substantially opposing interpretation of the relation between εὐδαιμονία and ἀρετή. His is an *instrumental* view, maintaining that, far from being constitutive of εὐδαιμονία in any way, ἀρετή is a mere means to our final end, something to be chosen only for the sake of something else, never for its own. Beginning with *Lysis* 220a7–b5, Irwin attributes to Socrates the 'Instrumental Principle':

> Socrates claims that whatever is loved for the sake of some further end is not really what we love, and that the only thing we really love is whatever we love without loving it for the sake of anything...Socrates' principle reduces anything chosen for the sake of an end to the status of a purely instrumental means.[26]

Based on this principle, he proceeds to argue:

> Socrates also suggests in the *Euthydemus* that we desire happiness for its own sake and desire everything else for the sake of happiness; and so he commits himself to the conclusion that we desire everything other than happiness only for the sake of happiness and not for its own sake. Now Socrates believes that virtue and virtuous action are desirable, as the *Euthydemus* says, for the sake of happiness. If, then, he accepts the Instrumental Principle, he must infer that virtues are purely instrumental to happiness, and are not to be valued for their own sakes.[27]

Irwin does recognize that one might be suspicious of such a view in light of Socrates' commitment to virtue's sufficiency for εὐδαιμονία, as expressed at *Apology* 30c6–d5, 41c8–d2; *Crito* 48b8–9; *Charmides* 173d3–5, 174b11–c3. If ἀρετή is sufficient for εὐδαιμονία, how can it be merely instrumental? Irwin's response is to consider ἀρετή to be an 'infallible instrumental means' to εὐδαιμονία: if action in accordance with ἀρετή invariably promotes εὐδαιμονία in all cases, there is then no conceptual requirement for virtue to be constitutive of its end. Since this objection can be answered in a way not incompatible with the Socratic position, if not explicitly endorsed; and further, passages from the *Lysis, Euthydemus* and *Gorgias* count as evidence of Socrates' acceptance of the Instrumental Principle as a fundamental axiom; Irwin concludes that reading ἀρετή as instrumental for εὐδαιμονία is the conceptually and textually consistent interpretation of the relation between the two.

The positions of Vlastos and Irwin, though certainly not exhaustive of the range of possible interpretations of Socratic virtue and εὐδαιμονία, represent the major lines of thought in the contemporary literature on this topic. My interest in presenting them is to evaluate some consequences each position has for the present inquiry into external goods. External goods, like the virtues, are a class of features of human life whose relation to happiness is of philosophic interest; and one's acceptance of a particular relation of virtue to happiness will have an impact on what one can and cannot say about the place of external goods on such an interpretation.

If, following Irwin, one accepts that virtue is simply *instrumental* for happiness, rather than constitutive, this position weakens the grounds for maintaining a sharp distinction between virtue and external goods, since we need only prove that external goods are instrumental for happiness to put them on equally respectable footing with the virtues. The primary distinction to be drawn, in this case, will be between a class of *consistently* instrumental goods and a class of *intermittently* instrumental goods—a difference of degree rather than of kind.[28] If, however, following Vlastos, one counts virtue as a necessary and sufficient component of happiness, this position preserves the privileged role of virtue—that which is not susceptible to chance misfortune—for happiness; yet it still allows the possibility for other factors to be components of the happy life—it allows other things to *matter* in the various ways that seem intuitively plausible to us as human beings in the world.

In either of these two interpretations of Socrates' position on εὐδαιμονία and its relation to ἀρετή, then, we end up with conceptual space for external goods to count as significant factors within the happy life: Irwin achieves this by 'demoting' the virtues to the rank of instruments, a role quite plausibly filled by external goods as well, on any but the most extreme intellectualist eudaimonism; Vlastos achieves it by arguing, via his Sovereignty Thesis, that happiness is legitimately enhanced by non-moral factors which, when enjoyed in conjunction with the necessary and sufficient ingredient of ἀρετή, constitute true ἀγαθά. Why this should be so is, I believe, explained by Socrates' conception of the specifically human: human nature, as distinct from the divine, frames and specifies what benefits us, and so too what counts as (a) good. These issues will constitute the focus of a later section of the chapter. Before we can begin to draw any conclusions about particular goods, however, we must first explore what Socrates had to say about the relation between εὐδαιμονία and τὸ ἀγαθόν generally.

εὐδαιμονία, *the Good, and* ὠφελεῖα. The relation of happiness and the good enjoys much less explicit argumentative support in Plato's work than, say, the relation of happiness and virtue. However, textual evidence suggests that treating εὐδαιμονία and τὸ ἀγαθόν as synonymous is not at all considered a significant philosophical issue, either by Socrates himself or by any of his contemporaries. Compare *Gorgias* 494e–495b, where Socrates, in the thick of argument with Callicles about the hedonist definition of the good, uses both εὐδαιμονία and τὸ ἀγαθόν as the items of contrast with ἡδονή and χαίρειν: 'the one who says, just like that, that those who enjoy themselves, however they may do it, are *happy*...But tell me now, too, whether you say that the pleasant and the *good* are the same,' 'ἐκεῖνος ὃς ἂν φῇ ἀνέδην οὕτω τοὺς χαίροντας, ὅπως ἂν χαίρωσιν, εὐδαίμονας εἶναι...ἀλλ' ἔτι καὶ νῦν λέγε πότερον φῇς εἶναι τὸ αὐτὸ ἡδὺ καὶ *ἀγαθόν*.' Again, in the *Euthydemus*: 'Do all of us humans wish to do well? Or [is] this question one of the ridiculous ones that I was afraid of just now? For I suppose it is stupid even to raise such questions: for who among humans does not wish to do well?'; 'ἆρά γε πάντες ἄνθρωποι βουλόμεθα *εὖ πράττειν*; ἢ τοῦτο μὲν ἐρώτημα ὧν νυνδὴ ἐφοβούμην ἓν τῶν καταγελάστων; ἀνόητον γὰρ δήπου καὶ τὸ ἐρωτᾶν τὰ τοιαῦτα· τίς γὰρ οὐ βούλεται ἀνθρώπων *εὖ πράττειν*;' (*Euthydemus* 278e).

Contemporary scholars have followed the ancients in equating happiness and the good. Vlastos identifies the 'Eudaemonist Axiom,' '[the premise] that happiness is desired by all human beings as the ultimate end (τέλος) of all their rational acts,' and notes 'neither Socrates nor Plato feels called upon to *argue* that happiness is man's good—they use the terms interchangeably.'[29] Brickhouse and Smith make the point thus:

> It is interesting that in saying that happiness—one's own happiness—is our ultimate goal, Socrates does not take himself to be making a deep or controversial philosophical claim. Not only does that principle seem to Socrates to be obviously true, but it seems obviously true to others when he brings it up. As a result, nowhere do we find him arguing for the *Principle of Eudaimonism*.[30]

This identification of happiness and the good is uncontroversial, and unargued-for, because it is axiomatic to the eudaimonist framework within which Socrates and the other ethical philosophers of the era work: Brickhouse and Smith's 'Principle of Eudaimonism,' that 'happiness is everyone's ultimate goal, and anything that is good is good only insofar as it contributes to this goal,'[31] like Vlastos' Eudaemonist

Axiom, articulates precisely the foundational premise on which the rest
of the ethical questions so interesting and relevant to Socrates and his
successors depend. And so, whether or not we want to challenge this
premise, we must first understand why Socrates himself, always so
careful in his assumptions, never does: the identification of εὐδαιμονία
with τὸ ἀγαθόν is axiomatic.

But what *is* τὸ ἀγαθόν? That is to say, how do we define it in general,
and thus recognize it in particular cases—τὰ ἀγαθά? We need this
information before we can attribute any evaluations of individual ἀγαθά
to Socrates; only once we have an essential definition of the concept can
we reliably begin to recognize and sort things that belong in the category
of good from those that do not.

First, Socrates clearly believes that τὸ ἀγαθόν is parsed in terms of
benefit or advantage, ὠφέλεια. While it is true that '[a]ny Greek would
have accepted' the equation of 'good' and 'benefit' (Long and Sedley
1987(1), 374), we find Socrates' explicit testimony on the point in
several places. At *Protagoras* 333d Socrates relates: ἄρ' οὖν, ἦν δ' ἐγώ,
ταῦτ' ἐστὶν ἀγαθὰ ἅ ἐστιν ὠφέλιμα τοῖς ἀνθρώποις; 'So then, I said,
these things are goods, which are beneficial to mankind?,' with
Protagoras assenting. Again in the *Euthyphro*, Socrates equates the good
with benefit: οὐκοῦν θεραπεία γε πᾶσα ταὐτὸν διαπράττεται; οἷον
τοιόνδε: ἐπ' ἀγαθῷ τινί ἐστι καὶ ὠφελίᾳ τοῦ θεραπευομένου, ὥσπερ
ὁρᾷς δὴ ὅτι οἱ ἵπποι ὑπὸ τῆς ἱππικῆς θεραπευόμενοι ὠφελοῦνται καὶ
βελτίους γίγνονται, 'So every instance of caring produces the same
thing? I mean: it is [aiming] toward some good and benefit of the one
helped, just as you see that horses cared for by horsecraft are benefited
and become better.'[32]

Upon this premise, Socrates grounds the further claim that whether
something is beneficial for a given individual depends on that
individual's φύσις, nature, i.e. what sort of being it is. Textual support is
again widespread. *Protagoras* 334a-c gives a list of examples illustrating
the point, 'foods and drinks and drugs and many other things' that are
advantageous to humans but disadvantageous to other beings, or
advantageous to some parts of a human but harmful to other parts.
Socrates' discussion of the difference between ἐμπειρία and τέχνη in the
Gorgias is more explicit on the topic: τέχνην δὲ αὐτὴν οὔ φημι εἶναι ἀλλ'
ἐμπειρίαν, ὅτι οὐκ ἔχει λόγον οὐδένα ᾧ προσφέρει ἃ προσφέρει ὁποῖ'
ἄττα *τὴν φύσιν* ἐστίν, 'I say that it [pastry baking] is not a craft but a
knack, because it does not have an account of *the nature* of whatever

things it applies by which it applies them' (*Gorgias* 465a3–5). At 501a2 medicine is contrasted as a proper τέχνη precisely because ἡ μὲν τούτου οὗ θεραπεύει καὶ τὴν φύσιν ἔσκεπται καὶ τὴν αἰτίαν ὧν πράττει, καὶ λόγον ἔχει τούτων ἑκάστου δοῦναι, 'it has investigated both *the nature* of the object it serves and the cause of the things it does, and is able to give an account of each of these.' When we adduce the premises that justice (and the other ἀρεταί) turn out to be τέχναι (465c) and further, that τέχνη is the practice and procedure for obtaining the good (500d), the connection between φύσις and τὸ ἀγαθόν is further reinforced.[33]

In spite of the widely accepted connection between benefit and the good, it would be disingenuous to insist on, or to attribute to Socrates, a Stoic-style 'οὐδὲν ἄλλο' criterion of benefit to qualify something as (a) good, for the following reason. No matter what one tries to get to meet such a criterion, one can always find at least one case wherein it fails to produce benefit, if one understands the term 'benefit' in any way related to or dependent on the world outside one's own consciousness or internal character.[34] If, in order to avoid this problem, one responds by defining ὠφέλεια in some narrowly intellectual or internal way, there are two problems that arise.

First, one loses at least some of the ground on which to argue that the various external goods aren't goods. One cannot argue, as the Stoics commonly do (e.g. D.L. 7.101–3), that health or wealth sometimes causes harm if 'harm' and 'benefit' are defined internally. Socrates would be prevented from making the argument, at *Republic* I.347c, that a good person can be compelled to rule through fear of the punishment (presumably a harm) of being ruled by someone worse than himself; nor could he claim, as at *Protagoras* 351b3, that a person does not live well if distressed or in pain. Second, an internal definition of ὠφέλεια commits one to a specifically intellectualist eudaimonism, with all the problems associated with such a position. Once we investigate Socrates' conception of human nature more fully, it will be clear, at least, that such an inflexible criterion of the good cannot be the Socratic position. Rather than the Stoics' οὐδὲν ἄλλο, Socrates rather accords with Aristotle's τὸ ἀεὶ ἢ τὸ ὡς ἐπὶ τὸ πολύ, 'always or for the most part' (Arist. *Meta.* 1027a21) approach to philosophy and the sciences generally.[35]

Divine Matters, Human Matters, and Socrates' Calling

The quotation from Cicero's *Tusculanae Disputationes* that begins this chapter paints a picture of Socrates as someone who has made a particular, conscientious choice. Unlike so many of his intellectual predecessors, whose inquiries were directed toward lofty, metaphysical subject matter such as the nature of heavenly bodies, the origins and elements of the natural world, mathematical principles and laws governing motion, and suchlike, Socrates 'philosophiam devocāvit ē caelō,' radically redescribing its function and purpose, and directing it at the benefit, or the good, of mortal human beings, their individual lives, and their communities. We are in no danger of hyperbole by claiming that this specifically human focus is a thoroughgoing, if not the defining, characteristic of Socratic philosophy; and Socrates acknowledges implicitly, at *Protagoras* 334a-c, that a necessary step in any investigation into the good for human beings is to understand human nature.

However, because of the great emphasis Socrates places on the primacy of knowledge or wisdom for happiness, it is easy to suppose that he envisions a sort of 'superhuman' ideal of happiness, based on the cultivation and exercise of the intellect, transcending the quotidian requirements and limitations of our physical circumstance. On such a view, whatever factors demand that we direct our attention and efforts toward the world of particulars are factors to be overcome—hindrances to a full attainment of happiness. A curious feature of this sort of view, however, is the implicit assumption it makes about human nature— namely, that it is essentially divine, only flawed; and thus that human happiness is essentially the same as divine happiness. We are Hephaistos—divine but lame.

Can such a view be correct? And if so, how can we reconcile it with Socrates' ubiquitous emphasis on *human* affairs, as well as his distinct rejection of inquiry into the *divine*? This section will investigate, first, what Socrates means when he distinguishes between the human and the divine; and second, what he says about human nature, and hence about the possibilities of human happiness. Ultimately, Socrates does not intend to, nor does he in fact, classify human nature as a defective version of divinity—rather, it is something unique unto itself, even inasmuch as it does contain a component of the divine. And so, neither is its proper εὐδαιμονία reducible, in principle or in practice, to a divine εὐδαιμονία, but must be explained and pursued on its own, ineradicably human, terms.

Divine Matters (τὰ δαιμόνια). The Socratic literature is suffused with an awareness of the divine, and of its relevance to human life. The *Apology* gives us Socrates' impassioned defense against Meletus' charge that he denies the existence of the gods (26b–28a), as well as the crucial role of the Delphic oracle (20e–23b) and his δαιμόνιον (31c-d) for his philosophical calling. The entirety of the *Euthyphro* is devoted to inquiring into the nature of ὸσία, piety, and its relation to the good; at 5a3–4, Socrates tells Euthyphro: ἔγωγε καὶ ἐν τῷ ἔμπροσθεν χρόνῳ τὰ θεῖα περὶ πολλοῦ ἐποιούμην εἰδέναι, 'in the past too I considered knowing about divine matters to be the most important,' an allusion to the account given in the *Phaedo* (96a–100b) of Socrates' early enthusiam for (and subsequent disillusionment with) the natural philosophy of Anaxagoras. The *Ion* concludes that the gods are the ultimate source of inspiration for poets, rhapsodes and the arts in general.

What are some characteristics of the divine? Xenophon's account gives us some clues. Socrates says:

Ἔοικας, ὦ Ἀντιφῶν, τὴν εὐδαιμονίαν οἰομένῳ τρυφὴν καὶ πολυτέλειαν εἶναι· ἐγὼ δὲ νομίζω τὸ μὲν μηδενὸς δεῖσθαι θεῖον εἶναι, τὸ δ' ὡς ἐλαχίστων ἐγγυτάτω τοῦ θείου, καὶ τὸ μὲν θεῖον κράτιστον, τὸ δ' ἐγγυτάτω τοῦ θείου ἐγγυτάτω τοῦ κρατίστου.

You seem, Antiphon, to imagine that happiness consists in luxury and extravagance. But I believe that to have no wants is divine; to have as few as possible comes next to the divine; and as that which is divine is supreme, so that which [is] nearest to the divine is nearest to the supreme.[36]

To be divine is τὸ μηδενὸς δεῖσθαι, to stand in need of nothing—to be self-sufficient. Socrates' acceptance of this feature of the divine is attested by the Platonic evidence as well. In dialogue with Euthyphro about the nature of θεραπεία, 'care,' which 'aims at the good and the benefit of the object cared for' (*Euthyphro* 13b5), and whether piety can properly be considered 'care of the gods' in the same way, viz. θεῶν ὠφέλεια τέ ἐστι θεῶν καὶ βελτίους τοὺς θεοὺς ποιεῖ, 'to benefit the gods and make them better' (13c6), Socrates and Euthyphro readily concur that piety is not care in this way, precisely because it is ridiculous to suppose that the gods stand in need of benefit from any external source.[37]

If this criterion applied to the human condition—if human beings could be considered self-sufficient in the relevant way(s)—this would supply a persuasive argument against drawing a sharp distinction between divine and human nature. However, Socrates indicates that self-sufficiency is a condition proper (ἴδιον) to the divine nature; and so we cannot credibly use it as a standard for the εὐδαιμονία proper to human beings.

Intimately tied to the characteristic of self-sufficiency is a second feature of the divine: the *locus* of value in divine pursuits, unlike human value, is something quite separate and separable from considerations of benefit, or ὠφέλεια. Xenophon's *Memorabilia* I.i.11–16 recounts both the fact of Socrates' move away from philosophical inquiry into τὰ θεῖα— even calling those who pursue it 'μωραίνοντας,' foolish (I.i.11)—and his justifications for this move. The following passage illustrates clearly the Socratic line of reasoning about the worth of such inquiry:

ἐσκόπει δὲ περὶ αὐτῶν καὶ τάδε, ἆρ' ὥσπερ οἱ τἀνθρώπεια μανθάνοντες ἡγοῦνται τοῦθ' ὅ τι ἂν μάθωσιν ἑαυτοῖς τε καὶ τῶν ἄλλων ὅτῳ ἂν βούλωνται ποιήσειν, οὕτω καὶ οἱ τὰ θεῖα ζητοῦντες νομίζουσιν, ἐπειδὰν γνῶσιν, αἷς ἀνάγκαις ἕκαστα γίγνεται, ποιήσειν, ὅταν βούλωνται, καὶ ἀνέμους καὶ ὕδατα καὶ ὥρας καὶ ὅτου ἂν ἄλλου δέωνται τῶν τοιούτων, ἢ τοιοῦτο μὲν οὐδὲν οὐδ' ἐλπίζουσιν, ἀρκεῖ δ'αὐτοῖς γνῶναι μόνον, ᾗ τῶν τοιούτων ἕκαστα γίγνεται. Περὶ μὲν οὖν τῶν ταῦτα πραγματευομένων τοιαῦτα ἔλεγεν.

And he asked about [natural philosophers] these things too: just as students of human matters, he said, think that they will apply that which they have learned in due course for their own sake and for any others they choose; just so, do those who inquire into heavenly phenomena think that, when once they have discovered the laws by which these are produced, they will create, at their will, winds, waters, seasons, and such things to their need, or do they have no such expectation, and is it enough for them only to know from where each of these arises? In this way, then, he spoke of those who concern themselves with these matters.[38]

The motivation underlying this criticism of the natural philosophers could not be much clearer. Philosophy is taken to be a purposeful pursuit, dedicated to achieving the good for particular human beings. Inquiry which has no avenue of tangible benefit for anyone, beyond 'knowing the causes' of phenomena, is, in the context of human benefit, a deficient enterprise; or, at least, one whose pursuit is by rights ancillary to the main business of philosophy, worthy of pursuit only once the important matters have been settled (I.i.12). In short, Socrates, according to Xenophon, αὐτὸς δὲ περὶ τῶν ἀνθρωπίνων ἀεὶ διελέγετο σκοπῶν, 'himself always inquired [by] investigating about human matters' (I.i.16); with the understanding that the characteristic of his method which makes it distinctly, and uniquely, human is its purposeful pursuit of ὠφέλεια in living. Inquiry into divine matters, encompassing knowledge for its own sake, ranges far beyond the Socratic conception of philosophy.

Plato presents a portrait of Socrates consistent with the preceding account. However much Plato's account of Socrates differs from Xenophon's in other areas, his description of Socrates' philosophical mission as specifically directed toward the lived human life, and sharply distinguished from the pursuit of abstracted, idealized or disconnected inquiry, reads from the same script. A broad point of agreement is that Socrates intensely cares about investigating the sorts of questions central to the human condition, rather than the abstruse and abstract inquiries and hypotheses of natural philosophy. On Socrates' rejection of inquiry into τὰ δαιμονία in the 'early' Platonic dialogues, we need look no further than the charges levelled by Meletus: Σωκράτης ἀδικεῖ καὶ περιεργάζεται ζητῶν τά τε ὑπὸ γῆς καὶ οὐράνια, 'Socrates commits injustice and engages in inquiries about things heavenly and those beneath the earth' (Plato *Apology* 19c), the sorts of inquiries quintessentially characteristic of the natural philosophers. Again, compare his rejection of Anaxagoras' natural philosophy in the *Phaedo* 96a–100b. After recounting that, as a youth, he was 'wonderfully keen on that wisdom which they call natural science' (96a), he tells Cebes that he became disillusioned with the field because this 'old method of investigation' (97b) led to skeptical confusion rather than any increase in knowledge or wisdom. Upon hearing someone reading Anaxagoras' work, Socrates believes that Anaxagoras is pursuing philosophical investigation in the right sort of way, since his work claimed:

...νοῦς ἐστιν ὁ διακοσμῶν τε καὶ πάντων αἴτιος, ταύτῃ δὴ τῇ αἰτίᾳ ἥσθην τε καὶ ἔδοξέ μοι τρόπον τινὰ εὖ ἔχειν τὸ τὸν νοῦν εἶναι πάντων αἴτιον, καὶ ἡγησάμην, εἰ τοῦθ' οὕτως ἔχει, τόν γε νοῦν κοσμοῦντα πάντα κοσμεῖν καὶ ἕκαστον τιθέναι ταύτῃ ὅπῃ ἂν βέλτιστα ἔχῃ...ἐκ δὲ δὴ τοῦ λόγου τούτου οὐδὲν ἄλλο σκοπεῖν προσήκειν ἀνθρώπῳ καὶ περὶ αὐτοῦ ἐκείνου καὶ περὶ τῶν ἄλλων ἀλλ' ἢ τὸ ἄριστον καὶ τὸ βέλτιστον.

...Mind directs and is the cause of everything. I was delighted with this cause and it seemed to me good, in a way, that Mind should be the cause of all. I thought that if this were so, the directing Mind would direct everything and arrange each thing in the way that was best....On these premises then it befitted a man to investigate only, about this and other things, what is best.[39]

Socrates goes on to explain his ultimate hopes for what Anaxagoras would finally achieve: ἑκάστῳ οὖν αὐτῶν ἀποδιδόντα τὴν αἰτίαν καὶ κοινῇ πᾶσι τὸ ἑκάστῳ βέλτιστον ᾤμην καὶ τὸ κοινὸν πᾶσιν ἐπεκδιηγήσεσθαι ἀγαθόν: καὶ οὐκ ἂν ἀπεδόμην πολλοῦ τὰς ἐλπίδας, 'Once he had given the best for each [natural phenomenon] as the cause for each and the general cause of all, I thought he would go on to explain the common good for all, and I would not have exchanged my hopes for a fortune' (98b). Socrates' hope was to find a philosophical explanation of the world whose ultimate achievement was an explanation of 'the common good for all'—that is, a metaphysics which rests on the basis of a conception of the good, one whose fundamental explanatory principle was located in considerations of Mind and the good, rather than principles or elements or random factors. Even though the Socrates of the *Phaedo* is generally considered the mouthpiece of Plato's middle period doctrines, rather than representative of Socrates himself, the motivation attributed to him here is by no means at odds with that found in the 'early' dialogues: the only times Socrates uses language that blurs the distinction between the divine and the human are in later, Platonic dialogues—e.g. θεοφιλῆς in *Symposium* 212a, ὁμοίωσις θεῷ[40] in *Theaetetus* 176b1–2. Contemporary scholars have noted the peculiarly human nature and focus of Socrates in Plato, as well. Vlastos comments on the decidedly non-mystical approach of the Socrates of the early dialogues: '[Socrates'] relation to the divine world is severely practical—ethical, not mystical...[His] relation to the god is never intimate. Of ecstatic union with his god, or *even of imitation of his god* there is never a hint.'[41]

Why does Socrates make this point so insistently? What philosophical significance is there in the distinction between the divine and the human, and the matters proper to investigating each? In short, how is philosophy 'in urbibus' significantly different from philosophy 'in caelō'?

Human Matters (τἀνθρώπινα). Even within the ancient reception of Socrates, the theme of the Socratic humanistic focus stands out in high relief. We have seen above that, in rejecting τὰ δαιμόνια, Socrates is specifically rejecting a sort of philosophical inquiry that is disconnected from a pursuit of the final goal of the human good as related to the lived experience. Our inquiry will benefit from examining what things are uniquely 'human' about this human-directed philosophy, and the 'human' good that is its professed *raison d'être*.

One not insignificant feature of the human condition is its limited nature. In the *Apology*, for instance, Socrates' commitment to the specifically human realm is evident. He tells the jury that his reputation is διὰ σοφίαν τινὰ, 'on account of a certain wisdom,' and specifies: ποίαν δὴ σοφίαν ταύτην; ἥπερ ἐστὶν ἴσως ἀνθρωπίνη σοφία, 'What kind of wisdom is this? It is perhaps a *human* wisdom.'[42] Nowhere in the undisputedly Socratic literature do we see any hint of a transcendent intellectualism, proclaiming man's ability to cast off the hindrances of his 'mere' human nature in pursuit of a 'pure' rationality. Aristotle testifies that 'Socrates did not, however, separate the universal or the definitions, but they [viz. Plato and his students] did, calling them the Forms of things' (*Metaphysics* 1078b29–32). Variations of this language, and this philosophic project of 'separation,' are characteristic of Plato and the Stoics (and even Aristotle himself, at least according to the contemporary intellectualist interpretation of his ethical works). On the contrary, the historical Socrates of both Xenophon and Plato approaches human beings as they are, in all their complexity, striving toward improving us without simplifying away our given, real-world messiness.

Characteristic of this messiness and Socrates' refusal to 'clean it up' conceptually is the fact that the two most interesting positive doctrines accepted as the Socratic legacy have been labeled 'the Socratic paradoxes': (a) virtue is knowledge and (b) no one does wrong intentionally (οὐδεὶς ἐκὼν ἐξαμαρτάνει) (*Meno* 77b ff., *Hippias Minor* 375d–376b, *Hippias Major* 296c, *Gorgias* 488a, 509e, *Apology* 25d–26a, *Protagoras* 345e, *Rep.* I.336e, 589c).[43] Each of these theses is a paradox because of some discrepancy in observed human practice, not a theoretic inconsistency. In the first case, Socrates begins to question the thesis, even though the preceding *elenchus* with Meno has in itself achieved a seemingly unequivocal identification, upon realizing that there do not seem to be any teachers of virtue in human society; in the second, our lived experience of ἀκρασία, and the testimony of history and psychology, directly challenge the ideal rational self-interest.

Xenophon's testimony gives us less philosophically detailed insight into Socrates' conception of the character of human nature. However, the general point is just as clearly made as in Plato, though in terms more broadly applicable to Socrates' thought and life. In particular, Xenophon shows Socrates addressing the question of the relation of the body and its care to one's proper concern for the soul and its cultivation. It is noteworthy that Socrates endorses a 'mēns sana in corpore sanō' conception of well-being. In the *Memorabilia* III.xii.5–6, Socrates, in conversation with Epigenes about the young man's poor physical health, says πρὸς παντα γάρ, ὅσα πράττουσιν ἄνθρωποι, χρήσιμον τὸ σῶμά ἐστιν...ἐπεὶ καὶ ἐν ᾧ δοκεῖς ἐλαχίστην σώματος χρείαν εἶναι, ἐν τῷ διανοεῖσθαι, τίς οὐκ οἶδεν, ὅτι καὶ ἐν τούτῳ πολλοὶ μεγάλα σφάλλονται διὰ τὸ μὴ ὑγιαίνειν τὸ σῶμα, 'in everything that men do the body is useful...indeed even that in which you see the least need of the body, in the process of thinking, who doesn't know that even in this case many people commit great mistakes on account of the body being in ill health.' Again at IV.vii.9, '[Socrates] also strongly urged his companions to take care of their health.' Xenophon's Socrates expresses his consideration for the physical self erhaps most explicitly at I.ii.4:

ἀλλὰ μὴν καὶ τοῦ σώματος αὐτός τε οὐκ ἠμέλει τούς τ' ἀμελοῦντας οὐκ ἐπήνει...τὸ δὲ ὅσα γ' ἡδέως ἡ ψυχὴ δέχεται, ταῦτα ἱκανῶς ἐκπονεῖν ἐδοκίμαζε. ταύτην γὰρ τὴν ἕξιν ὑγιεινήν τε ἱκανῶς εἶναι καὶ τὴν τῆς ψυχῆς ἐπιμέλειαν οὐκ ἐμποδίζειν ἔφη.

But he himself did not neglect the body, and reproved those who did... And he approved of taking as much hard exercise as is agreeable to the soul; for the habit not only insured good health, but *did not hamper the care of the soul*.[44]

Socrates shows that he is fully aware of the potential conflicts here, and their philosophical consequences. We cannot attribute his pragmatic, synthetic conception merely to the philosophical unsophistication of Xenophon as chronicler. Socrates acknowledges that physical care is subordinate to, and limited by, the care of the soul; and he speaks about the body's role in διανοεῖσθαι as χρεία, usefulness. Yet these facts do not permit one to relegate concern for the body to the status of irrelevance or indifference; rather, by recognizing a) that care for the body, when undertaken in moderation, will not interfere with care for the soul, and b) that bodily flourishing is a necessary condition for the proper exercise of one's rational faculty, Socrates sets up the parameters of a specifically human course of action for pursuing εὐδαιμονία that incorporates intellectual and bodily flourishing in a balanced and complementary mix, but maintains the privileged role of the rational faculty and its exercise.[45]

It is particularly and essentially human to partake of a sense of δικαιοσύνη, justice (*Protagoras* 323c). *Protagoras* 320d–323c recounts

Protagoras' myth of the distribution of the various abilities to human beings. Certainly Socrates takes issue with Protagoras' imprecision about ἀρετή, among other things, in this mythic exposition. However, one of the things to which he does not take exception is Protagoras' attribution of δικαιοσύνη to humanity as ἴδιον. Justice is standardly conceived as a quintessentially social virtue, one whose essence is bound up in application in the context of civil society.

What, if anything, underlies and gives common ground to the claims Socrates makes about what intrinsically constitutes the specifically human experience? Socrates' mythic account of death, at *Gorgias* 524b–527a, is useful in discovering his underlying conception of the relation of humans' physical and mental parts within human nature as a whole. Socrates describes death as the separation of soul and body, after which the three judges Minos, Aeacus, and Rhadamanthus evaluate the soul in light of its virtuous or vicious history. On an initial reading, this story might seem to support the 'σῶμα = σῆμα' conception of human embodiment—that we are essentially spiritual, and our physical parts are mere, ultimately disposable, impediments. After all, Socrates does refer to soul and body as two separable things (524b3), each with its own nature (524b6); and the final adjudication of one's life and eternal fate is made solely on the evidence of the soul, not the body (524e–525a). However, an overlooked aspect of this account is this: it is the soul *in its embodied state* that is judged. There is no possibility for a separated soul to take actions that affect its evaluation; a soul separated from a body is incapable of acting virtuously or viciously, since there is necessarily no context for action. Taking the broad view, one can see that it is the acknowledgement of the disparate elements that are relevant and causally efficacious in practice. Socrates places incredible faith in the potential of rational inquiry and character development as the best and most paradigmatically proper methods of pursuing εὐδαιμονία—there is no question about this fact. The crucial point to recognize is that this fact by no means necessarily precludes admitting that there are other factors that matter in our pursuit of happiness and the good, factors which, if ignored or devalued, will always and necessarily return to wreak havoc with any explanatory thesis that fails to take full account of them. Vlastos, as we have seen, recognizes this point in arguing against the so-called 'Identity Thesis' for virtue and happiness:

> if Identity were the true relation of virtue to happiness, *we would have no rational ground for preference between alternatives which are equally consistent*

with virtue—hence no rational ground for preference between states of affairs differentiated only by their non-moral values. And if this were true, it would knock out the bottom from eudaemonism as a theory of rational choice... if happiness were identical with virtue, our final reason for choosing anything at all would have to be only concern for our virtue; so the multitude of choices that have nothing to do with that concern would be left unexplained.[46]

Granted, as we have seen, Socrates accepts the general eudaimonistic thesis that all rational human action is teleological—explicitly defended at *Gorgias* 467d–468d, 499e7–8; *Lysis* 219c-d argues for a *terminus ad quem* for this teleology (cf. Arist. *EN* i.2 1094a18–22)—and that the practice of virtue is the *sine quā nōn* for happiness. These claims are well and uncontroversially documented. However, interpreting Socrates' overall conception of εὐδαιμονία *only* in light of the above two theses leads to the untenable consequences Vlastos recognizes: a strict identity of virtue and knowledge destroys the value of Socrates' eudaimonism as an explanation of, or guide for, practical human living. This produces no formal paradox, but it does produce a consequence antithetical to the intent of the entire Socratic project—a consequence Socrates himself would unquestionably reject. What remains, then, must be a eudaimonism that, while defending the centrality of wisdom and virtue for happiness, also embraces and accounts for, as far as possible, the realities of the human experience that fall outside those noble categories.

Later mentions of Socrates' approach to philosophy tend to cement the description given by his immediate contemporaries and successors. Aristotle, for instance, writes about Σωκράτους δὲ περὶ μὲν τὰ ἠθικὰ πραγματευομένου περὶ δὲ τῆς ὅλης φύσεως οὐθέν, 'Socrates, disregarding the physical universe and confining his study to moral questions.'[47] Cicero knows Socrates as 'the first who called philosophy down from heaven.'[48] Diogenes Laertius' *Lives* 2.16 and 2.45 portray Socrates as nothing if not concerned with human conduct. All the extant accounts concur on the essence of Socrates' philosophical project. What is justice? What is piety? What is beauty? And, underlying all these, what is the good life? These are the matters that engage and constitute Socratic inquiry—specifically ἀνθρώπινα, not δαιμόνια, matters.

External Goods (τὰ ἐκτός) and εὐδαιμονία

Given that Socrates' aim is to search out the sorts of things that truly count in living a human life, we have much evidence to support the idea that Socrates recognized a suitable place for external goods in his conception of the happy life. In the previous section I defended three proposals: a) Socrates held a conception of happiness concerned with specifically *human* matters, as separate from *divine* matters. b) He had a well-developed and articulated set of beliefs concerning what sorts of activities were characteristic of each category. c) Socrates considered it his own god-given duty, as well as the duty of philosophy and philosophers in general, precisely to promote the human, and *not* to inquire into the divine for its own sake, or at the expense of philosophy's primary task. Given these premises, the salient inquiry is to discover Socrates' views concerning the role within happiness of the specifically *human* components of life—those items that are important for physically embodied, composite, social, *and* rational beings, whose possibilities for rational conduct are inextricably commingled with considerations of their physical, physiological, psychological, and social environments.[49]

External Goods (τὰ ἐκτός) as Goods (τὰ ἀγαθά). Arguments concerning external goods, specifically how Socrates conceives of their relation to wisdom and their possible identification as goods proper, are found particularly in the *Euthydemus* and *Meno*. In these dialogues Socrates begins by establishing two complementary theses: that people take good fortune (εὐτυχία) to be 'the greatest of the goods,' and that wisdom can be identified with good fortune because it makes people more fortunate (*Euthydemus* 279c7-8; 279d6). The reason for this is because wisdom never makes a mistake 'but must necessarily do right and be lucky—otherwise she would no longer be wisdom' (*Euthydemus* 280a7-8). Inasmuch as wisdom rules and rightly conducts action, it provides people with good fortune and well-doing (εὐπραγία) (*Euthydemus* 281b). The commonly-held thesis that we do well through having many goods might, then, be true, on one important condition: that what people usually call 'goods'—wealth, health, and the other standard external goods—are not goods *simpliciter* and *per se*, but count as goods if and only if wisdom rules over them (*Euthydemus* 281a8–e1). We are not made happy by the mere presence of things such as wealth or beauty (*Meno* 87e-88a), because such things can harm us if not guided by wisdom. Similarly, if one takes away knowledge from crafts, such as medicine or shoemaking, no craft can be performed rightly: medicine cannot produce health, nor can shoemaking produce shoes, nor can the pilot's craft prevent loss of life at sea (*Charmides* 174c-d). The right use of these goods (wealth, beauty) and crafts (medicine, shoemaking, piloting) benefits us, and their wrong use harms us (*Meno* 88a-b); knowledge is what guarantees their right use. This distinction can be applied to the moral virtues as well. If we suppose that a moral good, such as courage, is a certain kind of recklessness or boldness, and that, accordingly, it is not accompanied by wisdom, it can indeed harm us. If we want to defend the thesis that external goods are beneficial components of the happy life, they must somehow be forms of wisdom, since 'all the qualities of the soul are in themselves neither beneficial nor harmful,' but when directed by wisdom or folly they become beneficial or harmful (*Meno* 88c-d)—and this holds true, *a fortiori*, of external goods as well.

The only way external goods could possibly participate in εὐδαιμονία, then, would be in a secondary and dependent relation to wisdom, never as fully autonomous or freestanding components. However, does this ancillary nature of external goods establish a much stronger conclusion—that external goods have *no* part in εὐδαιμονία, as some commentators would have us believe? Are we justified in concluding that wisdom is *entirely* constitutive of happiness, based on the premise that it, and nothing else, is the only necessary and sufficient component? We have seen that Vlastos vigorously defends a multicomponent model of εὐδαιμονία based on the Sufficiency Thesis, claiming that virtue is the 'sovereign' good, both necessary and sufficient for happiness, but that there are other components to happiness as well. These other components, such as health, wealth, and so on, though themselves neither necessary nor sufficient for happiness, still enhance happiness if present and used or enjoyed in conjunction with virtue. Does Socrates ever implicitly accept, or even explicitly admit, that any external good counts as a good proper? It will be illuminating to examine the textual evidence, to determine whether such an interpretation is viable.

One of the first issues to be addressed is the question of degrees of happiness. If we want to include external goods within the Socratic conception of εὐδαιμονία, and it is quite obvious that external goods vary tremendously over time for any given individual, it would seem that happiness must admit of degrees. Is this position compatible with the evidence? If not, there will be a significant argument against considering τὰ ἐκτός as goods proper. Although we do not have explicit textual support for a positive statement of this position, we do have strong indirect evidence in at least two dialogues. First, in the *Euthydemus*, Socrates asks the following question: [νοῦν μὴ ἔχων] οὐκ ἐλάττω πράττων ἐλάττω ἂν ἐξαμαρτάνοι, ἐλάττω δὲ ἁμαρτάνων ἧττον ἂν κακῶς πράττοι, ἧττον δὲ κακῶς πράττων ἄθλιος ἧττον ἂν εἴη; 'if [the man without wisdom] did less, would he not make fewer mistakes; and if he made fewer mistakes, would he not do less badly, and if he did less badly, would he not be less miserable?' (*Euthydemus* 281c1–3). Second, in the *Gorgias*, Socrates says: δεύτερον ἄρα ἐστὶν τῶν κακῶν μεγέθει τὸ ἀδικεῖν· τὸ δὲ ἀδικοῦντα μὴ διδόναι δίκην πάντων μέγιστόν τε καὶ πρῶτον κακῶν πέφυκεν, 'and so to commit injustice is the second of evils with respect to magnitude: but not to pay the penalty, once having committed injustice, is naturally the greatest and the foremost of all evils' (*Gorgias* 479d6–9). In both cases, the subject of Socrates' conversation is *unhappiness* or *doing badly*, not the opposite. However, what is critical to note is the use of comparative and superlative language: ἐλάττω, ἧττον, δεύτερον, μέγιστόν τε καὶ πρῶτον. Socrates, in these two separate contexts, is clearly embracing a conception of unhappiness that admits of degrees. One can be more or less badly off, and to be less badly off than one was previously is of course a more desirable state of affairs. Since this is so, it is by no means unwarranted to suppose, *ceteris paribus*, that Socrates conceives of *happiness* or *doing well* as admitting of degrees as well.[50] We should readily admit that this is a relatively unsupported and tenuous conclusion, and should be ready to reexamine it should occasion arise. But in the absence of textual evidence to the contrary, we can accept it as at least provisionally reasonable, especially if, as we will argue in what follows, this position accords well with the body of other evidence supporting a role for τὰ ἐκτός in εὐδαιμονία.[51]

Of course, the claim that εὐδαιμονία admits of degrees does not by itself permit us our intended conclusion. It does, however, contribute a telling piece of evidence against any 'unicomponent' model of Socratic eudaimonism, by showing the implausibility of a strict, οὐδὲν ἄλλο interpretation independent of circumstance.

Fortunately, we need not rely solely on indirect and circumstantial evidence. There are at least six references, in four Platonic dialogues, in

44

which Socrates explicitly identifies one or more of the external goods as goods proper: *Gorgias* 467e1–468b4 and 469b12–c2, *Lysis* 218e, *Meno* 78c and 87e–88a, and *Euthydemus* 279a-b. Bare textual references would be insufficient grounds on which to stake a claim, especially given the contested nature of this area of scholarship. However, combined with the rest of the evidence presented in this chapter, they represent a firm capstone to an overall interpretation of the Socratic eudaimonism that recognizes a proper role for τὰ ἐκτός as τὰ ἀγαθά, and as such, legitimate components of a properly human εὐδαιμονία when subordinated to, and used in conjunction with, the supreme ingredient of ἀρετή.

Euthydemus 279a4 expresses Socrates' guiding question to Clinias: 'ἀγαθὰ δὲ ποῖα ἄρα τῶν ὄντων τυγχάνει ἡμῖν ὄντα;,' 'but what sorts of existing things happen to be goods for us?' The lines that follow rely on consensus, and not argumentation, to enumerate the various options viable according to common opinion: τὸ πλουτεῖν, to be rich; τὸ ὑγιαίνειν, to be healthy; τὸ καλὸν εἶναι, to be noble; τἆλλα κατὰ τὸ σῶμα ἱκανῶς παρεσκευάσθαι, to have a sufficient supply of things for the body; εὐγένειαί, high birth; δυνάμεις, power; τιμαί, honors; τὸ σώφρονά εἶναι, to be self-controlled; τὸ δίκαιον εἶναι, to be just; τὸ ἀνδρεῖον εἶναι, to be courageous; σοφία, wisdom; and εὐτυχία, good fortune (which Socrates quickly seems to reduce to σοφία in 279d8 ff). Once Socrates and Clinias embark on their elenctic examination of these topics, they conclude that it is wisdom, and wisdom alone, which is the supreme good. The reasoning behind this conclusion (*pace* Socrates' protestation at 280b, οὐκ οἶδ' ὅπως) can be outlined thus:

P1. Only wisdom gives rise to correct use of the materials at one's disposal: τὸ ὀρθῶς ἐπιστήμη ἐστὶν ἡ ἀπεργαζομένη, it is right knowledge which makes [a craft] complete. (281a)

P2. It is only correct use of one's goods, never mere possession, that benefits or is advantageous to one: δεῖ ἄρα, ἔφην, ὡς ἔοικεν, μὴ μόνον κεκτῆσθαι τὰ τοιαῦτα ἀγαθὰ τὸν μέλλοντα εὐδαίμονα ἔσεσθαι, ἀλλὰ καὶ χρῆσθαι αὐτοῖς: ἢ οὐδὲν ὄφελος τῆς κτήσεως γίγνεται, So, I said, it is necessary, as it seems, that the one intending to be happy not only possess such goods, but also use them: or else there is no benefit of the possession. (280d)

P3. Deriving benefit from good things makes one happy: ἆρ' οὖν εὐδαιμονοῖμεν ἂν διὰ τὰ παρόντα ἀγαθά, εἰ μηδὲν ἡμᾶς ὠφελοῖ ἢ εἰ ὠφελοῖ; εἰ ὠφελοῖ, ἔφη, So then, are we happy through the presence of goods, if it doesn't benefit us or if it does? If it does, he said. (280c)

C. Thus only knowledge gives rise to, or produces, true happiness: οὐ μόνον ἄρα εὐτυχίαν ἀλλὰ καὶ εὐπραγίαν, ὡς ἔοικεν, ἡ ἐπιστήμη παρέχει τοῖς ἀνθρώποις ἐν πάσῃ κτήσει τε καὶ πράξει, So, as it seems, knowledge provides to men not only good fortune but also good action, in all possession and also in all practice. (281b)

This argument, taken with Socrates' comment at 281e—τί οὖν ἡμῖν συμβαίνει ἐκ τῶν εἰρημένων; ἄλλο τι ἢ τῶν μὲν ἄλλων οὐδὲν ὂν οὔτε ἀγαθὸν οὔτε κακόν, τούτοιν δὲ δυοῖν ὄντοιν ἡ μὲν σοφία ἀγαθόν, ἡ δὲ ἀμαθία κακόν; 'Then what is the result of our conversation? Isn't it that, of the other things, no one of them is either good or bad, but of these two, wisdom is good and ignorance bad?'—appears conclusively to reject the earlier catalogue of common-sense 'goods.' One suspects that the Stoics relied much on this text. However, the argument has in fact done nothing to reject the other goods out of hand, only to establish ἐπιστημή as the *sine quā nōn* of εὐδαιμονία. Let us look closely at a comment Socrates makes at 281d to summarize the argument's conclusions:

ἐν κεφαλαίῳ δ,' ἔφην, ὦ Κλεινία, κινδυνεύει σύμπαντα ἃ τὸ πρῶτον ἔφαμεν ἀγαθὰ εἶναι, οὐ περὶ τούτου ὁ λόγος αὐτοῖς εἶναι, ὅπως αὐτά γε καθ' αὑτὰ πέφυκεν ἀγαθὰ [εἶναι], ἀλλ' ὡς ἔοικεν ὧδ' ἔχει· ἐὰν μὲν αὐτῶν ἡγῆται ἀμαθία, μείζω κακὰ εἶναι τῶν ἐναντίων, ὅσῳ δυνατώτερα ὑπηρετεῖν τῷ ἡγουμένῳ κακῷ ὄντι, ἐὰν δὲ φρόνησίς τε καὶ σοφία, μείζω ἀγαθά, αὐτὰ δὲ καθ' αὑτὰ οὐδέτερα αὑτῶν οὐδενὸς ἄξια εἶναι.

From the top, then, Clinias, I said, it seems likely, with respect to all those things which we said to be goods at first, that the account for them is not about this, that they are by nature and through themselves goods, but as it seems thus: if ignorance is in control of them, [they] are greater evils than their opposites, inasmuch as they are more able to obey an evil master, but if practical wisdom and wisdom [are in control of them], they are greater goods, but themselves, through themselves, neither of them are at all valuable.[52]

Unlike his sweeping generalization a few lines later, that 'no one of them is either good or bad,' Socrates here still allows 'all those things which we said to be goods at first' properly in the category of goods and evils. To be sure, they are goods or evils only when ἡγῆται ἀμαθία or φρόνησίς τε καὶ σοφία, never αὐτὰ καθ' αὐτά. But then, in the context of human action, when *would* external goods ever be relevant αὐτὰ καθ' αὐτὰ, absent the direction of knowledge or its lack? In fact, once Socrates and Clinias establish p2) above, that mere possession never benefits, they have already ruled out the relevance of κτῆσις, and *a fortiori* of external goods considered αὐτὰ καθ' αὐτά.

At most, then, the argument above establishes that τὰ ἐκτός are not properly τὰ ἀγαθά when considered αὐτὰ καθ' αὐτά. But this is far from a decisive blow. In fact, we see, a few lines later, that this argument has *no* evidentiary force against considering external goods as goods *at all*, precisely because a parallel argument can be made against *whatever* one wishes to identify as goods. As Socrates prepares to move the argument forward, and examine the consequences of their previous conclusions, he makes the following comment: εὐδαίμονες μὲν εἶναι προθυμούμεθα πάντες, ἐφάνημεν δὲ τοιοῦτοι γιγνόμενοι ἐκ τοῦ χρῆσθαί τε τοῖς πράγμασιν καὶ ὀρθῶς χρῆσθαι, 'we all wish to be happy, and we appear to become so both through using things and using [them] rightly' (282a). The main thrust of the argument has been to establish the irrelevance of external goods considered αὐτὰ καθ' αὐτά. However, the formulation of happiness at 282a locates the emphasis on 'αὐτὰ καθ' αὐτὰ,' no matter what is under consideration: we become happy, first and foremost, through *using things*. Socrates insists on an ineradicable connection between εὐδαιμονία and πρᾶξις, and while ἐπιστημή is indeed a necessary (and sufficient) component of happiness, Socrates states emphatically at 282a that, like τὰ ἐκτός, *it too* would be irrelevant if considered αὐτὴ καθ' αὐτήν, divorced from τὸ χρῆσθαι τοῖς πράγμασιν. The true aim of 281d-e is not to marginalize external goods: rather, by saying that 'αὐτὰ δὲ καθ' αὐτὰ οὐδέτερα αὐτῶν οὐδενὸς ἄξια εἶναι,' Socrates intends to demonstrate the folly of considering *any* ingredients of εὐδαιμονία 'αὐτὰ καθ' αὐτά.'

Once we understand the argument of *Euthydemus* 280–281 according to this interpretation, we realize that, when Socrates explicitly identifies external goods as ἀγαθά in the dialogues—*Gorgias* 467e1–468b4 and 469b12–c2, *Lysis* 218e, *Meno* 78c and 87e–88a, and *Euthydemus* 279a–b—we do not need to shake our heads and chalk it up to human error, an unintended slip of the tongue, a troublesome textual contradiction. Socrates is quite conscientious in identifying external goods as goods—under the correct circumstances, firmly under the control of wisdom, and never αὐτὰ καθ' αὑτὰ—but goods nonetheless.

Conclusion

At first glance, the role played by external goods in Socrates' human inquiry is subject to serious challenge. Socrates famously held that 'virtue is knowledge,' as we have seen above, and that even someone who suffers the greatest misfortunes can truly be called happy, as long as he does not flag in exercising his knowledge. In addition to this doctrinal commitment, attributed to him by Plato, the extant accounts of Socrates' life all show that he demonstrated a singular unconcern for acquiring, enjoying, or retaining the sorts of external goods commonly held to be important: money, property, civic or military honors, or political influence. As we saw earlier, he tells Antiphon 'to have no wants is divine; to have as few as possible comes next to the divine; and as that which is divine is supreme, so that which approaches nearest to its nature is nearest to the supreme.'[53]

Yet we should not judge too hastily, nor leap to the conclusion that an extreme of asceticism represents the pinnacle of virtue *or* of happiness. After all, moderation, not deprivation, is the keyword we find so often in his discussions (*Gorgias* 492b, 504a, 507a; *Laches* 198a, 199d; *Protagoras* 323b; *Meno* 73b et al.), and Socrates himself never endorses nor practices detachment from, but rather throwing oneself into, the enjoyment of the goods of fortune when appropriate. Indeed, enjoyment is recognized as a part of practicing moderation: 'οὐκ οἶσθ', ὅτι ὁ μὲν ἥδιστα ἐσθίων ἥκιστα ὄψου δεῖται, ὁ δὲ ἥδιστα πίνων ἥκιστα τοῦ μὴ παρόντος ἐπιθυμεῖ ποτοῦ;' 'Do you not know that the one eating most pleasantly has the least need of sauce, and the one drinking most pleasantly has the least desire for drink that is not available?' (*Mem.* I.vi.5) A close reading of the evidence in Plato's accounts of Socrates provides a wealth of textual support for the thesis that Socrates, far from being completely unconcerned with external goods in his pursuit of the good life, rather positively recognizes them as, in fact, goods in the precise philosophical sense of that word, given his understanding of human nature and its relation to a specifically human conception of the good. Socrates' preoccupation with human affairs seems quite compatible with a view that he considers external goods to be legitimate, if ancillary, components of living a human life characterized by a specifically human εὐδαιμονία.

Notes

1   See C.P. Parker (1916) for his examination of the issues surrounding the discovery of the historical Socrates. Also useful (and more up-to-date) is Lacey in Vlastos 1971, 22–49.

2   cf. Vlastos 1991, 45: 'The question "Who are you talking about—Socrates *or* a 'Socrates' in Plato?" will dog your steps, barking at you, forcing you to turn and face it in self-defense. If you do mean the former, you must argue for it.'

3   The δίσσοι λόγοι are of course still another crucial piece of the puzzle of reconstructing the general atmostphere and influence of Socrates and Socratic methods. I do not rely on these texts in my arguments, not from a willful desire to ignore their value as source material, but simply from a lack of time and resources to deal properly with the multitude of interpretive, historical and philological problems that would necessarily arise were I to include them. An important modern work on the topic of the δίσσοι λόγοι is Taylor 1911, 91–128. More recent general works include Peter Scholz's 'Philosophy Before Plato: On the Social and Political Conditions of the Composition of the *Dissoi Logoi*' in Detel, Becker and Scholz 2003; Owen Goldin's 'To Tell the Truth: *Dissoi Logoi* 4 and Aristotle's Response' in Caston and Graham 2002; Thomas Robinson's 'The *Dissoi Logoi* and Early Greek Skepticism' in Preus 2001.

4   For a useful methodical and thorough overview of Aristophanes' portrayal of Socrates as a theatrical work, see Dover 1968, reprinted in Vlastos 1971, 50–77.

5   e.g. Verrall 1895, Chiappelli 1886.

6   Taylor 1911, 129ff. argues that the extent of the *Clouds'* value for the history of philosophy is that it 'so exactly confirms the statements of the *Phaedo* as to the entourage of Socrates...as to leave little doubt that the Platonic representation is curiously exact even down to matters of detail.'

7   Vander Waerdt 1994, 51.

8   Diogenes Laertius 7.2. Consider, too, the interesting thesis advanced by DeFilippo and Mitsis in Vander Waerdt 1994, 252–271, that Xenophon's *Memorabilia* was a 'crucial source of reflection' for early Stoic thinking, and Vander Waerdt's contention that 'Xenophon's interpretation of Socratic ethics provided a model that competed with Plato's for the allegiance of Socrates' Hellenistic heirs' (Vander Waerdt 1994, 12), a thesis mentioned approvingly by Striker in Vander Waerdt 1994, 241.

9   Zeller 1818, 50.

10 Baker 1916, 293.

11 Vlastos 1971, 32.

12 Marchant and Todd 2002, xxiii.

13 Since the thesis of this work is quite specific in its scope, many of the conflicts between Xenophon and Plato will turn out to be relevant in a very minor way, if at all, to the arguments made herein. When a serious disagreement arises, it will be taken note of and given attention within the textual discussion of the issue at hand. Though it is fair to give due weight to Plato's philosophical expertise on points of doctrine requiring precision of interpretation, Xenophon provides essential context for the

application of philosophy to the lived experience, and it is precisely this synthesis which, I am arguing, makes sense of Socratic eudaimonism.

14 Vlastos 1991, 45.

15 Cooper (ed.) 1997, xiv.

16 Vlastos 1991, 33.

17 The question of the relative dating of Plato's works, and its relevance for interpreting Socrates and Plato, will be revisited in chapter 2. Some of the core literature on this issue includes Ross 1951, ch.1; Brandwood 1958 and 1976; Young in Taylor 1994; Vlastos 1991, 45–80.

18 Vlastos 1991, 214–224.

19 Cf. *Meno* 72e for a brief investigation of ταὐτόν. As Vlastos notes, Aristotle's is the earliest extant in-depth analysis of the term.

20 Vlastos 1991, 217.

21 Vlastos 1991, 223. Socrates' use of the two terms in context lends further plausibility to the claim that, strictly speaking, we cannot consistently attribute to Socrates the belief that εὐδαιμονία and ἀρετή are *definitionally* ταὐτόν. See e.g. *Euthyphro* 5d ff.; *Rep.* I.354; *Charmides* 173 ff.

22 τὸ εὖ ζῆν, as at *Crito* 48b4, as well as τὸ εὖ πράττειν, are common synonyms for εὐδαιμονία (*Euthydemus* 278e and 282a, *Gorgias* 507b8–c7, *Republic* I.353e10–354a1); δικαιοσύνη is considered one of the five core ἀρεταί (*Protagoras* 349b2 and 369e4, *Laches* 198a8 ff., *Republic* I.332d–336a et al.).

23 Aristotle *EN* 1095a29–30: ἐξετάζειν τὰς δόξας μάλιστα ἐπιπολαζούσας ἢ δοκούσας ἔχειν τινὰ λόγον is a practice well-established.

24 Vlastos 1991, 214.

25 Cf. section 1.3 for further evaluation of this consequence.

26 Irwin 1995, 67,

27 Irwin 1995, 67.

28 Nevertheless, a rather significant chasm exists between the two classes, such that it is appropriate to wonder whether it is misleading so to classify them. One could, for instance, defend a third category, rather than grouping together such seemingly disparate goods as temperance and swiftness. This would involve a rather significant re-evaluation and -interpretation of the Platonic Socrates' ethics—certainly a worthy project, but one somewhat beyond the scope of the current work. I am indebted to Sherwin Klein for bringing this challenge to my attention.

29 Vlastos 1991, 203–204; also 302.

30 Brickhouse and Smith 2000, 128.

31 Brickhouse and Smith 2000, 128.

32 Also *Gorgias* 468b-e, 499d, 525b; *Hippias Major* 284d, 295d, 296e.

33 Section 1.3 will clarify the Socratic position on the necessity of recognizing the features of human beings that are essentially relevant to the sorts of conclusions about virtue and happiness that are appropriate to draw from them.

34 A fuller exploration and defense of this claim is presented in chapter 4.

35 Cf. also Aristotle *EN* I.iii 1094b12–27; I.vii 1098a26–29; II.ii 1103b35–1104a12; III.iii 1112b3–12.

36 Xen. *Mem.* I.vi.10.

37 Indeed, when Socrates and Euthyphro pursue the line of argument proceeding from conceiving of the relation between gods and humans as a 'sort of trading skill' (14e4), and try to uncover what benefits the gods might derive from such transactions, they find themselves arguing circularly for the initial, discarded premise that the pious is

what is dear to the gods (15b3). Compare Aristotle at *EN* 1178b8–24, who uses the terms γελοῖοι, ἄτοπον, and φορτικός in imagining the gods as enacting various virtuous activities.

38 Xenophon, *Memorabilia* I.i.15.
39 Plato, *Phaedo* 97c-d.
40 This concept will feature prominently in chapter 2.
41 Vlastos 1988, 97; emphasis mine.
42 Plato, *Apology* 20d, italics mine.
43 For an interesting parallel expression of this paradox in the non-philosophical literature of the time, cf. Gorgias *Palamedes* 26. See also Calogero 1957 for modern commentary.
44 Xen. *Mem.* I.ii.4; emphasis mine.
45 Just on its own, this argument establishes, at the very least, the *de facto* necessity of some minimal standard of external goods, and concern for their acquisition and maintenance, for any human being pursuing εὐδαιμονία. A subsequent section will present textual evidence in support of the further claim that, not only are concerns with τὰ ἐκτός necessary preconditions, but count as goods, ἀγαθά, proper.
46 Vlastos 1991, 225.
47 Aristotle, *Metaphysics* I.i, 987b1.
48 Cicero, *Tusculanae Disputationes* V.4.
49 Cf. Nussbaum's elegant formulation of this insight: 'Human cognitive limits circumscribe and limit ethical knowledge and discourse; and an important topic *within* ethical discourse must be the determination of an appropriate human attitude towards those limits' (Nussbaum 1986, 8).
50 See Vlastos 1991, 214–217.
51 The idea that εὐδαιμονία admits of degrees is far from novel or unique to Socrates; one need only refer to the contemporary scholarship on inclusivism and intellectualism in Aristotle's ethics to run up against this notion.
52 Plato, *Euthydemus* 281d-e.
53 Xen. *Mem.* I.vi.10.

Chapter 2
The Idealist: Plato in the Realm of Forms

διὸ καὶ πειρᾶσθαι χρὴ ἐνθένδε ἐκεῖσε φεύγειν ὅτι τάχιστα. φυγὴ δὲ ὁμοίωσις θεῷ κατὰ τὸ δυνατόν· ὁμοίωσις δὲ δίκαιον καὶ ὅσιον μετὰ φρονήσεως γενέσθαι.

Wherefore one should make all haste to escape from earth to heaven. And escape is becoming as like god as possible; and to become like god is to become just and pure, with understanding.

Plato, Theaetetus

Introduction

Investigating Plato's position on the role of external goods in εὐδαιμονία is unavoidably complicated. Unlike Socrates, who left no body of written work, and whose positions must be carefully reconstructed from secondary accounts, in Plato's case we suffer from no lack of written evidence. Quite to the contrary, we are confronted with twenty-six distinct works definitively attributable to Plato, of which eighteen are generally agreed to represent Plato's own philosophical positions. Of course, such an extensive corpus of work, written over the course of a lifetime of philosophical development and refinement, frequently falls short of complete internal consistency, even on issues of central import to Plato's thought. And so our very preponderance of textual evidence results in interpretive uncertainty, giving us conflicting accounts of Plato's thought, and no easily discoverable rubric for choosing any given interpretation at the expense of another. Commentary and analysis must, then, frequently concern themselves with aligning or somehow harmonizing Platonic texts which appear *prima facie* incompatible.

In the case of our present study, Plato describes two major directions of thought regarding the nature and attainment of εὐδαιμονία, mutually irresolvable into a single account. In the first case, εὐδαιμονία is consistently identified as δικαιοσύνη, justice, throughout Plato's work; however, beneath this broad claim we find significantly different characterizations of what justice entails. On one hand, several Platonic texts, including the *Philebus* and Book IV of the *Republic*, support, either implicitly or explicitly, a conception of εὐδαιμονία characterized by its central component, the state of harmony among the parts of the soul, which harmony is presented as δικαιοσύνη in the *Republic*. Relying as it does upon Plato's metaphysical thesis of the tripartite soul, this account of εὐδαιμονία stands in need of some method of accounting for the various goods which are appropriate to each part of the soul, and hence each area of human life; nor can it rest content with a unitary, intellectualist or abstracted account of happiness, as long as the human soul contains not only τὸ λογιστικόν, the 'rational' part, but also τὸ θυμοειδες and τὸ ἐπιθυμητικόν, the 'spirited' and 'appetitive' parts. On the other hand, in texts such as *Republic* Book X, *Theaetetus, Timaeus,* and others, we find Plato endorsing a much less humanistic, and more idealistic, philosophical analysis of the best kind of life: εὐδαιμονία described as ὁμοίωσις θεῷ, the state of being like a god. Within this stream of Plato's thought, the primacy of the soul *qua* rational is the focal point of his analysis; and the seeker of the best, and most philosophic, kind of life is enjoined to abandon, as far as possible, the merely mortal realm with its ethically trivial concerns.

As we conduct the present investigation, then, we must stand ready to address several serious and problematic questions. How does Plato's metaphysical analysis of the nature of the human soul circumscribe or guide our conclusions about his eudaimonism? Can Plato actually endorse a 'godlike' life as an expression of εὐδαιμονία proper to human beings given his understanding of what constitutes a proper function? How does Plato's commitment to order as expressive of justice tie in to his identification of justice and happiness, if happiness is essentially divine? It is only through addressing these questions that we can hope eventually to come to understand the role of external goods.

Plato's two different accounts of εὐδαιμονία correspond to two distinct philosophical descriptions he presents of human nature, life, and *proprium* good: the 'mixed' life and the 'highest' life. We will first examine Plato's so-called 'highest' form of life, εὐδαιμονία as ὁμοίωσις θεῷ, the account most typically associated with Plato's ethics. In reviewing the textual and commentary support for this account, we will find much to challenge any attempt at an inclusivist interpretation. When we turn to the portions of Plato's writings that deal with the 'mixed' life, however, we will begin to see that even the strongest arguments in support of the ὁμοίωσις θεῷ account of εὐδαιμονία cannot completely ward off serious doubts about Plato's commitment to a eudaimonistic intellectualism. I believe that, on balance, Plato's core metaphysical and ethical commitments are sufficient not only positively to preclude a plausible intellectualist reading, but also—remaining true to the spirit of Socrates' approach to philosophy—to constitute a pedagogically practical guide to the pursuit of εὐδαιμονία, one conceived as proper to humans as composite beings.

εὐδαιμονία as Justice (δικαιοσύνη)

The initial step Plato takes in conceptualizing happiness is to identify εὐδαιμονία as δικαιοσύνη, justice. This identification is quite implicit and widespread in Greek thought, an underlying assumption shared among many philosophers, although not always made an explicit doctrine. We can, however, find much textual evidence for this link in Plato's writings, from his early, 'Socratic' dialogues through his middle and later periods. In the *Crito*, the character of Socrates asks Crito, τὸ δὲ εὖ καὶ καλῶς καὶ δικαίως ὅτι ταὐτόν ἐστιν, μένει ἢ οὐ μένει; 'does it remain true, or not, that [living] well and [living] nobly and [living] justly are the same?,' with Crito replying in the affirmative (*Crito* 48b6). At 612b1–2 in Book X of the *Republic*, he makes the preliminary and general statement ἀλλ' αὐτὸ δικαιοσύνην αὐτῇ ψυχῇ ἄριστον ηὕρομεν, 'but we consider justice [to be] the best itself[1] for the soul itself.' Only a few lines further down, he elaborates upon this assertion:[2]

ὥστε ἐξ ἀπάντων αὐτῶν δυνατὸν εἶναι συλλογισάμενον αἰρεῖσθαι, πρὸς τὴν τῆς ψυχῆς φύσιν ἀποβλέποντα, τόν τε χείρω καὶ τὸν ἀμείνω βίον, χείρω μὲν καλοῦντα ὃς αὐτὴν ἐκεῖσε ἄξει, εἰς τὸ ἀδικωτέραν γίγνεσθαι, ἀμείνω δὲ ὅστις εἰς τὸ δικαιοτέραν.

so that having considered them, he is able to choose from all these things, considering according to the nature of the soul, the worse and the better life, calling the worse that which leads it [the soul] toward becoming more unjust, but [calling] better whichever [leads it] toward [becoming] more just.[3]

And in the final lines of the *Republic*, Plato caps his work with the following statement:

ἀλλ' ἂν ἐμοὶ πειθώμεθα, νομίζοντες ἀθάνατον ψυχὴν καὶ δυνατὴν πάντα μὲν κακὰ ἀνέχεσθαι, πάντα δὲ ἀγαθά, τῆς ἄνω ὁδοῦ ἀεὶ ἑξόμεθα καὶ δικαιοσύνην μετὰ φρονήσεως παντὶ τρόπῳ ἐπιτηδεύσομεν...καὶ ἐνθάδε καὶ ἐν τῇ χιλιέτει πορείᾳ, ἣν διεληλύθαμεν, εὖ πράττωμεν.

But if we are persuaded by me, we'll believe that the soul is immortal and able to endure every evil and every good, and we'll always hold to the upward path, practicing justice with reason in every way....Hence, both in this life and on the thousand-year journey we've described, we'll do well.[4]

At this point, Plato is using broad brushstrokes to paint the general outline of his conception of happiness; hence the imprecise language he uses here. Although he does not use exclusively forms of εὐδαιμονία or its cognates, instead speaking loosely about 'αὐτῇ ψυχῇ ἄριστον,' 'τὸν ἀμείνω βίον,' and 'εὖ πραττεῖν,' we need not be so pedantic as to take issue with his intended point: the practice of justice (however he will eventually define this) is a necessary part of living the good human life.[5]

Whatever the nature of the good human life turns out to be, we already know some basic facts about its structure. We know that it is intimately connected with justice—and in fact justice is either identical with, or at least a necessary component of it. We know that justice, like virtue generally, is a sort of practice, and is reliant upon the practical both for its development and for its exercise. And so we know already that the good human life is *ex hypothesi* a life consisting in at least some (as yet unspecified) practices, that is to say, some relations with the external world—εὖ πραττεῖν, a 'doing well.' There remains quite a long distance to traverse in the discovery of these relations, but we have already determined that the Plato who wrote the *Republic* has committed himself to an active, engaged conception of εὐδαιμονία. This is an important first step, since it seems to argue *ab initio* against an intellectualist reading of the *Republic*—a significant directional guidepost to Plato's ethics.

Now that we have seen Plato's identity of εὐδαιμονία with δικαιοσύνη, it remains to establish what this identification entails. The next section explores the notion of δικαιοσύνη in the two directions, mentioned above, we find in Plato's works. First we will examine the textual evidence for δικαιοσύνη as essentially a divine state, that of ὁμοίωσις θεῷ. We will then consider an alternate description Plato gives of the nature of justice, namely as ἁρμονία, harmony. We will find that neither of these trends of thought can be easily dismissed, and both offer critical understandings of Plato's thoughts about happiness, making the task of synthesis a challenging one. We hope to arrive at some plausible points of convergence, however, which might offer a means to clarify his understanding of happiness and its relation both to the life of contemplation and to the active life.

δικαιοσύνη as ὁμοιῶσις θεῷ

The use of religious language is pervasive in Plato's writing. This is unsurprising, given that a central aspect of what it means to seek the good life is to understand the proper relationship between man and his world, including, perhaps most importantly, between the human and divine aspects of reality. Matters of death and dying, just action, social cooperation, prosperity, even philosophical inquiry—these necessarily involve an awareness of, and respect for, forces beyond the merely mortal, in the cultural context within which Plato works.[6]

This pervasive awareness of the divine takes two major forms in Athens of the classical period, according to Morgan:[7] what he calls the 'Delphic theology,' and the Orphic-Bacchic-Pythagorean-Eleusinian world. The former is characterized primarily by an awareness of and respect for the definite boundaries between the mortal and the divine, summed up by the traditional maxims of the Pythia: 'nothing too much' and 'know thyself.'[8] The latter posits a continuum between the mortal and the divine based largely on the theoretical supposition of the immortality of the human soul, and emphasizes the possibility of transcending mortality, and achieving divinity, in some fashion, usually via ecstatic ritual. These two religious traditions reflect the competing trends in Plato's conception of εὐδαιμονία; but Plato does not uncritically embrace either of them. Rather, he navigates a course which is intended to assimilate and subsume the best of each within a specifically rational framework. We can see many elements in Plato's ethics with an affinity to the 'Delphic' mode: the focus on politics—that is, applied, rather than theoretical, ethics; elenctic investigation; concern with virtues of character, and not solely those of the intellect. Likewise, from the ecstatic religious tradition, Plato appropriates the concept of the immortality of the human soul;[9] the mystical, mysterious nature of the pursuit of philosophy (cf. e.g. Diotima's speech in the *Symposium*); and, most interestingly for our purposes, the possibility of achieving εὐδαιμονία through ὁμοίωσις θεῷ, the state of being like a god.

We find the best life, or the best kind of life, referred to or linked to the divine in numerous places throughout Plato's writings: at *Symposium* 207c–209e, and again at 212a; at *Apology* 41c-d; at *Timaeus* 90a3–d8, to name a few. In *Phaedrus* 252c–253c we see ὁμοίωσις θεῷ in the context of a mythic use of the traditional Olympian gods as representative of the various kinds of moral character:

> καὶ οὕτω καθ' ἕκαστον θεόν, οὗ ἕκαστος ἦν χορευτής, ἐκεῖνον τιμῶν τε καὶ μιμούμενος εἰς τὸ δυνατὸν ζῇ, ἕως ἂν ᾖ ἀδιάφθορος καὶ τὴν τῇδε πρώτην γένεσιν βιοτεύῃ...καὶ ἐφαπτόμενοι αὐτοῦ τῇ μνήμῃ ἐνθουσιῶντες ἐξ ἐκείνου λαμβάνουσι τὰ ἔθη καὶ τὰ ἐπιτηδεύματα, καθ' ὅσον δυνατὸν θεοῦ ἀνθρώπῳ μετασχεῖν.[10]

> So it is with each of the gods: everyone spends his life honoring the god in whose chorus he danced, and emulates that god in every way he can, so long as he remains undefiled and in his first life down here...and as they are in touch with the god by memory they are inspired by him and adopt his customs and practices, so far as a human being can share a god's life.[11]

In addition to these instances in which Plato describes the best life as divine or divinely-inspired, we see his disposition to privilege the divine in human life in other ways as well. At 589c6 in the *Republic* Book IX, we find Socrates telling Glaucon that 'fine things are those that subordinate the beastlike parts of our nature to the human—or better, perhaps, to the divine (μᾶλλον δὲ ἴσως τὰ ὑπὸ τῷ θείῳ),' placing the original basis for the conventions about what is fine and what is shameful in the contrast between the beastlike and the divine. Similarly, at 590c-d, the slavish individual 'ought to be the slave of that best person who has a divine ruler within himself (ἔχοντος ἐν αὐτῷ τὸ θεῖον ἄρχον)' because 'it is better for everyone to be ruled by divine reason (ὑπὸ θείου καὶ φρονίμου).' With regard to justice as the ruling virtue of human life, *Laws* Book IV 716c tells us that it is god 'who is preeminently the "measure of all things"... and on this principle the moderate man is god's friend, being like him, whereas the immoderate and unjust man is not like him.'[12] In sum, then, it seems plausible to admit, with Sedley, that the significant number of passages dealing directly or indirectly with the notion of ὁμοίωσις θεῷ can count as 'evidence of its growing prominence in Plato's thought around the end of his middle period' (Fine 797).

The central text in which Plato sings the praises of ὁμοίωσις θεῷ, however, is the 'digression' in *Theaetetus* 172b–177c. The topic of argument is whether truth and falsity, knowledge and ignorance are objective or relative, as Protagoras claimed, to the individual's or community's opinions. After showing that Protagoras' 'man is the measure' criterion leads to self-refuting relativism, Socrates guides the discussion to the position that there are at least *some* areas of knowledge in which *some* individuals are more and less in conformity with the truth.

On the cusp of a turn in the argument, Socrates is apparently distracted by an offhand comment made by Theodorus at 172c2 to the effect that, as philosophers, they have sufficient time to pursue arguments at their leisure. This launches Socrates into a rhapsodic digression on the differences between the life of the philosopher and that of the practical man, with the life of the philosopher, unsurprisingly, turning out to be much more authentic and conducive to human happiness.[13] At the conclusion of this comparison, Theodorus regretfully claims that 'if your words convinced everyone as they do me, there would be more peace and less evil on earth' (176a3–4). In response, Socrates cautions:

ἀλλ' οὔτ' ἀπολέσθαι τὰ κακὰ δυνατόν, ὦ Θεόδωρε—ὑπεναντίον γάρ τι τῷ ἀγαθῷ ἀεὶ εἶναι ἀνάγκη—οὔτ' ἐν θεοῖς αὐτὰ ἱδρῦσθαι, τὴν δὲ θνητὴν φύσιν καὶ τόνδε τὸν τόπον περιπολεῖ ἐξ ἀνάγκης. διὸ καὶ πειρᾶσθαι χρὴ ἐνθένδε ἐκεῖσε φεύγειν ὅτι τάχιστα. φυγὴ δὲ ὁμοίωσις θεῷ κατὰ τὸ δυνατόν: ὁμοίωσις δὲ δίκαιον καὶ ὅσιον μετὰ φρονήσεως γενέσθαι.

[i]t is not possible, Theodorus, that evil should be destroyed—for there must always be something opposed to the good; nor is it possible that it should have its seat in heaven. But it must inevitably haunt human life, and prowl about this earth. That is why a man should make all haste to escape from earth to heaven; and escape means becoming as like god as possible; and a man becomes like god when he becomes just and pure, with understanding.[14]

This passage lays out some metaphysical suppositions about the existence of the Good, among which are the claims that (a) evils necessarily exist; (b) it is impossible for them to exist ἐν θεοῖς, among the gods; and so (c) evils necessarily περιπολεῖ, 'prowl around,' human nature and this τόπος. We will have much to say later about human nature and how it determines the good for us; for now let us simply note some consequences attendant upon this picture.

Socrates tells us that evils are a necessary condition of mortality, and that our very nature is beset with them; but we can hope for φυγή, escape, if we become just and pure μετὰ φρονήσεως, in accordance with φρόνησις, as much as possible. Our achievement of the Good, and true happiness, is directly proportional to our ability to leave behind the sullied mortal realm and approach the pure realm of the Good, true wisdom, the Forms. The *Timaeus* passage shows us that it is not our entire human nature which permits us the potential for achieving happiness, but one part only—τὸ θεῖον, the divine part.

Only a few lines later, Socrates clarifies exactly what it would mean to become like god: θεὸς οὐδαμῇ οὐδαμῶς ἄδικος, ἀλλ' ὡς οἷόν τε δικαιότατος, καὶ οὐκ ἔστιν αὐτῷ ὁμοιότερον οὐδὲν ἢ ὃς ἂν ἡμῶν αὖ γένηται ὅτι δικαιότατος, 'in god there is no sort of wrong whatsoever; he is supremely just, and the thing most like him is the man who has become as just as it lies in human nature to be' (176c3-4). Finally, he explicitly identifies this ὁμοίωσις as the goal of human life: ἡ μὲν γὰρ τούτου γνῶσις σοφία καὶ ἀρετὴ ἀληθινή, ἡ δὲ ἄγνοια ἀμαθία καὶ κακία ἐναργής, 'it is the realization of this that is genuine wisdom and goodness, while the failure to realize it is manifest folly and wickedness' (176c6-7). As Sedley has put it, 'the *Theaetetus* digression portrays the philosopher as essentially unworldly, unconcerned with the here-and-now thanks to the breadth of his intellectual horizons and his preoccupation with universal, objective values instead of localized ones.'[15]

ὁμοίωσις θεῷ is a recurring motif elsewhere in Plato's works as well. *Republic* Book X recounts Socrates' discussion with Glaucon about the nature of justice and injustice, and whether justice is truly more desirable and beneficial than the seeming advantages of injustice. In judging the relationship between the just man and the favor or disfavor of the gods, Socrates says that οὐ γὰρ δὴ ὑπό γε θεῶν ποτε ἀμελεῖται ὃς ἂν προθυμεῖσθαι ἐθέλῃ δίκαιος γίγνεσθαι καὶ ἐπιτηδεύων ἀρετὴν εἰς ὅσον δυνατὸν ἀνθρώπῳ ὁμοιοῦσθαι θεῷ, 'the gods never neglect anyone who eagerly wishes to become just and who makes himself as much like a god as a human can by adopting a virtuous way of life' (*Republic* 613a6-7).

We see, then, that from Plato's earliest writings onward consistently through his latest, a sense of the interconnectedness of the divine and the human underlies his attempts to describe the good life. Even more specifically, we find explicit references to the concept of ὁμοίωσις (or μιμούμενος or μετεχεῖν) θεῷ in the *Republic*, *Phaedrus*, and *Theaetetus*—the idea that the just and virtuous, hence the happy, life is desirable precisely inasmuch as it emulates and approximates that of a god. Such a life is characterized by quintessentially philosophical values—φρόνησις, σοφία, ἀρετὴ ἀληθινή, ὀσία, συμμετρία. Yet the picture is not complete: there is another facet of δικαιοσύνη Plato recognizes as philosophically valuable, and hence which merits our close attention—justice as harmony of the soul. It is to this characterization of justice that we turn next.

Justice as Harmony (ἀρμονία)

Harmony of the soul is the touchstone of Plato's conception of the human ideal, as we see represented in this passage from the *Republic*:

δεῖν δέ γέ φαμεν τοὺς φύλακας ἀμφοτέρα ἔχειν τούτω τὼ φύσει. -δεῖ γάρ. – οὐκοῦν ἡρμόσθαι δεῖ αὐτὰς πρὸς ἀλλήλας; -πῶς δ' οὔ; -καὶ τοῦ μὲν ἡρμοσμένου σώφρων τε καὶ ἀνδρεία ἡ ψυχή; -πάνυ γε....ἐπὶ δὴ δύ' ὄντε τούτω, ὡς ἔοικε, δύο τέχνα θεὸν ἔγωγ' ἄν τινα φαίην δεδωκέναι τοῖς ἀνθρώποις, μουσικήν τε καὶ γυμναστικὴν ἐπὶ τὸ θυμοειδὲς καὶ τὸ φιλόσοφον, οὐκ ἐπὶ ψυχὴν καὶ σῶμα, εἰ μὴ εἰ πάρεργον, ἀλλ' ἐπ' ἐκείνω, ὅπως ἂν ἀλλήλοιν συναρμοσθῆτον ἐπιτεινομένω καὶ ἀνιεμένω μέχρι τοῦ προσήκοντος.

Now, we say that our guardians must have both these natures [the spirited and the philosophic]. –They must indeed. –And mustn't the two be *harmonized* with each other? –Of course. –And if this *harmony* is achieved, the soul is both moderate and courageous? –Certainly....It seems, then, that a god has given music and physical training to human beings not, except incidentally, for the body and the soul but for the spirited and wisdom-loving parts of the soul itself, in order that these might *be in harmony* with one another, each being stretched and relaxed to the appropriate degree.[16]

Most of the *Republic* is focused explicitly on discovering the nature of justice. In Book IV, Socrates and Glaucon come to the conclusion that fulfilling the various proper functions of the parts of the city is precisely what constitutes justice, and is the content of this fourth cardinal virtue after having exhausted wisdom, moderation, and courage (433b-e). For, Socrates explains, justice is τοῦτο...ὃ πᾶσιν ἐκείνοις τὴν δύναμιν παρέσχεν ὥστε ἐγγενέσθαι, καὶ ἐγγενομένοις γε σωτηρίαν παρέχειν, ἕωσπερ ἂν ἐνῇ, 'the power that makes it possible for [moderation, courage, and wisdom] to grow in the city and that preserves them when they've grown for as long as it remains there itself' (433b-c). For evidence of this preservative or prophylactic role, Socrates adduces two examples, one positive and one negative. For the first, he goes to the legal profession:

σκόπει δὴ καὶ τῇδε εἰ οὕτω δόξει· ἆρα τοῖς ἄρχουσιν ἐν τῇ πόλει τὰς δίκας προστάξεις δικάζειν; -τί μήν; -ἢ ἄλλου οὑτινοσοῦν μᾶλλον ἐφιέμενοι δικάσουσιν ἢ τούτου, ὅπως ἂν ἕκαστοι μήτ᾽ ἔχωσι τάλλότρια μήτε τῶν αὑτῶν στέρωνται; -οὔκ, ἀλλὰ τούτου. -ὡς δικαίου ὄντος; -ναί. -καὶ ταύτῃ ἄρα πῃ ἡ τοῦ οἰκείου τε καὶ ἑαυτοῦ ἕξις τε καὶ πρᾶξις δικαιοσύνη ἂν ὁμολογοῖτο.

Look at it this way if you want to be convinced. Won't you order your rulers to act as judges in the city's courts? –Of course. –And won't their sole aim in delivering judgments be that no citizen should have what belongs to another or be deprived of what is his own? –They'll have no aim but that. –Because that is just? –Yes. –Therefore, from this point of view also, *the having and doing of one's own would be accepted as justice*.[17]

The phrase ὅπως ἂν ἕκαστοι μήτ᾽ ἔχωσι τάλλότρια μήτε τῶν αὑτῶν στέρωνται articulates Plato's conception of justice as distributive, that is, concerned first and foremost with the appropriate allocation of goods among citizens based upon criteria of desert (compare one of the definitions of δικαιοσύνη at *Definitions* 411d: 'the state that distributes to each person according to what is deserved'); and Plato's criteria rest upon his previously articulated notions of φύσις. It should be unsurprising that Plato's conception of justice rests so firmly upon a platform of οἰκείωσις, given the overarching trajectory of the *Republic* as a whole, which elaborates on the basic theme of the integration of the various distinct natures of human beings into the body politic in such a way as to aim at the highest good for society. The division of souls into 'gold,' 'silver,' and 'bronze,' and the delineation of the types of education and duties proper to each, show us that Plato rejects the notion of a 'one-size-fits-all' system of justice—there are different expectations and obligations that count as just for individuals and groups whose essential natures are relevantly different. The only way for Plato to synthesize this picture, not to be left with an incoherent *satura* of incompatible and casuistic justices, is to formulate such a meta-framework of justice as the *harmonizing* of these various and disparate natures-based obligations under the final τέλος of the good of the city.

Socrates' second example to Glaucon reinforces his identification of justice with harmony by soliciting agreement about the nature of its opposite, injustice. He offers the following scenario:

But I suppose that when someone, who is by nature a craftsman or some other kind of money-maker, is puffed up by wealth, or by having a majority of votes, or by his own strength, or by some other such thing, and attempts to enter the class of soldiers, or one of the unworthy soldiers tries to enter that of the judges and guardians, and these exchange their tools and honors, or when the same person tries to do all these things at once, then I think you'll agree that these exchanges and this sort of meddling bring the city to ruin. –Absolutely. – Meddling and exchange (πολυπραγμοσύνη καὶ μεταβολή) between these three classes, then, is the greatest harm that can happen to the city and would rightly be called the worst thing someone could do to it. –Exactly. –And wouldn't you say that the worst thing that someone could do to his city is injustice (ἀδικίαν)? –Of course. –Then, that exchange and meddling is injustice. Or to put it the other way around: For the money-making, auxiliary, and guardian classes each to do its own work (οἰκειοπραγία, ἑκάστου τούτων τὸ αὐτοῦ πράττοντος) in the city, is the opposite. That's justice (δικαιοσύνη), isn't it, and makes the city just? –I agree. Justice is that and nothing else. (*Republic* 434a-d)

The undermining or perversion of harmonious relations among the several parts of the city is μεγίστη τε βλάβη and μάλιστα κακουργία— the greatest harm and ill-doing it is possible to wreak upon the well-being of a city. When an individual usurps the position and duties of another, for which he is unsuited by nature, it strikes a triple blow. The first and most obvious result is that, since his nature and training have not equipped him for the position, he will carry out its duties less well, and with less understanding of them, than would the person trained for it. Second, his own appropriate function and duties suffer: whether they are performed, in his absence, by someone unqualified for them, or by himself as he continues performing them in addition to his new ones, they will be degraded either due to spreading his attention too thin in the latter case, or by leaving them in the hands of an unqualified person in the former. Third, his assumption of duties unsuited to him by nature and by training will have the effect of subverting the educational system of the city, which is designed precisely to match citizens to appropriate social roles based on their natures and abilities, and to provide the education and training best suited for each. After all, if a merchant can achieve rule of the city merely by amassing wealth and popularity, what need is there to undergo the arduous training of a guardian?[18]

Once Socrates and Glaucon have come to agreement concerning the nature of justice as it appears in the city, they examine the parallel issue of justice in the individual. Informed by the metaphysical account of the tripartite soul set forth earlier, taken together with Plato's idea that the individual and the city are relevantly similar, and thus that discovering the features of the latter can guide us appropriately to learning about the former, Socrates argues:

καὶ δίκαιον δή, ὦ Γλαύκων, οἶμαι φήσομεν ἄνδρα εἶναι τῷ αὐτῷ τρόπῳ ᾧπερ καὶ πόλις ἦν δικαία....ἀλλ' οὔ πῃ μὴν τοῦτό γε ἐπιλελήσμεθα, ὅτι ἐκείνη γε τῷ τὸ ἑαυτοῦ ἕκαστον ἐν αὐτῇ πράττειν τριῶν ὄντων γενῶν δικαία ἦν....μνημονευτέον ἄρα ἡμῖν ὅτι καὶ ἡμῶν ἕκαστος, ὅτου ἂν τὰ αὐτοῦ ἕκαστον τῶν ἐν αὐτῷ πράττῃ, οὗτος δίκαιός τε ἔσται καὶ τὰ αὐτοῦ πράττων.

we'll say that a man is just in the same way as a city...and we surely haven't forgotten that the city was just because each of the three classes in it was doing its own work...then we must also remember that each one of us in whom each part is doing its own work will himself be just and do his own.[19]

The rational part of the soul, in a just individual, will have received training and education specifically designed to promote its ruling nature—philosophy and mathematics, ethics, politics and rhetoric. The spirited part of the soul will have benefited from physical training, as well as exposure to arts and music designed to soothe it and make it amenable to submitting to the rule of the rational (441e–442a). The appetitive part of the soul doesn't seem to get much attention, or require any sort of specialized training: its proper role seems primarily to submit to the dictates of the two higher parts. Nevertheless Socrates does state, if in passing, that it, too, has its own work to do, τὰ αὐτοῦ πράττῃ (442a), though the nature of this work is not mentioned, presumably as of minimal ethical importance[20]. To illustrate the plausibility of this parallel between the just city and the just individual, Socrates finally asks a hypothetical skeptic to consider some 'ordinary cases' that support the parallel: if some individual had a nature and training similar to what was described for the city, he would be of a character least likely to participate in various kinds of crimes and injustices because αὐτοῦ τῶν ἐν αὐτῷ ἕκαστον τὰ αὐτοῦ πράττει ἀρχῆς τε πέρι καὶ τοῦ ἄρχεσθαι, 'every part within him does its own work, whether it's ruling or being ruled' (443a-b).

Compare *Gorgias* 504–5, where Callicles is challenging Socrates about the nature and purpose of oratory. In a brief but important digression from the main flow of the argument, Socrates attempts to convince Callicles that, just as health and strength result from organization (τάξις) and order (κόσμος) within the body, so too do justice and self-control result from organization and order within the soul. The way in which Socrates describes and explains these two terms, and their relation to 'the good man,' very strongly indicate a close, if not an explicit, supportive connection with his conception of justice as the harmony of parts. Socrates first explains:

φέρε γάρ, ὁ ἀγαθὸς ἀνὴρ καὶ ἐπὶ τὸ βέλτιστον λέγων, ἃ ἂν λέγῃ ἄλλο τι οὐκ εἰκῇ ἐρεῖ, ἀλλ᾽ ἀποβλέπων πρός τι· ὥσπερ καὶ οἱ ἄλλοι πάντες δημιουργοὶ [βλέποντες] πρὸς τὸ αὑτῶν ἔργον ἕκαστος οὐκ εἰκῇ ἐκλεγόμενος προσφέρει [πρὸς τὸ ἔργον τὸ αὑτῶν,] ἀλλ᾽ ὅπως ἂν εἶδός τι αὐτῷ σχῇ τοῦτο ὃ ἐργάζεται. οἷον εἰ βούλει ἰδεῖν...ὡς εἰς τάξιν τινὰ ἕκαστος ἕκαστον τίθησιν ὃ ἂν τιθῇ, καὶ προσαναγκάζει τὸ ἕτερον τῷ ἑτέρῳ πρέπον τε εἶναι καὶ ἁρμόττειν, ἕως ἂν τὸ ἅπαν συστήσηται τεταγμένον τε καὶ κεκοσμημένον πρᾶγμα.

the good man, the man who speaks with regard to what's best, [will] say whatever he says not randomly but with a view to something, just like the other craftsmen, each of whom keeps his own product in view and so does not select and apply randomly what he applies, but so that he may give his product some shape...see how each one places what he does into a certain organization, and compels one thing to be suited for another and to fit to it until the entire object is put together in an organized and orderly way.[21]

He next elicits Callicles' agreement (one of the few unreluctant and unqualified assents given by the latter!) that, for artifacts and bodies generally, τάξις and κόσμος constitute something good for them, and even for the soul as well.[22] Having secured this agreement, Socrates proposes that, just as the state of organization of the body is called 'healthy,' from which bodily excellence results, ταῖς δέ γε τῆς ψυχῆς τάξεσι καὶ κοσμήσεσιν νόμιμόν τε καὶ νόμος, ὅθεν καὶ νόμιμοι γίγνονται καὶ κόσμιοι· ταῦτα δ᾽ ἔστιν δικαιοσύνη τε καὶ σωφροσύνη, 'the name for the states of organization and order of the soul is 'lawful' and 'law,' from whence people become law-abiding and orderly: and these [states] are justice and self-control' (*Gorgias* 504d). Here, as in the *Republic*, Plato's conception of justice rests squarely upon the rationally ordered and organized operation of parts. Although he does not here use the term ἁρμονία, but instead τάξις and κόσμος, it is clear that the sentiment is identical. At *Laws* 896e, the gods' activity is to make order prevail in the world, an account quite similar to the Demiourgos of the *Timaeus* (Armstrong 192–3). And although the nature of the Good is ineffable, the closest Plato comes to describing it is to say that it is like order or harmony (*Gorgias* 503–4, *Philebus* 64–65).[23]

What can we derive from this trend? Plato's core conception of justice is the harmonious synthesis of the multiple and distinct elements of the city or individual soul, recognizing the different proclivities, abilities, and tendencies of each part and encouraging them to operate within their own proper sphere. Plato's is not a theory seeking to eliminate 'unwanted' or 'inferior' behaviors—he nowhere claims that, for instance, it is wrong for an individual to have an interest in making money, any more than he claims that it would be wrong for a city to have cobblers and carpenters in addition to guardians. The emphasis is squarely upon channeling each of the desires and tendencies within our souls, guiding them, by means of rational direction, to flourish in their proper place and proportion to produce the greatest good for the city, or the individual, overall. τὸ δέ γε ἦν ἄρα, ὦ Γλαύκων—δι' ὃ καὶ ὠφελεῖ—εἴδωλόν τι τῆς δικαιοσύνης, τὸ τὸν μὲν σκυτοτομικὸν φύσει ὀρθῶς ἔχειν σκυτοτομεῖν καὶ ἄλλο μηδὲν πράττειν, τὸν δὲ τεκτονικὸν τεκταίνεσθαι, καὶ τἆλλα δὴ οὕτως, 'Indeed, Glaucon, the principle that it is right for someone who is by nature a cobbler to practice cobblery and nothing else, for the carpenter to practice carpentry, and the same for others is a sort of image of justice—that's why it's beneficial' (*Republic* 443d). Plato makes much the same point in the *Timaeus*, one of his later works, where he maintains:

καθάπερ εἴπομεν πολλάκις, ὅτι τρία τριχῇ ψυχῆς ἐν ἡμῖν εἴδη κατῴκισται, τυγχάνει δὲ ἕκαστον κινήσεις ἔχον, οὕτω κατὰ ταύτὰ καὶ νῦν ὡς διὰ βραχυτάτων ῥητέον ὅτι τὸ μὲν αὐτῶν ἐν ἀργίᾳ διάγον καὶ τῶν ἑαυτοῦ κινήσεων ἡσυχίαν ἄγον ἀσθενέστατον ἀνάγκη γίγνεσθαι, τὸ δ' ἐν γυμνασίοις ἐρρωμενέστατον· διὸ φυλακτέον ὅπως ἂν ἔχωσιν τὰς κινήσεις πρὸς ἄλληλα συμμέτρους.

[t]here are, as we have said many times now, three distinct types of soul that reside within us, each with its own motions. So now too, we must say in the same vein, as briefly as we can, that any type which is idle and keeps its motions inactive cannot but become very weak, while one that keeps exercising becomes very strong. And so we must keep watch to make sure that their motions remain proportionate to each other.[24]

It may be tempting to suppose that, although each part of the soul apparently has its own motions, Plato intends to convey that the ruling, rational part of the soul, with the help of the spirited part, compels the lower part, causing it to move when required, and otherwise leaving it quiescent or dormant, moving only at the prompting of its masters. But this is not Plato's position. He states, only a few lines before the above passage, τῶν δ' αὖ κινήσεων ἡ ἐν ἑαυτῷ ὑφ' αὑτοῦ ἀρίστη κίνησις—μάλιστα γὰρ τῇ διανοητικῇ καὶ τῇ τοῦ παντὸς κινήσει συγγενής—ἡ δὲ ὑπ' ἄλλου χείρων: χειρίστη δὲ ἡ κειμένου τοῦ σώματος καὶ ἄγοντος ἡσυχίαν δι' ἑτέρων αὐτὸ κατὰ μέρη κινοῦσα.

Now the best of the motions is one that occurs within oneself and is caused by oneself. This is the motion that bears the greatest kinship to understanding and to the motion of the universe. Motion that is caused by the agency of something else is less good. Worst of all is the motion that moves, part by part, a passive body in a state of rest.[25]

In the well-ordered soul, it seems, τὸ ἐπιθυμητικόν, no less than τὸ θυμοειδές and τὸ λογιστικόν, must needs be more than an anemic and inert ugly stepchild, deprived of the things that are its own objects of desire from fear that it will overindulge. It must, with the guidance of reason, be active, and of its own accord pursue its proper activities. In section 3 below, we will examine in depth some of the consequences of Plato's commitment to ἁρμονία considered in light of the nature of the soul and its parts, and how these will shape our understanding of the possible courses the happy human life can take.

Justice as πρᾶξις

Of course, the intellectualist might argue that, thus far, nothing in Plato's treatment of δικαιοσύνη acknowledges any role whatsoever for external goods in εὐδαιμονία. Indeed, the most telling statement Plato makes seems to reject externals as irrelevant to justice: justice 'isn't concerned with someone's doing his own externally, but with what is inside him, with what is truly himself and his own' (*Republic* IV 443c6–8). When the soul itself is harmonized, this internal state is sufficient for justice, and hence for happiness. Insofar as Plato conceives of the soul as (at least conceptually, and likely actually) separable from the body, likewise his conception of justice seems to be essentially unrelated to the merely accidental features of the soul's embodiment. Just actions, and virtuous relations with one's world and society, the intellectualist can claim, are merely the natural result of placing the just individual in imperfect surroundings; though they are indeed the best sort of actions, nevertheless they are still merely imperfect expressions of the soul's harmony, maimed or limited by the soul's embodied state. On such a view, just πράξεις have no part in any *essential* description of justice; in an ideal world, an internal harmony of soul would be sufficient to characterize the just man.

It is important to recognize that this conclusion rests upon a specific picture of the soul as essentially self-sufficient and self-contained, rather than as essentially connected to or dependent upon anything else. This description accords well with Plato's ideal or divine rational soul, as exemplified by a god; the action of such a being is entirely directed toward the Forms, that is, can be entirely encapsulated under the practice of θεωρία, contemplation, which is wholly a relation of the soul to the Forms. For a soul whose nature is wholly self-sufficient, the purely internal ἁρμονία of that soul, and the expression of that ἁρμονία through θεωρία, suffice to constitute the entirety of its proper εὐδαιμονία. We will confront the question of Plato's conception of the soul's nature in section 3 below.

However, there is another very prominent notion of justice, as πρᾶξις, that runs throughout Plato's works, which we cannot ignore. At the very least, we must give some account of why it fails to embody Plato's mature doctrine; at most, we may be compelled to admit some form of this conception into Platonic δικαιοσύνη alongside a purely internal ἁρμονία.

We know that, from the beginning of the discussion in the *Republic*, Plato clearly intends to move beyond what has been dubbed 'conventional' or 'vulgar' justice—what Cephalus defines as truth-telling and the paying of debts (*Rep.* 331), Polemarchus as giving others their due (331–2), and Glaucon as a sort of compromise or social contract (358–9). Plato aims to characterize the nature of justice as more than simply a particular set of actions.[26] It is also clear that his concept of justice will not perfectly overlap conventional justice. Yet, both for reasons of plausibility and of motivation, the Platonically just person must turn out to be conventionally just much, if not most, of the time.[27] After all, a significant aim of Plato's writing is pedagogical—he is engaged in the project of convincing the skeptic, represented here in the character of Thrasymachus, that justice is not merely an instrumental good, but is good both 'for its own sake and also for the sake of what comes from it' (357b6–7).[28]

Beside the pragmatic reasons we can adduce for correlating Plato's conception of justice with the conventional notion of just or virtuous action, we see a more essential connection between Platonic justice and πρᾶξις in the well-known description of the philosopher-king at *Republic*

V 473, and in the philosopher's 'paradox' in the allegory of the Cave: the apparent tension between the claims upon the philosopher's allegiance of θεωρία, the 'highest' and most divine form of life, and of ruling the city, the active life that will result in the happiest city. At least in the *Republic*, Plato recognizes the claim of the city on the philosopher as a legitimate and serious competitor to pure θεωρία: in Book IV, Socrates reminds Adeimantus that, although the life of the guardians does not make them, individually or collectively, as happy as they might be, 'we aren't aiming to make any one group outstandingly happy but to make the whole city so, as far as possible' (420b4–5). Seemingly, the 'highest good' of the 'highest part' of the city is not necessarily the 'highest good' of the city as a whole—sometimes the guardian class is required to sacrifice its own individual best interest for the sake of the whole. Does this have any bearing on how we should understand the relation of the 'highest good' of the 'highest part' of the soul to the 'highest good' of the soul entire? We will explore this topic below.

Before we say anything about the harmony among the parts of the soul, however, we first need to focus on the nature of these parts themselves, and the particular states attendant upon them—the pleasures and goods that are proper to them.

The Nature of the Soul

Plato consistently reminds us that the good for any given thing is determined by the nature of that thing. And so no investigation into the good for human beings can be effective or complete absent an account of the nature of the human soul. We have seen that Plato follows two distinct trends in describing εὐδαιμονία—elevating it to an innately divine state on the one hand (as we saw earlier), and treating it as essentially the balancing and harmonizing of the parts of the soul on the other. The prevailing trend in Plato's works is to identify the human soul as tripartite, consisting of τὸ λογιστικόν, τὸ θυμοειδές, and τὸ ἐπιθυμητικόν (*Rep.* 340d3, 435e–441c, 550b1, 571c4, 605b5; *Phaedo* 108a7; *Theaetetus* 145a7; *Laws* 731b3; *Definitions* 413a7). Yet this bare metaphysical position is compatible with either conception of δικαιοσύνη—ἁρμονία or ὁμοίωσις θεῷ—as we see in this passage from the *Timaeus*, which expresses a conception of 'the most excellent life

68

offered to humankind' based upon the essential divinity of the human soul:

τὸ δὲ δὴ περὶ τοῦ κυριωτάτου παρ' ἡμῖν ψυχῆς εἴδους διανοεῖσθαι δεῖ τῇδε, ὡς ἄρα αὐτὸ δαίμονα θεὸς ἑκάστῳ δέδωκεν, τοῦτο ὃ ...πρὸς δὲ τὴν ἐν οὐρανῷ συγγένειαν ἀπὸ γῆς ἡμᾶς αἴρειν...ἐκεῖθεν γάρ, ὅθεν ἡ πρώτη τῆς ψυχῆς γένεσις ἔφυ, τὸ θεῖον τὴν κεφαλὴν...τῷ μὲν οὖν περὶ τὰς ἐπιθυμίας ἢ περὶ φιλονικίας τετευτακότι...σφόδρα πάντα τὰ δόγματα ἀνάγκη θνητὰ ἐγγεγονέναι...τῷ δὲ περὶ φιλομαθίαν καὶ περὶ τὰς ἀληθεῖς φρονήσεις ἐσπουδακότι καὶ ταῦτα μάλιστα τῶν αὐτοῦ γεγυμνασμένῳ φρονεῖν μὲν ἀθάνατα καὶ θεῖα, ἄνπερ ἀληθείας ἐφάπτηται, πᾶσα ἀνάγκη που, καθ' ὅσον δ' αὖ μετασχεῖν ἀνθρωπίνῃ φύσει ἀθανασίας ἐνδέχεται, τούτου μηδὲν μέρος ἀπολείπειν, ἅτε δὲ ἀεὶ θεραπεύοντα τὸ θεῖον ἔχοντά τε αὐτὸν εὖ κεκοσμημένον τὸν δαίμονα σύνοικον ἑαυτῷ, διαφερόντως εὐδαίμονα εἶναι. θεραπεία δὲ δὴ παντὶ παντὸς μία, τὰς οἰκείας ἑκάστῳ τροφὰς καὶ κινήσεις ἀποδιδόναι. τῷ δ' ἐν ἡμῖν θείῳ συγγενεῖς εἰσιν κινήσεις αἱ τοῦ παντὸς διανοήσεις καὶ περιφοραί· ταύταις δὴ συνεπόμενον ἕκαστον δεῖ, τὰς περὶ τὴν γένεσιν ἐν τῇ κεφαλῇ διεφθαρμένας ἡμῶν περιόδους ἐξορθοῦντα διὰ τὸ καταμανθάνειν τὰς τοῦ παντὸς ἁρμονίας τε καὶ περιφοράς, τῷ κατανοουμένῳ τὸ κατανοοῦν ἐξομοιῶσαι κατὰ τὴν ἀρχαίαν φύσιν, ὁμοιώσαντα δὲ τέλος ἔχειν τοῦ προτεθέντος ἀνθρώποις ὑπὸ θεῶν ἀρίστου βίου πρός τε τὸν παρόντα καὶ τὸν ἔπειτα χρόνον.

Now we ought to think of the most sovereign part of our soul as god's gift to us...it raises us up away from the earth and toward what is akin to us in heaven...for it is from heaven, the place from which our souls were originally born, that the divine part suspends our head....So if a man has become absorbed in his appetites or his ambitions...all his thoughts are bound to become merely mortal....On the other hand, if a man has seriously devoted himself to the love of learning and to true wisdom, if he has exercised these aspects of himself above all, then there is absolutely no way that his thoughts can fail to be immortal and divine, should truth come within his grasp. And to the extent that human nature can partake of immortality, he can in no way fail to achieve this: constantly caring for his divine part as he does, keeping well-ordered the guiding spirit that lives within him, he must indeed be supremely happy. Now there is but one way to care for anything, and that is to provide for it the nourishment and the motions that are proper to it. And the motions that have an affinity to the divine part within us are the thoughts and revolutions of the universe. These, surely are the ones which each of us should follow. We should redirect the revolutions in our heads that were thrown off course at our birth, by coming to learn the harmonies and revolutions of the universe, and so bring into conformity with its objects our faculty of understanding, as it was in its original condition. And when this conformity is complete, we shall have achieved our goal: that most excellent life offered to humankind by the gods, both now and forevermore.[29]

Even if the soul is tripartite, having parts with an affinity to the realm of Forms and other parts whose natures are proper to the mortal realm, the intellectualist can claim that it is only the 'divine'-linked part of the soul that counts toward the achievement of happiness.[30]

Whether we can legitimately assent to this account, on which true happiness results exclusively from the cultivation of the divine part of the soul, will be a topic we explore later. But first we should investigate the following question: Given that Plato recognizes three distinct parts of the human soul, and that the ἁρμονία of these parts is a central description of justice, hence happiness, for humans, how do the proper characteristics of each part determine the good for each part, and for the human being as a whole?

Two items in particular seem to be relevant to the discussion at hand. First, we will examine Plato's account of pleasure—its nature, its relation to εὐδαιμονία, and its various forms. We will see that Plato differentiates between 'true' and 'false' pleasures, and that there does seem to be a place in the happy human life for at least 'true' pleasures. We will also see that pleasures vary in relation to the part of the soul with which we experience them; and this variation gives the pleasures of each part of the soul very different characteristics and relations both to the soul and—most significantly—to the *objects* of the soul's pleasure. In the consideration of these objects we will determine whether external goods have a legitimate place in the just and happy life.

Second, we will examine Plato's account in the *Philebus* of the nature of the particular goods in relation to the Good itself. From this, we will see that, not only do we arrive at the conclusion that the proper goods of the different parts of the soul themselves differ, but we see that this variegation is compatible with how Plato conceives of the Good itself, namely, as itself a mixture of elements.

Pleasures and Their Proper Goods

What does Plato intend when he talks about pleasures and their role in the εὐδαίμων life? It is of crucial importance to our project to pin down what Plato means: if he defines pleasure in a purely intellectualist way, this will make a critical difference in whether our central thesis is supportable. On the other hand, if Plato's preferred conception of pleasure is found to be explicitly externals-related, we will be able to adduce his account of pleasure as a further piece of evidence in favor of a 'mixed' life.

In *Republic* IX, Plato defines pleasure as a motion (583e7) of 'filling' (585b1–e3) in the soul (583e9–10, 584c4–5); and pleasures are terminated by the restoration of 'natural' order (*Philebus* 32b3–4). While the strongest and most intense pleasures are an impediment to intelligence and reason (63d4), nevertheless the experience of moderate pleasures seems appropriate to, nor does it appear to conflict with, the conduct of a truly good life; especially since, as Plato defines them, they arise as a natural consequence and effect of the restoration of one's natural balance. Plato suggests that different pleasures are enjoyed depending upon the different activities (such as being temperate or intemperate) in which one takes pleasure; thus pleasures are partially determined by their object (*Philebus* 37a–38a). Just as opinions differ depending on what the opinion is about, pleasures differ depending upon the activity in which pleasure is taken; we might therefore say that pleasures are *representative* states. In explaining the different kinds of pleasure in the *Philebus*, like Aristotle after him, Plato maintains that pleasures differ in kind as their respective activities differ;[31] but Plato's account is more substantive than this. He argues (*Phil.* 36c–44b) that the pleasures can be true or false depending upon whether the object in which one takes pleasure (τό γε ᾧ τὸ ἡδόμενον ἥδεται) is itself true or false. And if pleasures themselves can be true or false, they can differ *qua* pleasures, and even oppose one another.

Clearly, false pleasures will have no place in the Platonic account of the best life; but by contrast, Plato enjoins us to treat the true and pure pleasures as kin to νοῦς and φρόνησινς: ἀλλ' ἅς τε ἡδονὰς ἀληθεῖς καὶ καθαρὰς [ἃς] εἶπες, σχεδὸν οἰκείας ἡμῖν νόμιζε (*Phil.* 63e2). What makes pleasures true or pure? They are 'based on imperceptible and painless lacks, while their fulfillments are perceptible and pleasant' (*Phil.* 51b4–5), and they are 'unmixed with pain' (51e2, 52b4–5). While the truest examples of pleasure are those related to pure colors, shapes, sounds and smells (*Phil.* 51b2–4), as well as the pleasure of learning (51e6–52b6), Plato imagines νοῦς and φρόνησινς, in describing the nature of the best life, telling us καὶ...τὰς μεθ' ὑγιείας καὶ τοῦ σωφρονεῖν, καὶ δὴ καὶ συμπάσης ἀρετῆς πόσαι καθάπερ θεοῦ ὀπαδοὶ γιγνόμεναι αὐτῇ συνακολουθοῦσι πάντῃ, ταύτας μείγνυ, 'also mix in the pleasures of health and of temperance and all those that commit themselves to virtue as to a god and follow it around everywhere' (63e).

Plato states that 'to be filled with things that are naturally fitting is pleasant' (*Rep.* 585d11). This passage decisively establishes a direct link between the appropriateness of a pleasure and the *nature* in question. Certainly, Plato's intended focus and emphasis are on τὸ λογιστικόν, that which is uniquely human and most divine. But this passage leaves conceptual space for admitting pleasures of types other than intellectual, *if* such pleasures can be shown to be 'naturally fitting' to the human soul.

Plato has established that the reasoning part of the soul is more accurate and truer than the other two parts. Thus, one who follows the guidance of reason, and not the judgments of the spirit or the appetite, will be best able to choose those replenishments which have the least deception and thus the truest pleasures in *each* sphere of life, *not just* in matters of the rational soul:

> Then may we not confidently declare that about both the gain-loving and the victory-loving part of our nature all the desires that follow knowledge and reason and pursue *their* [i.e. *their own, not* those of knowledge and reason] pleasures in conjunction with these, take only those pleasures which reason approves, they will receive the truest pleasures so far as that is possible for them, since they follow truth, and also the pleasures *that are proper to them and their own,* if for everything that which is best may be said to be most its 'own'. Then when the entire soul accepts the guidance of the wisdom-loving part and is not filled with inner dissension, the result for each part is that it in all other respects keeps to *its own* task and is just, and likewise that each enjoys *its own proper pleasures* and the best pleasures and, so far as such a thing is possible, the truest. (*Republic* IX, 586d–587a)

Once again, Plato argues for the superiority of the well-ordered soul with reason in command. And it is this same order of the soul which makes a person just and good (see *Rep.* 441d ff.). But Plato's position that any non-experienced good is a 'lack' is, as Frede puts it,

> his ultimate explanation of why human beings would and could not choose a life without pleasure, even though a life of total imperturbability would, in principle, be 'more divine.' Such a life is simply not open to human beings...human beings never live in permanent possession of the good, in a state of continued perfect self-sufficiency....Plato, the philosopher whose striving for perfection constituted the basis of his lifelong attachment to Socrates, would not deny that love and pleasure make us human; he came to see that and why they cannot and should not be eradicated but even deserve to be cultivated. This is just what the Philebus was designed to confirm; our needy state is precisely what makes us human, but it is also what makes us all too human. It is a necessary ingredient of our mortal condition.[32]

It should not strike us as strange or surprising that Plato should accept a mixture of various types of pleasure as compatible with the most suitable state of affairs for the human soul. Since each part of the soul can be 'filled with what is naturally fitting,' each part of the soul has the capacity to experience proper pleasures—subject, of course, to the guidance, but not to the usurpation, of reason, as we shall explore further below.[33]

τό λογιστικόν: *Ascendant or Transcendant?* One of the reasons Plato gives to explain why the reason-loving part of the soul deserves to rule is the inherent superiority of its pleasures and the objects of its desire, as we saw in the section above. However true his arguments toward this end may be, I believe that this reason is not his most convincing, nor is it sufficient from the perspective of human psychology, pedagogy, or motivating someone actually to live according to reason. One of the most *compelling* reasons it seems best to give mastery to the reason-loving part of the soul is because of its inherent loyalty to *order*—that is, acting and deciding to ensure that each part of the soul, each appetite, each need, receives what is proper and best for it. Complementarily, one of the most compelling reasons the rule of the appetitive or spirited part of the soul seems so repugnant and undesirable is because, in a position of rule, these parts of the soul lack restraint or a sense of order, and so make decisions only based upon what is good and proper *for themselves*, allowing the other parts of the soul to suffer the ill effects and excesses that result. Plato clearly recognizes that the human soul is not all 'of a piece,' with his analyses of the rational, spirited, and appetitive parts. Part of this distinction among the parts of the soul is the fact that each part has characteristics, and needs, that are ἴδιον to itself, and which constitute its own ἴδιον nature. Plato's picture of the man leading the best life is not a picture of someone who has somehow successfully 're-worked' his appetitive and spirited parts until they have taken on the nature and characteristics of the rational part. Such a man would surely be, in Aristotle's words, 'either a beast or a god': Plato's goal is not to excise the non-rational parts of the soul, but to bring them under the direction of the rational, *so that they can benefit from and enjoy their own proper goods and pleasures*, both individually and as constitutive of the higher goods and pleasures capable of being enjoyed only by a whole, rationally ordered human being.[34]

The τέλος of εὐδαιμονία

We mentioned at the beginning of this chapter that, in view of the competing trends within Plato's treatment of εὐδαιμονία, we recognized value in both; and that our project is not to reject one of these trends in favor of the other, but rather to attempt to achieve a kind of harmony between them. Yet the previous section seems strongly to support a picture of δικαιοσύνη as composite, rather at the expense of the essentially divine state of soul we found in passages such as the *Theaetetus* digression, the *Phaedrus*, or the *Timaeus*. Is there a way to balance the weight of these arguments, so that we can still make sense of justice, and happiness, as ὁμοίωσις θεῷ?

The section to follow will address this question, and attempt to present evidence that an affirmative answer is possible, by focusing more precisely both on the nature of ὁμοίωσις and on its τέλος. In the former case, we will determine to what extent Plato's expectations of ὁμοίωσις truly conflict with the more humanistic aspect of justice presented earlier; in the latter, we will consider the possibility that even ὁμοίωσις can take as its proper τέλος the consideration, not only of Forms, but also of matters of applied moral thought.

The Goal of ὁμοιῶσις θεῷ: κατὰ δυνατόν. The divine is frequently assumed to be the ideal τέλος: *Rep.* 589c, 590c-d. Our conception of what the divine life, and its purposes or supreme fulfillment, are like is often most like what is expressed, for example, in the *Timaeus*:

> If a man has seriously devoted himself to the love of learning and to true wisdom, if he has exercised these aspects of himself above all, then there is absolutely no way that his thoughts can fail to be immortal and divine, should truth come within his grasp....The motions that have an affinity to the divine part within us are the thoughts and revolutions of the universe. These, surely are the ones which each of us should follow. We should redirect the revolutions in our heads that were thrown off course at our birth, by coming to learn the harmonies and revolutions of the universe, and so bring into conformity with its objects our faculty of understanding, as it was in its original condition. And when this conformity is complete, we shall have achieved our goal: that most excellent life offered to humankind by the gods, both now and forevermore.[35]

By bringing ourselves into conformity with the κόσμος and its λόγος, and with the Forms as the true objects of our understanding, we achieve 'that most excellent life,' in which we transcend experience of the imperfections of the transient, perceptible world in exchange for contemplation of the perfections of the eternal realm. Insofar as this state is *per se* good and desirable, there is no further thing for the sake of which we need strive; we achieve the *terminus ad quem* of rational desire—the Good itself—just as the gods enjoy, undisturbed by the concerns and obligations of virtuous actions or relations.

Or do we? Is the picture of the divine life as just described acceptable as it stands? In fact, as Sedley notes, the nature of the cognitive state achieved through ὁμοίωσις was by no means agreed upon even among the near contemporaries of Plato's time or later antique philosophers. Aristotle famously considers it ridiculous to suppose that the gods would instantiate moral virtues like temperance or courage. Similarly, Plotinus locates supreme happiness not in the harmony of the three parts of the soul, i.e. moral virtue, but rather in the purely intellectual ideal state of τὸ λογιστικόν alone (*Enneads* 1.2). Contemporary scholars, including Sedley, find compelling the latter account, and agree that there is 'good textual warrant...for reading Plato's ideal of ὁμοίωσις θεῷ as one which leaves moral virtue behind and focuses instead on pure intellectual development'.[36]

On the other hand, as preserved in Aristotle's *Topics*, Xenocrates said εὐδαίμονα εἶναι τὸν τὴν ψυχὴν ἔχοντα σπουδαίαν, 'the one having a morally good soul is happy'.[37] What grounds are there for supposing that Plato's ideal, divine state is moral, rather than purely intellectual? It will help us to answer this question if we consider the possible aspects in which we might 'be like' the divine. In fact there seem to be two: in our capacities and in our actions. In terms of our capacities, our human soul is like the divine in its innate rationality and in its immortality. Within the tradition of Platonic philosophy, there is little debate on this count. When we turn to consider how our actions might imitate the actions of the divine, however, we find divergence. For although the essential mark of the divine intellect is precisely its rational thought, when Plato discusses the paradigmatic example of divinity, the 'world soul' in the *Timaeus*, we see that it is first and foremost concerned with the *sensible* world: it is its governing principle, and its goal is achieving the harmony and the good of the κόσμος in all of its parts, from the celestial to the mundane, from the orbits of the planets to the cycle of seasons to the ordered life of a city.[38] If we are to become like god, and god uses his rational capacity toward the goal of ordering the sensible world, does it make sense for us to cultivate our rationality, but then refrain from putting it to use in our lives? This sense of the obligation of the rational individual toward others, or toward the world at large, is a persistent echo throughout even the most intellectualist portions of Plato's work, and even, later, in Aristotle. If it is a good thing for an individual to achieve εὐδαιμονία, how much more divine is it to achieve happiness for an entire city or society?

It is worthwhile to note that, in each case wherein Plato mentions ὁμοίωσις θεῷ, he invariably includes some phrase meaning 'as much as possible': κατὰ τὸ δυνατόν at *Theaetetus* 176a5–b3; καθ' ὅσον δυνατὸν...ἀνθρώπῳ at *Phaedrus* 252d1–3, 253a2–4; ὅτι δικαιότατος at *Theaetetus* 176c3–4; εἰς ὅσον δυνατὸν ἀνθρώπῳ at *Republic* 613a6–7; καθ' ὅσον...ἀνθρωπίνη φύσει at *Timaeus* 90a3–d8; κατὰ τὸ δυνατόν at *Symposium* 207d1. One interpretation of this phrasing, the most commonly understood, is that it is Plato's way of recognizing the limits of human fallibility in our quest for the divine life—that, because we are *not* gods, because we have bodies and irrational parts of our souls, we cannot ever fully achieve divine εὐδαιμονία, but only some approximation thereof within the limits imposed by our embodied state. This is true, and it is indeed important to let this fact guide our attempts to achieve our goals. However, I believe that there is another interpretation of κατὰ τὸ δυνατόν which clarifies Plato's intended conception of the divine and its relation to the active life. Rather than merely a reminder of our limitations, κατὰ τὸ δυνατόν is also Plato's way of suggesting that our capacity to emulate the divine extends *beyond* perfecting the intellectual virtues—the achievement of individual εὐδαιμονία. Our nature and circumstance as embodied beings permits us a *further* field in which to become like a god—in molding the imperfect, changeable sensible world to the λόγος and κόσμος, just as the world soul itself does.

Harmony and External Goods. Of course, Plato quickly makes clear that ἡ δικαιοσύνη ἀλλ' οὐ περὶ τὴν ἔξω πρᾶξιν τῶν αὑτοῦ, ἀλλὰ περὶ τὴν ἐντός, ὡς ἀληθῶς περὶ ἑαυτὸν καὶ τὰ ἑαυτοῦ, 'justice [is] *not* concerned with doing one's own *with respect to externals, but with respect to what's inside*, what's truly himself and his own' (*Rep.* 443c, emphases mine). The fundamental essence of justice is the harmony of the parts of the soul—an internal matter. Merely to regulate and harmonize one's social activities—taking moderate exercise, participating in commerce, serving one's military duties, farming, and serving on a jury—does not justice make.[39] As Fine puts it, '[a] person is just, on Plato's view, when the parts of her soul are in psychic harmony, in the sense that each part of her soul fulfils its proper function' (Fine 501). Plato has already referred to the sort of externally-measurable justice proper to a city as merely an εἴδωλόν τι τῆς δικαιοσύνης, 'a sort of image of justice.' Does this faint identification indicate anything about how Plato views the relation between the harmony of the parts of the soul and its external results? Do we, after all, find ourselves facing yet again the traditional intellectualist position—that the best life is constituted by an internal state of the soul, unconnected to the states of affairs in which we find ourselves as corporeal creatures?

Reading closely a few lines further goes far to dispel this fear, and to grasp the subtleties of Plato's position on integrating the soul's harmony with the necessary results of this internal state. The intellectualist would cite 443c6–e1 as the defining text. However, this would be a selective reading; Plato's full account goes on, through 443e7; the just man 'puts himself in order,' and 'harmonizes the three parts' of his soul, becoming 'entirely one, moderate and harmonious'—but

οὕτω δὴ *πράττειν* ἤδη, ἐάν τι *πράττῃ* ἢ περὶ χρημάτων κτῆσιν ἢ περὶ σώματος θεραπείαν ἢ καὶ πολιτικόν τι ἢ περὶ τὰ ἴδια συμβόλαια, ἐν πᾶσι τούτοις ἡγούμενον καὶ ὀνομάζοντα δικαίαν μὲν καὶ καλὴν *πρᾶξιν* ἢ ἂν ταύτην τὴν ἕξιν *σῴζῃ* τε καὶ *συναπεργάζηται*, σοφίαν δὲ τὴν ἐπιστατοῦσαν ταύτῃ τῇ πράξει ἐπιστήμην.

Only then does he *act*. And when he does anything, whether acquiring wealth, taking care of his body, engaging in politics, or in private contracts—in all of these, he believes that the *action* is just and fine that *preserves* this inner harmony and *helps achieve it*, and calls it so, and regards as wisdom the knowledge that oversees such actions.[40]

Action is integral to the harmony that is justice. It is no mere peripheral side-effect—it helps to *achieve* the inner harmony of the soul, and once achieved also *preserves* it. The examples Socrates cites—acquiring wealth, caring for the body, engaging in politics, making private contracts—go beyond the bare minimum we might expect to be grudgingly admitted in an intellectualist account, the concessions the contemplative hermit must make to his imperfect flesh. No: these acts are the acts of a fully-engaged social being, one who recognizes and affirms the totality of his embodied and social nature *qua* human being, and understands that his εὐδαιμονία springs from this totality, a totality unified and synthesized from τὸ λογιστικόν, τὸ θυμοεῖδες, and τὸ ἐπιθυμητικόν, and from the expression of each of these in the context of a complete, lived human life.[41]

Adkins offers an intriguing argument supporting the view that the life of practical moral and political activity must be, by Plato's own standards, just as properly ἴδιον to human beings, and just as legitimate an expression of εὐδαιμονία, as the life of θεωρία, contemplation.[42] In the *Republic* Book I, Plato defines the ἔργον, function, of something as 'that which *only* it or it *better than anything else* can perform' (353a, emphasis mine). A few lines later, he specifies that the human ψυχή has an 'ἔργον which one could not accomplish with anything else in the world, as for example management, rule, deliberation, and the like' (353d). The language used in these two passages is a standard way of expressing a thing's ἴδιον characteristic; in this case, we see that the ἔργον of the human soul, that function which nothing else can fulfill, is constituted by 'management, rule, deliberation, and the like.' In the early *Republic*, at least, Plato has committed himself to identifying the ἔργον of the human soul specifically as various πράξεις, or forms of σοφροσύνη.

This view of the active life is confirmed from another angle. The ἔργον, function, of something is 'that which *only* it or it *better than anything else* can perform.' On either of these two criteria, the life of contemplation fails to qualify as the ἔργον, that is to say, the ἴδιον function, of human beings or the human soul, since θεωρία is not only practiced by god but practiced more completely. Contemplation of the Forms is consistently identified as a 'divine' activity; yet if we accept this, we must also accept that no human being can claim contemplation as his ἔργον so long as we abide by Plato's definition above. The argument can be made that, insofar as the highest part of our soul is, in a sense, and in Plato's opinion, divine, contemplation is indeed the proper function of the human soul, at least as represented by the best part. But consider: if we 'abstract away' the 'lower' parts of the soul, and consider the 'essential' human soul as only its rational part, what remains whereby we could identify this entity as a human being? Without the spirited and appetitive parts, and without the context of embodiment, such a soul would be indistinguishable from a god. We know that Plato considers contemplation to be one of the best, if not the best, activity for which we should strive; can we equally confidently claim that he wants us to strive to better ourselves by seeking to achieve the ἔργον of another being through denial of our own φύσις? Or is it more likely, as his endorsement of the active practical moral and political life throughout the *Republic* and elsewhere indicates, that he recognizes that human beings 'cannot live as if they were disembodied νοῦς, and must acknowledge the necessity of *all* the ἀρεταί of the embodied totality as constituents of εὐδαιμονία'?[43] Given the relation of justice and εὐδαιμονία, if we consider that justice, insofar as it is an ἀρετή, is the ability of something to perform its ἴδιον ἔργον well (*Rep.* I 353c4), it is clear that the end of justice, and hence happiness for human beings, is bound up in the active life.[44]

We have seen (in section 2.2) that several Platonic texts, most notably the *Philebus* and Book iv of the *Republic*, supply evidence that Plato conceived of εὐδαιμονία as a state of harmony among the parts of a city or an individual. The *Republic* presents this harmony as δικαιοσύνη, justice, the pre-eminent virtue whose presence, in either city or soul, permits the growth and flourishing of all the others. This account of εὐδαιμονία shares its metaphysical presuppositions with the theory of justice upon which it rests; specifically, it conceives of the nature of the soul as composite. Thus, it stands in need of some way to account for the various goods which are appropriate by nature to each part of the soul, and hence each area of human life; nor can it rest content with an undifferentiatedly intellectualist account of happiness, so long as the human soul contains not only τὸ λογιστικόν, but τὸ θυμοειδές and τὸ ἐπιθυμητικόν.

Plato's metaphysics of the soul, combined with his commitment to identifying happiness as justice, lead him necessarily to an explanation of happiness, and the happy life, as mixed—characterized not by a single, unique, and homogeneous state, but rather by an appropriately balanced blend of multiple aspects of human life—certainly concerned with developing abstract, intellectual thought and approaching the realm of the Forms, but no less concerned with virtues as practiced in social relations, under the circumstances in which we find ourselves. This initial recognition of the composite nature of the soul leads necessarily to the realization that the ἴδιον goods (in Plato's preferred terms, τὰ ἑαυτοῦ or τὰ τοῦ οἰκείου) of τὸ θυμοειδές and τὸ ἐπιθυμητικόν cannot be the same goods as those of τὸ λογιστικόν, any more than those ἴδιον to the cobbler are identical to those of the guardian. And indeed, we find in the *Philebus* Plato's account of the Good and goods, which identifies distinct types of goods which are appropriate to the several parts of the soul—pleasures among them. Upon investigating Plato's treatment of pleasure in *Republic* IX and elsewhere, there emerges a sophisticated tiered ranking of pleasures; and although a great many external pleasures, even most of them, are rejected as false and irrelevant (even harmful) to εὐδαιμονία, Plato does draw a clear connection between true pleasures and the φύσις of the soul (*Rep.* 585d11). A thing's *proper pleasures* (as determined by its φύσις) are *true* pleasures; and true pleasures are characteristic of, even constitutive of, a life of εὐδαιμονία:

> θαρροῦντες λέγωμεν ὅτι καὶ περὶ τὸ φιλοκερδὲς καὶ τὸ φιλόνικον ὅσαι ἐπιθυμίαι εἰσίν, αἳ μὲν ἂν τῇ ἐπιστήμῃ καὶ λόγῳ ἑπόμεναι καὶ μετὰ τούτων τὰς ἡδονὰς διώκουσαι, ἃς ἂν τὸ φρόνιμον ἐξηγῆται, λαμβάνωσι, τὰς ἀληθεστάτας τε λήψονται, ὡς οἷόν τε αὐταῖς ἀληθεῖς λαβεῖν, ἅτε ἀληθείᾳ ἑπομένων, καὶ τὰς ἑαυτῶν οἰκείας, εἴπερ τὸ βέλτιστον ἑκάστῳ, τοῦτο καὶ οἰκειότατον;

> Then can't we confidently assert that those desires of even the money-loving and honor-loving parts that follow knowledge and argument and pursue with their help those pleasures that reason approves will attain the truest pleasures possible for them, because they follow the truth, and the ones that are most their own, if indeed what is best for each thing is most its own?[45]

Therefore, given that the φύσεις of τὸ θυμοειδές and τὸ ἐπιθυμητικόν are necessarily relative to external objects and states of affairs, we can see that identifying εὐδαιμονία as a kind of ἁρμονία is quite apt: just as harmony is by definition a state relative between two or more distinct tones, so εὐδαιμονία is found ultimately to be a relative state among the three separate natures of the parts of the soul—the pure, intellectual, abstract Forms-related activities, pleasures, and goods of τὸ λογιστικόν, as well as the impure, corporeal, particular τύχη-related activities, pleasures and goods of τὸ θυμοειδές and τὸ ἐπιθυμητικόν. For an explicit discussion and endorsement of this conclusion, we need not rely solely on speculative interpretation. In fact, we can turn to Plato's own writings for such support: the next section will present a compelling vision of Plato's considered position on εὐδαιμονία as an active life from the *Philebus*.

A Picture of the 'Mixed' Life

The *Philebus* is commonly held to be one of Plato's last works, and is also generally agreed to be the work that represents Plato's most mature positions on the question of identifying the good human life overall. Unlike the earlier, 'Socratic' dialogues, the *Philebus* portrays the character of Socrates not in a state of perpetual inquiry and ἀπορία, but rather propounding a definite set of views through the development of the conversation: Protarchus tells him 'we should not take it that the aim of our meeting is universal confusion; if we cannot solve the problem, you must do it, for you promised' (*Philebus* 20a3–4), and Socrates proves more than willing to oblige him. Over the course of the discussion, Socrates describes and endorses a particular account of the best human life: one that reflects the heterogeneous nature of the human soul, incorporating both pure knowledge and pleasure, each in its proper place.

Philebus, Socrates' first interlocutor, represents the position that pleasure constitutes the good for humans (though through most of the dialogue it is Protarchus who converses on behalf of this position, with Philebus contributing occasional supporting comments). Socrates tells us 'Philebus holds that what is good for all creatures is to enjoy themselves, to be pleased and delighted, and whatever else goes together with that kind of thing' (*Philebus* 11b3–4). On the other hand, Socrates is committed to defending the thesis that 'not these, but knowing, understanding, and remembering, and what belongs with them, right opinion and true calculations, are better than pleasure and more agreeable to all who can attain them; those who can, get the maximum benefit possible from having them' (*Philebus* 11b6–c3). Given these initial competing positions, Socrates gives the guiding structure of the inquiry: 'each of us will be trying to prove some possession or state of the soul to be the one that can render life happy for all human beings' (*Philebus* 11d3–4).

The first section of the dialogue (11a–20) sets up and takes us through several difficulties faced by both the proponents of pleasure and of reason before we can legitimately endorse one as being truly the good for humans. But before the reader (or the discussants) can get too comfortable with a rehashing of the well-established conflict between pleasure and reason, however, Socrates introduces a novel course for the discussion to take. At 20b3, when the discussion has hit a seemingly insoluble knot, after an involved discussion of unity and plurality, limit and unlimitedness, Socrates interjects, as a divinely-inspired memory, 'a doctrine that once upon a time I heard in a dream—or perhaps I was awake—that I remember now, concerning pleasure and knowledge, that neither of the two is the good, but that there is some third thing which is different from and superior to both of them.' Since, if we can identify some third item other than reason or pleasure as being identical with the good, it makes moot the project of pinning down the precise characteristics of pleasure (which had led to the previous difficulties), since it would be thereby disqualified from its candidacy for the good.

With the tangle of metaphysics safely bypassed, the main discussion of the identity of the human good is free to continue. Socrates and Protarchus first come to agreement on some characteristics of whatever turns out to be the good: it 'is necessarily bound to be perfect (τελείος)' (*Philebus* 20d1)—in fact 'the most perfect thing of all' according to the enthusiastic Protarchus!—and is *sufficient* (ἵκανος): in setting up a fair comparison between the life of pleasure and the life of reason, Socrates reminds us that 'if either of the two is the good, then it must have no need of anything in addition. But if one or the other should turn out to be lacking anything, then this can definitely no longer be the real good we are looking for' (*Philebus* 20e5–6). Compare *Republic* VI 505b–c, where pleasure and knowledge are both rejected individually as definitions of the good:

άλλὰ μὴν καὶ τόδε γε οἶσθα, ὅτι τοῖς μὲν πολλοῖς ἡδονὴ δοκεῖ εἶναι τὸ ἀγαθόν, τοῖς δὲ κομψοτέροις φρόνησις. -πῶς δ' οὔ; -καὶ ὅτι γε, ὦ φίλε, οἱ τοῦτο ἡγούμενοι οὐκ ἔχουσι δεῖξαι ἥτις φρόνησις, ἀλλ' ἀναγκάζονται τελευτῶντες τὴν τοῦ ἀγαθοῦ φάναι. -καὶ μάλα, ἔφη, γελοίως. -πῶς γὰρ οὐχί, ἦν δ' ἐγώ, εἰ ὀνειδίζοντές γε ὅτι οὐκ ἴσμεν τὸ ἀγαθὸν λέγουσι πάλιν ὡς εἰδόσιν; φρόνησιν γὰρ αὐτό φασιν εἶναι ἀγαθοῦ, ὡς αὖ συνιέντων ἡμῶν ὅτι λέγουσιν, ἐπειδὰν τὸ τοῦ ἀγαθοῦ φθέγξωνται ὄνομα. -ἀληθέστατα, ἔφη. -τί δὲ οἱ τὴν ἡδονὴν ἀγαθὸν ὁριζόμενοι; μῶν μή τι ἐλάττονος πλάνης ἔμπλεῳ τῶν ἑτέρων; ἢ οὐ καὶ οὗτοι ἀναγκάζονται ὁμολογεῖν ἡδονὰς εἶναι κακάς; -σφόδρα γε.

Furthermore, you certainly know that the majority believe that pleasure is the good, while the more sophisticated believe that it is knowledge. –Indeed I do. – And you know that those who believe this can't tell us what sort of knowledge it is, however, but in the end are forced to say that it is knowledge of the good. – And that's ridiculous. –Of course it is. They blame us for not knowing the good and then turn around and talk to us as if we did know it. They say that it is knowledge of the good—as if we understood what they're speaking about when they utter the word 'good.' –That's completely true. –What about those who define the good as pleasure? Are they any less full of confusion than the others? Aren't even they forced to admit that there are bad pleasures? –Most definitely. (*Rep.* 505b–c)

The centrally interesting feature of this section, and of the *Philebus* dialogue as a whole, is precisely Plato's characterization of the best human life as a 'mixture' or 'combination' of reason and pleasure. Just as one living the life of pure, unadulterated pleasure 'would thus not live a human life but the life of a mollusk' (*Phil.* 21c), neither does the life of pure reason qualify as the good life, ἣν γὰρ ἂν ἱκανὸς καὶ τέλεος καὶ πᾶσι φυτοῖς καὶ ζώοις αἱρετός, οἷσπερ δυνατὸν ἦν οὕτως ἀεὶ διὰ βίου ζῆν, 'since otherwise it would be sufficient, perfect, and worthy of choice for any of the plants and animals that can sustain [it], throughout their lifetime' (22b). The exact character of this 'mixture' is investigated in some depth as the dialogue progresses; however, the salient point to note is the definite non-intellectualist consequence of Plato's position. It is frequently emphasized that Plato, following Socrates, identifies virtue and the good with knowledge; it is not as frequently noted that he does not thereby mean to devalue applied knowledge or science. When discussing the method of mixing knowledge and pleasure together in the well-balanced life, Socrates asks Protarchus which sciences should be included in the mix—the purest and truest only, or some of the others as well:

Soc. [O]ne kind [of science] deals with a subject matter that comes to be and perishes (τὰ γιγνόμενα καὶ ἀπολλύμενα), the other is concerned with what is free of that, the eternal and self-same (ὡσαύτως ὄντα ἀεί). Since we made truth our criterion, the latter kind appeared to be the truer one....If we took from each sort the segments that possess most truth and mixed them together, would this mixture provide us with the most desirable life (τὸν ἀγαπητότατον βίον), or would we also need less-true ones? **Prot.** We should do it this way, it seems to me. **Soc.** Suppose, then, there is a person who understands what justice itself is and...all the rest of what there is....Will he be sufficiently versed in science if he knows the definition of the circle and of the divine sphere itself but cannot recognize the human sphere? **Prot.** We would find ourselves in a rather ridiculous (γελοίαν) position if we were confined entirely to those divine kinds of knowledge (ἐν ταῖς θείαις...ἐπιστήμαις), Socrates! **Soc.** But how about music: Ought we also to mix in the kind of which we said a little earlier that it is full of lucky hits and imitation (στοχάσεώς τε καὶ μιμήσεως) but lacks purity (καθαρότητος ἐνδεῖν)? **Prot.** It seems necessary to me, if in fact our life is supposed to be at least some sort of *life* (εἴπερ γε ἡμῶν ὁ βίος ἔσται καὶ ὁπωσοῦν ποτε βίος). (*Philebus* 62ba4–5)

The answer agreed upon by Socrates and Protarchus is the broader alternative: the best human life needs even the applied sciences, those fields of knowledge whose objects are the imperfect, impermanent products of generation and corruption, and even the sorts of pursuits that involve chance, if our life is to be a meaningful lived experience: in the end, μὴ ζητεῖν ἐν τῷ ἀμείκτῳ βίῳ τἀγαθὸν ἀλλ' ἐν τῷ μεικτῷ, 'we ought not to seek the good in the unmixed life but in the mixed one' (*Philebus* 61b3–4).[46]

Also compare 491a6–492a3 in *Republic* Book VI. Here Socrates acknowledges the traditional external goods as potentially corrupting influences upon a soul of the best nature which has received a bad upbringing. This seems an unsurprising claim on its face—in fact, it even appears to favor a traditional intellectualist interpretation. However, Socrates has grouped the external goods together (ἔτι τοίνυν, 'furthermore') with ἓν ἕκαστον ὧν ἐπῃνέσαμεν τῆς φύσεως, 'each of the things we praised in that nature' (491b3–4)—courage, moderation, and the other virtues—as sources of corruption in the absence of proper education. If, as Socrates here indicates, it is an anomaly— θαυμαστότατον, 'most surprising' (491b3), and ἄτοπον, 'strange' (491b6)—for these things to be corrupting influences on the naturally noble soul, the implication is that they are usually beneficial.

Conclusion

So, in support of Plato's 'mixed' life, we have seen the following textual evidence. First, *Republic* X identifies δικαιοσύνη as the highest good for human beings—i.e., εὐδαιμονία. *Republic* III and IV define δικαιοσύνη as ἁρμονία among the classes of citizens within the just city. Book IV explicitly extends this description to the δικαιοσύνη of the individual as well, based on Plato's general principle of treating the city and its characteristics as reflective of the individual, only 'writ large.' The tripartite division of the ψυχή provides the metaphysical basis for defining δικαιοσύνη as the ἁρμονία among the parts of the soul, a definition supported in both *Republic* IV and in the *Timaeus*. Then, lines 443e1–6 at the end of Book IV clarify that this psychic harmony is achieved, preserved, and expressed through πράξεις, and explicitly such πράξεις as are characteristic of a being whose φύσις is essentially social and composite. Finally, the *Philebus* and *Republic* VI explicitly reject the traditional dichotomy of knowledge and pleasure as the top candidates for the good life on the grounds that each is alone insufficient to constitute happiness; in the stead of these Socrates creates and defends an account of happiness that combines both knowledge in the highest sense *and* impure, external, and even chance-based pleasures. Plato certainly strenuously maintains the supremacy of reason over pleasure in any head-to-head comparison of the two, even in these texts; but, of the options available to human beings to conduct their lives, the pure intellectualist ideal takes no better than second place. For all its advantages over pleasure, it is still not sufficient on its own to constitute a good life. For that, we need connection to and activity within the external world.

Notes

1   Cf. C.D.C. Reeve's translation, 'justice itself is the best thing for the soul itself.' I take issue with his use of αὐτό to modify δικαιοσύνην on grammatical grounds: αὐτὸ is clearly the accusative neuter singular form, modifying the predicative substantive ἄριστον. On Reeve's translation, the implication is that 'justice itself'—i.e., Justice— is the best thing for the soul, rather than, say, just practices or just relations. Such a translation is automatically biased in favor of an intellectualist interpretation of Plato's meaning, in addition to being grammatically heterodox.

2   Likewise, at *Rep.* 619a and 621c-d justice and happiness are conjoined in similar fashion.

3   *Republic* x 618d7–e1. This passage also picks out a point I consider to be important for properly understanding Plato's eudaimonism, and on which I will rely through the course of this chapter. The nature of the soul is what determines 'the worse and the better life' (cf. also 490e3–4). This point, and the consequences it entails, will be the focus of section 3 below.

4   *Republic* x 621c1–d3.

5   Plato does not here specify whether εὐδαιμονία is constituted *exclusively* by δικαιοσύνη. Contemporary commentary contains many astute and complex arguments on all sides (for a representative and judicious survey of the literature, see Irwin, *Plato's Ethics* ch. 12; Dahl 1991, 'Plato's Defence of Justice,' *Philosophy and Phenomenological Research* 51, 809–834; Fine 2000, 483–515). Irwin has argued that justice or virtue is the *dominant* component of εὐδαιμονία, but is not necessary and sufficient for it (Fine 498), whereas Annas holds the opposite position, maintaining that justice *is* sufficient for happiness (Fine 498). We touch on this debate only as it is necessary to do so to properly understand the context of our argument, and Plato's eudaimonism generally; I will not defend a position here. What *is* crucial to note in this context, however, is the point that Fine makes, and which I defend, namely, that the *Republic* rejects a purely cognitive theory of virtue—virtue requires, at least, appropriate affective training (Fine 500).

6   For some scholarship on the religious traditions and cultural milieu in which Plato worked, see Burkert, *Greek Religion*; Morgan, *Platonic Piety: Philosophy and Ritual in Fourth Century Athens*; E.R. Dodds, *the Greeks and the Irrational*.

7   Morgan 1990, 231.
8   The danger of hubris, overstepping one's proper place, grows from this conception.
9   See e.g. *Laws* x 900 et seq., where the Athenian stranger, leading a discussion with Clinias on the existence and nature of the gods, mentions 'a kind of family tie between you and the gods' (899d7) and 'your kinship with the gods' (900a6–7).
10 It may be noteworthy, and is certainly suggestive, that this verb is also frequently used to describe the 'participation' of objects in Forms, both in Plato and in Aristotle.
11 *Phaedrus* 252d1–3, 253a2–4.
12 Also cf. *Protagoras* 330c1–331e8, where Socrates and Protagoras both agree that there is some kind of resemblance between justice and ὁσιότης—though they do not arrive at a completely satisfactory account of this resemblance here. For a stronger defense of the actual identity of δικαιοσύνη and ὁσιότης, see Sedley in Fine, 794–5.
13 A nearly identical comparison of the two types of life yields a quite different conclusion in the hands of Callicles at *Gorgias* 484c-e.
14 Plato, *Theatetus* 176a5–b3.
15 Fine 2000, 794.
16 Plato, *Rep.* III 410e–411e, emphases mine.
17 Plato, *Rep.* IV 433e–434a, emphasis mine.
18 For Plato's opinion on the consequences of a flawed system of public education see esp. *Rep.* vi 492e1–493a1.
19 Plato, *Republic* 441d-e.
20 Although 434d does explicitly include the money-making class performing its proper function—i.e., making money—in the account of justice.
21 Plato, *Gorgias* 503d–504a.
22 It is of interest in this context to note the definition of τάξις at *Definitions* 413d: 'functional similarity in all the mutual elements of a whole; due proportion in a society; cause of all the mutual elements of a whole; due proportion in respect of learning.'
23 Cf. Dahl 827–30.
24 Plato, *Timaeus* 89e5–90a2.
25 Plato, *Timaeus* 89a2–6.
26 For a good account of why, see Dahl 810–17, Sachs 50–51.
27 See Dahl 814–15, Kraut (1973) 207 et seq.
28 Consider, too, Plato's commitment to the idea that even the 'inferior' souls of non-philosophers are capable of achieving a certain degree of the ἁρμονία of the soul: see Kraut (1973) 216–22.
29 Plato, *Timaeus* 90a3–d8, emphases mine.
30 On the other hand, Plato in some places indicates that the ψυχή is simple, and thus εὐδαιμονία must be simple: the entire *Phaedo*, *Rep.* X 611a8–c1. Of course, this unicomponent εὐδαιμονία would then be divinely constituted, given the innate immortality of the soul.
31 At *EN* x.5 1175b1–24, Aristotle argues for the distinction between kinds of pleasure as follows: While the pleasure of one kind of activity (for example, reading) adds to that activity, pleasures from other activities tend to distract from, rather than augment, that activity—the pleasure of a delicious smell wafting by, for instance, will likely interfere with my concentration. Since these two types of pleasure act differently upon my activity of reading (the former complements, the latter detracts), the pleasures themselves must be of different kinds.
32 Kraut 1992, 453–456.

33 Another intriguing direction of support for a conception of Plato's eudaimonism as essentially mixed, one which I have not been able to explore here, is found in his description of *the Good itself* as a kind of mixture: οὐκοῦν εἰ μὴ μιᾷ δυνάμεθα ἰδέᾳ τὸ ἀγαθὸν θηρεῦσαι, σὺν τρισὶ λαβόντες, *κάλλει* καὶ *συμμετρίᾳ* καὶ *ἀληθείᾳ*, λέγωμεν ὡς τοῦτο οἷον ἓν ὀρθότατ' ἂν αἰτιασαίμεθ' ἂν τῶν ἐν τῇ συμμείξει, καὶ διὰ τοῦτο ὡς ἀγαθὸν ὂν τοιαύτην αὐτὴν γεγονέναι (*Philebus* 64d-e). Of the three ingredients, it is interesting to note that συμμετρία, measure, is identified as the defining characteristic of the 'first rank' of goods at *Phil.* 66a ff.—especially since συμμετρία is an essentially *relational* property.

34 Cf. *Republic* IV 420b4–5, where the goal is to make the *entire* city happy, not just the guardian class. By analogy, we can reasonably expect Plato to agree that the goal of the happy life for the individual is to make the *entire* soul happy, and not just τὸ λογιστικόν.

35 Plato, *Timaeus* 90b3–d8.

36 Fine 2000, 806.

37 *Top.* 112a36–8. Some Middle Platonists also endorse this view, including Stobaeus (*Eclogai* 2.49.8–25) and Alcinous (*Didaskalikos* 28).

38 The same sentiment is expressed at *Laws* X 899d–903a: the gods necessarily concern themselves with human affairs, virtues, etc.

39 Cf. Sachs 47–48, Dahl 813: though Platonic justice entails conventional justice, the reverse is not true.

40 *Rep.* 443e1–6, emphases mine.

41 Cf. *Symposium* 209a6–7, where Diotima claims that 'by far the greatest and most beautiful part of wisdom deals with the proper ordering of cities and households, and that is called moderation and justice.'

42 Adkins 1978, 302 et seq.

43 Adkins 1978, 300.

44 Cf. *Crito* 47d3–48a1.

45 Plato, *Rep.* 586d3–e1.

46 Although the predominant trend in Platonic commentary has been toward an intellectualist interpretation, note is often taken, even by intellectualist commentators, of the necessity to acknowledge a tension here, albeit usually as a preliminary to explaining it away. Cf. e.g. R.C. Lodge (1924) 488–9: 'We have, then, in Plato's thought, two strata [idealism and pragmatism] which are logically incompatible....A study of the Dialogues shows convincingly that in Plato's own thinking the two standpoints...are combined, and their combination is present in his most fundamental conceptions [e.g. the philosopher-king]....The only satisfactory way out of this difficulty would be to insist that the complete interpenetration of Idea and action-systems represents the highest human life.' Lodge, of course, claims that such a 'complete interpenetration' fails on logical grounds as a viable alternative. On this idea of 'complete interpenetration,' compare the Stoic concept of κρᾶσις δι' ὅλου in chapter 4 below.

Chapter 3
The Philosopher: Aristotle in Two Worlds

ὑπὲρ ἀγαθοῦ ἄρα, ὡς ἔοικεν, ἡμῖν λεκτέον, καὶ ὑπὲρ ἀγαθοῦ οὐ τοῦ ἁπλῶς, ἀλλὰ τοῦ ἡμῖν · οὐ γὰρ τοῦ θεῶν ἀγαθοῦ · ἀλλ' ὑπὲρ μὲν τούτου καὶ ἄλλος λόγος καὶ ἀλλοτρία ἡ σκέψις.

It is about good, then, as it seems, that we must speak, and about good not without qualification, but relatively to ourselves. For we have not to do with the good of the gods. To speak about that is a different matter, and the inquiry is foreign to our present purpose.

Aristotle, *Magna Moralia*

Introduction

In his discussion of εὐδαιμονία in Book i of the *Nicomachean Ethics* (*EN*), Aristotle writes εἰ δ' οὕτως, ἄθλιος μὲν οὐδέποτε γένοιτ' ἂν ὁ εὐδαίμων · οὐ μὴν μακάριός γε ἂν Πριαμικαῖς τύχαις περιπέσῃ, 'if it [the preceding discussion] is so, the εὐδαίμων could never become wretched; but he would not be μακάριος should he suffer misfortunes like Priam's'.[1] The connection between happiness and external goods is nowhere as evident as in the work of Aristotle. For several decades, one of the primary academic contests in Aristotelian study has been that between exclusivist and inclusivist interpretations of Aristotle's ethics. There is some ironic humor in the fact that study of the philosopher of whose goals and methods the ideal of harmony was most characteristic should be marked by the seeming incompatibility of quarreling interpretive camps. On the one side, intellectualists such as Hardie, Heinaman, Kraut, Kenny, Crisp, and Adkins have argued that contemplation is solely constitutive of εὐδαιμονία; on the other, inclusivists, among them Irwin, Cooper, Akrill, Roche, Gurtler, and White, cite evidence that Aristotle included external goods as ingredients in the life of the εὐδαίμων.[2] The various explanations of εὐδαιμονία Aristotle gives in the *Nicomachean*

Ethics have indeed challenged commentators to interpret his virtue ethics in a unified and coherent way. Throughout the *EN*, the *Magna Moralia*, the *Eudemian Ethics* and elsewhere, Aristotle maintains that εὐδαιμονία is the highest and most τελεῖος³ end of human life. He provides a thorough account of the concept in Book i of the *EN*, where he defines εὐδαιμονία in terms of human function, that is, rational activity, and seems reasonably satisfied with his account. Yet an important question remains insufficiently resolved, namely, what role, if any, external goods have in εὐδαιμονία. In some passages, Aristotle explicitly argues that the exercise of at least some virtuous actions requires external goods; for example *MM* ii.8, 1207b16: ἄνευ γὰρ τῶν ἐκτὸς ἀγαθῶν, ὧν ἡ τύχη ἐστὶ κυρία, οὐκ ἐνδέχεται εὐδαίμονα εἶναι, 'for without external goods, of which chance is ruler, it is not possible to be happy.' Elsewhere, he equally clearly maintains that it would be 'too discordant' for the highest human good to be left to chance (τύχη), and that εὐδαιμονία is something within our power to achieve, regardless of our circumstances: τὸ δὲ μέγιστον καὶ κάλλιστον ἐπιτρέψαι τύχῃ λίαν πλημμελὲς ἂν εἴη (*EN* i.9, 1099b24).

However, certain common external goods (such as are necessary for the exercise of the virtues) are indisputably present or absent according to the vagaries of chance. Since few, if any, individuals are completely furnished with all requisite external goods, any acceptable eudaimonistic theory must somehow allow more than the elite few to attain εὐδαιμονία, in spite of their lack of external goods.⁴ These are indeed significant passages which make Aristotle's intent opaque to interpretation. Yet, although Aristotle never presents a unified account of external goods in the *EN*, there is strong evidence that he does thoroughly understand the need for some such account to resolve this tension.

I will use as the core definition of εὐδαιμονία the one Aristotle gives at 1177a17, and at 1101a14–16: τί οὖν κωλύει λέγειν εὐδαίμονα τὸν κατ᾽ ἀρετὴν τελείαν ἐνεργοῦντα καὶ τοῖς ἐκτὸς ἀγαθοῖς ἱκανῶς κεχορηγημένον μὴ τὸν τυχόντα χρόνον ἀλλὰ τέλειον βίον;, 'what therefore prevents one from calling εὐδαίμων a person acting in accordance with τέλειος excellence and sufficiently supplied with external goods, not for a chance span of time but for a τέλειος life?' Furthermore, as stated in Book ii of the *EN*, an agent acts virtuously πρῶτον μὲν ἐὰν εἰδώς, ἔπειτ᾽ ἐὰν προαιρούμενος, καὶ προαιρούμενος δι᾽ αὐτά, τό δὲ τρίτον καὶ ἐὰν βεβαίως καὶ ἀμετακινήτως ἔχων πράττῃ, 'first if he acts knowingly, next if he acts having chosen to do so, and having chosen them for their own sakes, and thirdly if he acts from a firm and unchangeable character'.[5]

These two passages above, taken together, reveal a threefold recipe for εὐδαιμονία: a firm (βέβαιος) and unchangeable (ἀμετακίνητος) character, an activity (ἐνέργεια) in accordance with complete excellence (κατά τέλειαν ἀρετήν), and a sufficient (ἱκανός) supply of external goods. Of these three ingredients, the first two present no difficulties for understanding εὐδαιμονία as self-sufficient. Aristotle explicitly stipulates that the agent's character be steadfast and not subject to change; and that he (Aristotle) holds the activity of εὐδαιμονία to the same standard of immutability is clearly outlined in the following passage:

περὶ οὐδὲν γὰρ οὕτως ὑπάρχει τῶν ἀνθρωπίνων ἔργων βεβαιότης ὡς περὶ τὰς ἐνεργείας τὰς κατ᾽ ἀρετήν · μονιμώτεραι γὰρ καὶ τῶν ἐπιστημῶν αὗται δοκοῦσιν εἶναι...ὑπάρξει δὴ τὸ ζητούμενον τῷ εὐδαίμονι, καὶ ἔσται διὰ βίου τοιοῦτος.

...no function of man has so much permanence [βεβαιότης] as activities in accordance with excellence; for these appear to be longer lasting even than the sciences;...the εὐδαίμων therefore will possess the element of stability in question, and will remain εὐδαίμων all his life.[6]

Both the character and the activity itself of the εὐδαίμων point to the immutability of εὐδαιμονία.

The third element, a sufficient supply of external goods, is the point at which the possibility of impermanence arises. However, we must take great care when dealing with the notion of sufficiency. It is tempting to understand 'sufficient' as 'complete,' conflating ἱκανός and τέλειος; on such a view, the εὐδαίμων would have a full measure of each external good necessary for a truly 'blessed' life. However, a more careful reading yields the interesting possibility that there may be some threshold standard of external goods which is not quite complete (τέλειος), yet is still sufficient (ἱκανός) to support εὐδαιμονία. I believe that this standard is precisely what Aristotle means in chapter 10 of EN Book i, where he allows that the εὐδαίμων makes the best of whatever circumstances he encounters, and in his account in Book x of the contemplative εὐδαίμων, who still requires τὰ πρὸς τὸ ζῆν ἀναγκαία, 'the necessities of life' (1177a29), even if not to the same extent as the virtuous individual; and again, when he states that καὶ γὰρ ἀπὸ μετρίων δύναιτ' ἄν τις πρόττειν τὰ κατὰ τὴν ἀρετήν, 'even with moderate advantages one can act in accordance with excellence' (1179a4).

This chapter will comprise five sections. Section one introduces one of Aristotle's central characteristics of εὐδαιμονία, namely, self-sufficiency, or αὐταρκεῖα. Based upon Aristotle's function argument and his teleological analysis of human action and life generally, we see that the optimal expression of living well must indeed lack nothing requisite for happiness, if it is truly to be considered the best form of life.

The second section deals with external goods and their relation to chance, τύχη, and the question of fairness in ethical evaluation. We will examine Aristotle's argument that chance, and the goods that are dependent upon it, are not properly ethically evaluable. Resulting from this, we can recognize two distinct concepts in Aristotle's ethical writings: one which describes a fully self-sufficient and complete state, and is thus a properly ethically evaluable concept; and another which is rather an encomium, being dependent upon an abundance of external goods which is due to chance circumstance.

In section three I focus on Aristotle's characterization of εὐδαιμονία as an ἐνέργεια, and the tension, inherent in the above two positions, which arises from this description. Although chance is properly not ethically evaluable, nevertheless insofar as εὐδαιμονία is an ἐνέργεια, it *requires* τὰ ἐκτός for its actualization, for progressing beyond a mere δύναμις. This tension raises serious structural problems for any intellectualist interpretation of Aristotle. I believe an inclusivist position is better situated and equipped to resolve this tension.

In the fourth section, I argue that the two concepts from section two—the happy life and the fortunate life—can be usefully employed adequately and consistently to explain Aristotle's treatment of external goods. I propose that identifying these two lives as εὐδαιμονία and μακαρία, respectively, is consistent with the linguistic evidence from Homer through the later Aristotelian commentators, and that the distinction has well-grounded precedent in Aristotle's own use of the terms.

In the fifth section, I present an approach toward resolving the tension between εὐδαιμονία as αὐταρκής and as ἐνέργεια. Relying upon Aristotle's descriptions of the conditions of a human life, or βίος, I argue that εὐδαιμονία can be dependent upon a minimal standard of external goods, thus maintaining the intuition that a virtuous man being tortured on the rack is not εὐδαίμων in the full sense, while still being formally αὐτάρκης, self-sufficient insofar as no addition to it will serve to improve it.

εὐδαιμονία as Self-Sufficient (αὐτάρκης)

Book I of the *Nicomachean Ethics* contains Aristotle's characteristically systematic approach to discovering in what, exactly, εὐδαιμονία consists. He identifies several features as essential to it. Εὐδαιμονία is ψυχῆς ἐνέργεια...κατ' ἀρετήν...τὴν ἀρίστην καὶ τελειοτάτην, 'an activity of soul...in accordance with...the best and most τέλειος excellence' (*EN* i.7, 1098a16); it is τὸ εὖ ζῆν καὶ τὸ εὖ πράττειν, 'living well and doing well' in general (*EN* i.8, 1098b21).[7] The life of the εὐδαίμων is in itself pleasant (*EN* i.8, 1099a5); and it can be attained διά τινος μαθήσεως καὶ ἐπιμελείας, 'through some training and attention' (*EN* i.9, 1099b18).

A great deal of emphasis, however, is placed particularly upon the permanence, completeness, and self-sufficiency (αὐταρκεῖα) of the activity of happiness. It is τέλειον [καὶ] αὔταρκες (*EN* i.7, 1097b20), and τέλος καὶ τέλειον...πάντῃ πάντως (*EN* i.10, 1101a18); and it must be ἔτι δ' ἐν βίῳ τελείῳ (*EN* i.7, 1098a18). It is considered ὑπειληφέναι καὶ μηδαμῶς εὐμετάβολον, 'thoroughly established and not at all changeable' (*EN* i.10, 1100b3); changes after one's death, even though they can to a degree affect one's εὐδαιμονία, are never enough to reverse it (*EN* i.11, 1101b6). The permanence of εὐδαιμονία ensures that ὑπάρξει δὴ τὸ ζητούμενον τῷ εὐδαίμονι, καὶ ἔσται διὰ βίου τοιοῦτος, 'that which is sought will belong to the εὐδαίμων, and he will be such [i.e. εὐδαίμων] throughout his life'.[8]

All of these descriptions, which emphasize the nature of εὐδαιμονία as complete and self-contained, create a picture of εὐδαιμονία as free of the influence of contingent circumstance. The individual who is properly brought up, has the appropriate disposition, and thereby chooses to act in accordance with virtue, actually acts so, and desires and enjoys acting so—this person will enjoy the best and most excellent sort of life. He will not be subject to conflicts of desires, as are those who pursue various external goods (*EN* i.8, 1099a12), but will instead aim at and achieve those goods which are not only pleasant to himself, but pleasant by nature: οὐδὲν δὴ προσδεῖται τῆς ἡδονῆς ὁ βίος αὐτῶν ὥσπερ περιάπτου τινός, ἀλλ' ἔχει τὴν ἡδονὴν ἐν ἑαυτῷ, 'the life of these [those who are lovers of excellence] does not need pleasure as a sort of ornament, but has pleasure within itself'.[9]

Understanding self-sufficiency is an integral part of any complete account of εὐδαιμονία. If εὐδαιμονία is indeed the best form of life, this entails that no other form of life is better than it; but if there were any additional item X which, if added to εὐδαιμονία, would make life better, εὐδαιμονία would no longer be the best form of life, but εὐδαιμονία-plus-X would be better than εὐδαιμονία (*EN* i.7, 1097b15–20). Thus there can be no X which is not included within εὐδαιμονία, yet which would have the capacity to benefit or improve a life. If X is not an ingredient in εὐδαιμονία, then X is not a good, even though its presence might seem to enhance a life, and its absence to debilitate.

External Goods and Chance: Fairness in Ethical Evaluation

Why not, then, include external goods within εὐδαιμονία? This would meet the criterion of self-sufficiency, and would permit us to recognize the apparent influence external goods or their lack have upon the human life. However, Aristotle consistently recognizes the fact that the presence or absence of external goods, whether property, wealth, health, praiseworthy offspring, or a properly-functioning brain, is a matter over which individuals exercise only a limited degree of control. This being the case, εὐδαιμονία, insofar as it is an ethical concept, must in fact be qualitatively different from a life characterized by good fortune—the old 'ought implies can' dictum. Where εὐδαιμονία is intended to be an undebatably ethical concept, external goods, because of their intrinsic connection with τύχη, cannot be ethically substantive. As Aristotle puts it in the *Magna Moralia*, ἔστιν δ' ἡ εὐτυχία καὶ ἡ τύχη ἐν τοῖς μὴ ἐφ' ἡμῖν οὖσιν, μηδ' ὧν αὐτοὶ κύριοί ἐσμεν καὶ δυνατοὶ πρᾶξαι. διὸ τὸν δίκαιον, ᾗ δίκαιος, οὐθεὶς λέγει εὐτυχῆ οὐδὲ τὸν ἀνδρεῖον οὐδ' ὅλως τῶν κατ' ἀρετὴν οὐδένα, 'Good fortune, indeed fortune generally, is among those things not in our power, nor of which we ourselves are masters and able to make happen. For which reason no one calls fortunate the just man insofar as he is just, nor the brave man, nor any one at all of those [living] according to excellence'.[10]

Why does it matter that the individual's εὐδαιμονία be completely within his control, and exclude factors attributable to chance? Simply because we cannot praise or blame someone for things beyond his control; and εὐδαιμονία, as the highest expression of human ethical behavior, is the quintessential object of ethical evaluation. Another reason is the general intuition that any given individual has as good a shot at leading an ethically praiseworthy life as any other. It would seem monstrously unfair of the world to offer some few individuals the opportunity to lead ethical lives, while consigning the majority not merely to *materially* unsatisfactory lives, but to moral turpitude, in spite of their own best intentions. This would be moral determinism at its most heavy-handed.

In order to maintain εὐδαιμονία as a properly ethical concept, that is, a type of living which we can properly attribute specifically to the will of the individual, and for which we can properly and fairly assign praise or blame, it seems that we cannot subsume the results of τύχη under εὐδαιμονία. Rather, Aristotle understands the life characterized by 'lucky breaks' as a sort of felicitation:[11] it may presuppose εὐδαιμονία, but its inclusion of chance and its consequences puts it properly outside the realm of ethical evaluation, the realm wherein εὐδαιμονία is of paramount concern to us. We might be tempted to ask whether Aristotle is wrong in naming εὐδαιμονία the highest human good, as he explicitly does. If the life of a virtuous individual with good fortune exceeds εὐδαιμονία *simpliciter* in certain respects, shouldn't he—and we— consider the former to be the highest human good? However, in judging or evaluating human actions, as a theory of virtue ethics does, the domain of the evaluation is that which is within our ability to affect. The aspects in which the life of good fortune surpasses εὐδαιμονία are precisely aspects over which we have an intrinsic lack of control— external circumstances are always at least in part in the domain of chance or fortune, τύχη, an element that, while always present and efficacious in ethical matters, is not ethically evaluable.

How, then, to construe μακαρία? In order for someone to be μακάριος, he must not only possess the minimum elements of a human life, but must also happen to enjoy the best possible circumstances: wealth and prosperity, political power, good reputation, virtuous friends and family, physical strength and beauty.[12] As Aristotle points out, τὰ δὲ μεγάλα καὶ πολλὰ γιγνόμενα μὲν εὖ μακαριώτερον τὸν βίον ποιήσει (καὶ γὰρ αὐτὰ συνεπικοσμεῖν πέφυκεν, καὶ ἡ χρῆσις αὐτῶν καλὴ καὶ σπουδαία γίγνεται), 'a multitude of great events, should they come about, will make life more blessed (for they themselves are such as to add beauty to life, and the way one deals with them can be noble and good)' (*EN* i.10 1100b25-6). Μακαρία demarcates the highest attainable overall state of human flourishing: for the μακάριος, *all* possible factors in his life, not just ethical factors, are as good as they can get.

There are certain senses in which μακαρία is, in fact, 'better' than εὐδαιμονία. It would be quite in opposition to Aristotle's goal in his ethical writings—that is, to give a rational and normative account of the observed phenomena of human life—to claim that the sorts of goods characteristic of μακαρία are not truly goods; it is precisely insofar as they *are* goods that their presence elevates the life of the μακάριος to the realm of the blessed (as at 1100b25 above). However, there is a crucial distinction to be made here, one which explains why μακαρία does not qualify as the highest human good in the way that εὐδαιμονία does. The relevant difference between μακαρία and εὐδαιμονία, the former's characterization in terms of external goods dependent upon chance factors outside the control of the agent, is exactly what eliminates μακαρία from consideration as the highest human good. Aristotle's ethics is, after all, a science, dealing with human acts and our knowledge of them. And, as he establishes in the *Physics*, the activities of chance or fortune, even though they may be active in significant ways in human life, are nonetheless, by their very nature, not the sort of thing that can be described in terms of inquiry. This is because inquiry deals with τὰ μὲν ἀεὶ ὡσαύτως γινόμενα τὰ δὲ ὡς ἐπὶ πολύ, things that happen always or for the most part (*Phys.* ii.5, 196b10), while chance events, by definition, happen only unpredictably, unbound by any rational account. Also, the effects of chance are not within the control of human agency; and so a normative account of the human good will not properly have a place for an ethical evaluation of the workings of fortune. Μακαρία does presuppose εὐδαιμονία—an individual who is not εὐδαίμων cannot be μακάριος—but its essential reliance on chance makes it unfit to serve as a proper ethical guideline. That is why, on this account, it is most properly conceived of as a felicitation rather than a term of (ethical) commendation.

Εὐδαιμονία *per se* does not necessarily include external goods dependent upon chance or fortune—it can be (and most often is) expressed in less than ideal circumstances. However, I argue that εὐδαιμονία *per se* is just as desirable as μακαρία, even though the latter necessarily carries with it certain benefits the former may lack. For in both cases, the state of the soul is the same, particularly with respect to potentiality.[13] Both the εὐδαίμων and the μακάριος are such that, given proper circumstances, they will act in accordance with virtue. The difference lies in the fact that, for the μακάριος, such circumstances are, in fact, *always* given to him fully, whereas for the εὐδαίμων, they are not. The εὐδαίμων is no worse off than the μακάριος in any ethical sense, or in terms of evaluating his character, though he is worse off in respect of enjoying the goods of fortune.

The distinction I draw, then, between εὐδαιμονία and μακαρία is that the former, being stable and immutable, requires external goods only sufficient for the living of a human life, while the latter indicates the presence of εὐδαιμονία plus an abundance and full complement of external goods. I will show, in section 3.4 below, that such a distinction, while not consistently nor definitively upheld by Aristotle, is nevertheless strongly supported by textual evidence elsewhere in ancient literature, and enjoys some plausible support within the Aristotelian corpus as well.

εὐδαιμονία as Activity

One of the unambiguous features of εὐδαιμονία in Aristotle is that it is an ἐνέργεια, an activity. In his discussion of ἐνέργεια in Book ix of the *Metaphysics*, Aristotle tells us that ἐλήλυθε δ᾽ ἡ ἐνέργεια τοὔνομα...ἐπὶ τὰ ἄλλα ἐκ τῶν κινήσεων μάλιστα, 'the name 'activity' has been extended from motions mostly to other things' (1047a31), but that, more loosely, we connect it with fulfillment generally (ἡ πρὸς τὴν ἐντελέχειαν συντιθεμένη, 1047a30) and with τὸ ὑπάρχειν τὸ πρᾶγμα, the existence of the thing (1048a31). It is prior to potentiality (1049b5), in formula (1049b12–17), in time (1049b18–1050a3), in substance (1050a4–b6), and in a higher, more eternal sense (1050b7–28). Unsurprisingly for such a fundamental concept, Aristotle gives no strict definition: δῆλον δ᾽ ἐπὶ τῶν καθ᾽ ἕκαστα τῇ ἐπαγωγῇ ὃ βουλόμεθα λέγειν, καὶ οὐ δεῖ παντὸς ὅρον ζητεῖν ἀλλὰ καὶ τὸ ἀνάλογον συνορᾶν, 'that which we wish to say is apparent in each case by induction, and we must not seek a definition of everything but [should] accept the analogy' (*Meta.* ix.6, 1048a35–36). Among the several particular cases he offers for us to grasp the concept, he distinguishes between incomplete and complete actions—those which lack and those which contain within themselves the end to which they are directed. The former class includes such processes as making something thin, learning, walking, and building, which he calls (incomplete) movements. The latter class, in contrast, he identifies as actualities (ἐνέργειαι); and the paradigmatic examples of this latter sort are seeing, understanding, living well, and being happy (1048b18–34). This discussion foreshadows Aristotle's more explicit argument later in the *EN*:

εἴπομεν δὴ ὅτι οὐκ ἔστιν ἕξις· καὶ γὰρ τῷ καθεύδοντι διὰ βίου ὑπάρχοι ἄν, φυτοῦ ζῶντι βίον, καὶ τῷ δυστυχοῦντι τὰ μέγιστα. εἰ δὴ ταῦτα μὴ ἀρέσκει, ἀλλὰ μᾶλλον εἰς ἐνέργειάν τινα θετέον, καθάπερ ἐν τοῖς πρότερον εἴρηται, τῶν δ' ἐνεργειῶν αἱ μὲν εἰσὶν ἀναγκαῖαι καὶ δι' ἕτερα αἱρεταί, αἱ δὲ καθ' αὑτάς, δῆλον ὅτι τὴν εὐδαιμονίαν τῶν καθ' αὑτὰς αἱρετῶν τινὰ θετέον καὶ οὐ τῶν δι' ἄλλο.

We said, then, that it [εὐδαιμονία] is not a state; for it might belong to someone who was asleep throughout his life, living the life of a plant, or to someone suffering the greatest misfortunes. If these consequences are unacceptable, we must rather posit happiness as an activity, as was said in the earlier discussion, and [if] some activities are necessary and desirable for the sake of something else,while others are so in themselves, it is clear that εὐδαιμονία must be placed among those desirable in themselves, not among the others.[14]

The fact that Aristotle is so consistent and insistent on this point is a reasonable indication that the point that εὐδαιμονία is an activity is an essential part of his conception of εὐδαιμονία, and we would do well to consider the implications it contains. Human activity takes place in the context of the natural world. This is simply an unavoidable feature of our nature as physical beings. Even our contemplative activity, divine in nature as it may be, nevertheless is dependent upon certain features of our physical existence. We will explore some of these implications next.

ἐνεργεῖα and External Goods

The above conception of εὐδαιμονία as self-sufficient seems fully compatible with the account Aristotle gives, in *EN* i chapters 8 and 12 and outlined in the last section, that the potentiality or state (δύναμις), the simple possession (κτῆσις) of virtue, is not sufficient to constitute εὐδαιμονία (1098b32–1099a5, 1101b10–1102a4). Rather, εὐδαιμονία is the *activity* of soul according to complete excellence. Someone who possesses the potentialities of certain virtues but does not actively express them, such as, in Aristotle's own examples, someone asleep, or a spectator at the Olympic games, cannot truly be said to be εὐδαίμων.

However, a significant consequence of this stipulation is that at least some minimal level of external goods becomes necessary for the exercise of at least some virtues. For example, the virtue of magnanimity requires one to have property with which to be generous; friendship requires worthy friends; and courage requires circumstances, such as battles, in which to express bravery (*EN* i.8, 1099a32 et seq.). In addition, there are certain minimal external goods with which everyone must be supplied in order even to have a life at all—dependable food, shelter, and so on: without these being adequately provided, it will not be possible to achieve εὐδαιμονία.[15] And finally, as noted both here (1097b11 et al.) and in the *Politics* (*Pol.* i.7, 1253a2), man is a ζῷον πολιτικόν by nature; and as such, a complete human life cannot be limited to the individual, but must include his own immediate circumstances: καὶ γονεῦσι καὶ τέκνοις καὶ γυναικὶ καὶ ὅλως τοῖς φίλοις καὶ πολίταις, 'parents and children and wife and altogether friends and fellow-citizens' (*EN* i.7, 1097b10). This necessary connection of the individual's good with his family and peers directly informs the discussion in chapter 10, where Aristotle examines whether and to what extent one's εὐδαιμονία is affected by the character and deeds of one's ancestors and descendants. All of these considerations suggest—indeed, require—an understanding of εὐδαιμονία that extends beyond one's own virtues.

What makes this understanding problematic is that it seems incompatible with Aristotle's initial characterization of εὐδαιμονία as stable, permanent, or somehow insulated from contingent circumstance.[16] As Heinaman notes, and as we have seen above, self-sufficiency is a formal requirement of εὐδαιμονία for Aristotle,[17] both in Book i (εὐδαιμονία is described as αὔταρκες at 1097b20, and ὑπειληφέναι καὶ μηδαμῶς εὐμετάβολον at 1100b3) and in Book x (εὐδαιμονία is described as οὐδενὸς ἐνδεὴς and αὔταρκες at 1176b5). At 1097b14–15, the self-sufficient (τὸ αὔταρκες) is defined as ὃ μονούμενον αἱρετὸν ποιεῖ τὸν βίον καὶ μηδενὸς ἐνδεᾶ, 'that which alone makes life desirable and lacking nothing.' If εὐδαιμονία is truly self-sufficient, it is unclear how it can be lacking in any respect, according to the above definition. Yet it is apparent that εὐδαιμονία, when we understand it as Aristotle defines it, 'activity of soul in conformity with virtue,' in itself lacks many items which make our life desirable. Food itself, for example, has no part of εὐδαιμονία thus defined, even though it can be used virtuously, for example, temperately.

The Case for Distinguishing εὐδαιμονία and μακαρία

In *The Fragility of Goodness*, Nussbaum is concerned with the intersection of virtue, εὐδαιμονία, and chance. Her rich and complex account draws on considerations not only of the Greek philosophical tradition, but also tragedy and literature in general. When she turns her attention to Aristotle's treatment of the dialectical argument between the position that chance is the source of human happiness and the position that happiness is immune to reversal by luck, she acknowledges (in Aristotelian fashion) the positions that precede her in answering this question, and devotes herself to responding to them. Among these interlocutors are W.D. Ross and H.H. Joachim, whom Nussbaum identifies as the most recent in a tradition (characterized as Kantian) which attributes to Aristotle a distinction between εὐδαιμονία, happiness, and μακαρία, or blessedness. After presenting their arguments, Nussbaum rejects them, arguing convincingly that the textual support in Aristotle's major works, especially the *EN*, is essentially nonexistent. She presents a line-by-line analysis of the passages in which Aristotle uses the two terms, arguing that, in each case, the reasonable interpretation points to a consistent, unified account of εὐδαιμονία, rather than to one of two distinct concepts. On Nussbaum's account, εὐδαιμονία and μακαρία are completely synonymous terms.

I wish to challenge Nussbaum's dismissal of this position on three grounds. First, when we look at the historical use of the two terms in the works of earlier authors, including the pre-Socratics, there is significant and widespread evidence for understanding εὐδαιμονία and μακαρία as terms with distinctive semantic histories which consistently inform their use throughout Greek literature, rather than as mere synonyms which an author might use for the sake of stylistic variation. A reading of the earliest extant Aristotle commentators reveals a well-established tradition of interpreting Aristotle in terms of an ethically significant distinction between his account of εὐδαιμονία taken in isolation and when understood in the context of a lived human life, with external circumstance playing a role in one's understanding of εὐδαιμονία.

Finally, when examining the Aristotelian texts themselves, many of the passages offered by Nussbaum, though they are intelligible according to her account, are also consistent when understood as I argue.

We do find that there is, in fact, plentiful evidence for drawing meaningful distinctions between the terms εὐδαιμονία and μακαρία in the works of earlier Greek writers, from Homer down through the early 5th century BCE. The 1969 work of Cornelius de Heer, *Μακάρ, Εὐδαίμων, Ὄλβιος, Εὐτύχης*, provides a systematic analysis of the four main word-groups clustered around the general concept of happiness in ancient Greek. I shall rely on this work to examine the two relevant to the discussion here, starting with εὐδαιμονία.

***Homeric and Early Greek Uses of* εὐδαιμονία *and* μακαρία.** The history of εὐδαιμονία and its cognates is especially varied. de Heer admits that the term εὐδαίμων, as he says, 'has had the most spectacular career; in Hesiod [where it first appears in the extant literature] its meaning is simple; in the 5th century it portrays a wide range of hopes and fears which beset its time'.[18] In spite of the word's wide variation in sense over time, we do find several core senses consistently associated with the εὐδαιμονία group. First, as early as Sappho (late 7th century BCE) and Theognis (6th century BCE), we find an association suggested between εὐδαιμονία and ἀρετή:

ὁ πλοῦτος ἀνεὺ ἀρετάς οὐκ ἀσινῆς παροῖκος ·
ἃ δ' ἀμφοτέρων κράσις εὐδαιμονίας ἔχει τὸ ἄκρον

wealth without excellence [is] not a harmless neighbor;
but the combination of both holds the highest point of happiness. (Sappho 148)

and

Εὐδαίμων εἴην καὶ θεοῖς φίλος ἀθανάτοισιν,
Κύρν'· ἀρετῆς δ' ἄλλης οὐδεμιῆς ἔραμαι.

would that I were happy and dear to the deathless gods,
Cyrnus; I yearn for no other excellence. (Theognis 653–654)

Of course, we need no reminder of the danger involved in casting ἀρετή as a narrowly ethical concept. Still, for our purposes, it is important to note this association, especially in contrast with other terms, such as ὄλβια and μακαρία, from whose semantic vocabulary ἀρετή is conspicuously absent.

A second important thread of meaning associated with εὐδαιμονία, that it demarcates the apex of specifically human achievement, finds expression in Pindar:

οὔτε παλιγγλόσσος πόλις,
ἅτις οὐ Πήλεος ἄει κλεος ἠ-
ρωος, εὐδαίμονος γαμβροῦ θεῶν

nor is there a city so alien,
which [has] not [heard of] the eternal renown of the hero Peleus,
the happy son-in-law of the gods (Pindar, *Isthmian Odes* 6, 25 ff)

and

θεός εἴη
ἀπήμων κέαρ; εὐδαίμων δε καὶ ὑμνή-
τος οὗτος ἀνήρ γίγνεται σοφοῖς,
ὅς ἂν χέρσιν ἤ ποδῶν ἀρεταί κρατήσαις
τὰ μέγιστ᾽ ἀεθλῶν ἕλῃ τόλμαι τε καὶ σθένει

a god
may be untouched by ruin; but such a man becomes
happy and lauded among the wise,
who by his powerful hands or by the excellence of his feet seizes
the greatest of prizes with daring and power (Pindar, *Pythian Odes* 10, 21–25)

As de Heer puts it, 'the poet puts the fundamental difference between gods and men in a sharp perspective. Freedom from grief is godlike; all man can hope to achieve is to be εὐδαίμων, and ὑμνητός by the poets…to be εὐδαίμων is the peak of human hopes and ambitions'.[19] Εὐδαιμονία is explicitly disengaged from divine overtones (at least in the sense that its application is appropriate to mortals rather than to gods—its source is still undeniably divine); it is what marks the upper boundary of what is possible for human beings to achieve, given their subjection to chance fortune. In the first case, the quotation from the *Isthmian Odes*, even Peleus, son-in-law of the gods, is emphatically εὐδαίμων, when praised in close connection with the gods. This characterization of εὐδαιμονία as particularly human and not, or at least not fully, divine is in sharp contrast with μακαρία, as we shall see.

A third notable aspect of the εὐδαιμονία group, the possibility of permanence, is illustrated in Pindar's *Nemean Ode 7*:

εἰ γὰρ σφίσιν ἐμπεδοσθένεα βίοτον ἁρμόσαις
ἤβαι λιπαρῷ τε γήραι διαπλεκοῖς
εὐδαίμον' ἔοντα, παιδῶν δὲ παίδες ἔχοιεν ἄει
γέρας τὸ περ νύν καὶ ἄπειρον ὄπιθεν...

for if you accord to them a firm-settled life
in youth, and weave into a comfortable old age
being happy, and that their children's children might always
have honor both now and forever hereafter... (Pindar, *Nemean Odes* 7, 98–101)

In this prayer to Heracles, the poet associates εὐδαιμονία with at least the possibility of permanence (with his use of ἐμπεδοσθενέα and ἄρειον). Although he does not conflate merely human εὐδαιμονία with the blessed state of the gods, nevertheless he acknowledges that, with the cooperation of the divinity, even mortals can attain a lasting happiness.

Let us now examine the main features of the μακαρία group. From Homer onward, by far the most common use of μακαρία is in connection with the gods. Of the 18 times the word μάκαρ or one of its forms appears in the *Iliad*, 16 times it is used as an epithet for a god. This association of μακαρία with the divine is a primary component of the word's sense. A regular theme in Homer is the association of μακαρία with θεοί and/or with other words, such as ἀθάνατος, which carry connotations of the divine. However, overlaid on this core of divine application, there is also clearly established precedent for naming mortals as μάκαρες as well: at first, in Homer, the dead (*Odyssey* 2.483ff.; 5.306; 11.483) and/or heroes—Agamemnon, Priam, Achilles (*Iliad* 2.67ff; 3.181ff; *Odyssey* 1.217; 6.154ff.; 6.158); but later, in Pindar, for example, even a relatively unknown mortal, the chariot-driver Carrhotus, earns the right to be named μακάριος (Pindar, *Pyth.* 5.46ff). That the difference between the lives of the Olympians and those of mortals is conceived as one of degree more than of kind makes the transition plausible. The application of μάκαρ words to mortals, however, always retains a strong sense of divine favor and exceptionalness.

Besides divinity or its approximation, what else does μακαρία entail? What are some of its specific characteristics? Unlike εὐδαιμονία, there is no extant association of μακαρία with ἀρετή. However, we do find that μάκαρες enjoy something else, namely, external prosperity and bounty.[20] As de Heer writes, 'The name μάκαρ evokes a sense complex which is associated with the divine world....This resemblance [that is, of a mortal to the gods] is rooted in certain phenomena, such as...the possession of wealth and its concomitant, a life of ease' (de Heer 14).

Finally, insofar as μακαρία is associated with the life of the gods, permanence is an intrinsic feature; but insofar as it is applied to mortals and related to wealth and its consequences, it lacks the full permanence originally implied in the concept as divine. The *locus classicus* of this ambivalence is the case of Priam, mentioned both in the *Iliad* Book 24 (24.543ff.) and, of course, by Aristotle in *EN* i.10.

To sum up, then, the literary evidence leading up to Aristotle suggests that εὐδαιμονία is considered a specifically human, and not divine, goal; there is a close connection between it and ἀρετή; and there is a possibility of permanence associated with it. By contrast, μακαρία is essentially and originally divine, gradually applied to mortals by extension and through comparison to the divine; one of its core components is an association with the possession of wealth or goods; and, because of its dependence on external circumstance (as applied to mortals), it has only a qualified association with permanence or security.

***Post-Aristotelian Uses of* εὐδαιμονία *and* μακαρία.** An examination of philosophers and philosophical commentators subsequent to Aristotle yields further evidence supporting an interpretation of his work according to this distinction. The canonical interpretation of Aristotle by his successors reflects the account of εὐδαιμονία given in *EN* i.10, 1101a14–17: τί οὖν κωλύει λέγειν εὐδαίμονα τὸν κατ' ἀρετὴν τελείαν ἐνεργοῦντα καὶ τοῖς ἐκτὸς ἀγαθοῖς ἱκανῶς κεχορηγημένον μὴ τὸν τυχόντα χρόνον ἀλλὰ τέλειον βίον; 'what then prevents one from saying that the person is εὐδαίμων who is active in accordance with complete virtue and sufficiently equipped with the external goods not for a chance period of time but for a complete life?' Take, for example, the point Alexander of Aphrodisias makes in his argument against the Stoics in his *de Anima*:

ἔτι διττῆς οὔσης τῆς ἐνεργείας καθ' ἑκάστην τέχνην, τῆς μὲν ἐν προηγουμένοις, ὡς τῷ αὐλητῇ, εἰ ὑγιαίνοι τε τῷ σώματι καὶ αὐλούς, οἵους βούλεται ἔχοι καὶ μηδὲν ἔξωθεν αὐτὸν ἐνοχλοῖ, τῆς δὲ ἐν ἀβουλήτοις καὶ ἐναντίοις τῶν προειρημένων, ὥσπερ ταῖς ἄλλαις τέχναις τὸ τέλος ἐν ταῖς περὶ τὰ βουλητὰ καὶ ἐν προηγουμέναις ἐνεργείαις, οὕτως καὶ ἐπὶ τῆς ἀρετῆς, εἴ γε καὶ αὕτη τέχνη.

Activity in accordance with craft covers in each case two things. On the one hand there is activity in primary circumstances (ἐν προηγουμένοις), as for the flute-player if he is healthy in body and has flutes of the kind he wishes for and nothing external troubles him; on the other hand there is activity in circumstances he does not wish for (ἐν ἀβουλήτοις), that is, in circumstances the opposite of those just mentioned. So, just as the ends of the other crafts lie in activities with wished for things and in primary circumstances, so also for virtue, supposing it too is a craft.[21]

Here we see the standard Aristotelian characterization of virtuous activity as an activity, in particular a craft, aiming at an end. Alexander, like Aristotle, accepts the efficacy of external circumstances in virtuous activity: and further, he explicitly addresses two separate cases under which virtuous activity takes place: primary (or preferred) circumstances and unwished-for circumstances, with the clear implication that this is a significant distinction, producing a relevantly different account of virtuous activity depending upon which circumstances apply to a given case. This distinction is made by Arius Didymus as well, when he defines εὐδαιμονία as 'the προηγουμένη (preferred) use of complete virtue in a complete life.'[22]

Again, in Book v of the *de Finibus*, Cicero reports the position of Antiochus of Ascalon that there is a distinction between the *vita beata* and the *vita beatissima* based on the inclusion of external goods in addition to the virtues. In dialogue with Piso, Cicero says:

...sed haec cum corporis bona sint, eōrum conficientia certe in bonīs numerābis, amicōs, liberōs, propinquōs, divitiās, honorēs, opēs. Contrā hoc attende mē nihil dicere, [illud dicere], si ista mala sunt, in quae potest incidere sapiens, sapientem esse nōn esse ad beātē vivendum satis. Immō vero, inquit, ad beātissime vivendum parum est, ad beātē vero satis. Animadverti, inquam, tē istō modō paulō ante ponere, et sciō ab Antiochō nostrō dicī sīc solēre...

...but since these bodily things are goods, you shall certainly number among goods the things productive of these: friends, children, relatives, riches, honors, power. Notice that I say nothing against this, if misfortunes into which a wise man may fall are as you say evils, to be wise is not enough for happiness. No indeed, he said, it is not enough for living most blessedly, but indeed it is enough for living blessedly. I noticed, I replied, you made that distinction a little time ago, and I am aware that our master Antiochus is fond of saying the same...[23]

Cicero goes on to take note of the logical consistency, but practical absurdity, inherent in the Academic tradition of identifying a single degree of (virtuous) happiness.

Aristotelian Uses of εὐδαιμονία ***and*** μακαρία. With this background, we can now return to Aristotle and an analysis of the specifically philosophical use to which he puts these terms. Aristotle certainly recognizes this tension between the two accounts of εὐδαιμονία: or at least, it would be only reasonable to presume that, after having given such extensive attention to both of them, he would also recognize their incompatibility. Evidence of this realization seems implicit in chapter 10:

> τὸν γὰρ ὡς ἀληθῶς ἀγαθὸν καὶ ἔμφρονα πάσας οἰόμεθα τὰς τύχας εὐσχημόνως φέρειν καὶ ἐκ τῶν ὑπαρχόντων ἀεὶ τὰ κάλλιστα πράττειν, καθάπερ καὶ στρατηγὸν ἀγαθὸν τῷ παρόντι στρατοπέδῳ χρῆσθαι πολεμικώτατα καὶ σκυτοτόμον ἐκ τῶν δοθέντων σκυτῶν κάλλιστον ὑπόδημα ποιεῖν, τὸν αὐτὸν δὲ τρόπον καὶ τοὺς ἄλλους τεχνίτας ἅπαντας. εἰ δ᾽ οὕτως, ἄθλιος μὲν οὐδέποτε γένοιτ᾽ ἂν ὁ εὐδαίμων.

> For the man who is truly good and wise, we think, bears all the chances of life becomingly and always makes the best of circumstances, as a good general makes the best military use of the army at his command and a shoemaker makes the best shoes out of the hides that are given him; and so with all the other crafts. But if this is the case, the happy man can never become miserable.[24]

If it is true, as it seems to be, that there are certain necessary external circumstances without which one cannot attain εὐδαιμονία,[25] nevertheless perhaps this can be made compatible with the earlier account of the self-sufficiency of εὐδαιμονία by situating this self-sufficiency within the context of the individual's given circumstances. While the presence of external goods may be required, it is still up to the virtuous individual to establish his relations to his circumstances, whatever they may be, in accordance with virtue, which is still entirely within his own power. It is within this possible compromise position that Aristotle seems closest to drawing a clear distinction between εὐδαιμονία and μακαρία. Unfortunately, this move does not fully respond to the deeper problem involved. Even if the εὐδαίμων exercises his virtues in relation to whatever the given circumstances are, the fact still remains that there is some minimum threshold of necessary external goods, and if his given circumstances fail to meet this minimum, he will be unable to achieve εὐδαιμονία. The proposed solution simply makes εὐδαιμονία dependent upon some set of minimum conditions—a reasonable answer, but one which fails fully to resolve the tension: on this view, εὐδαιμονία is not *really* self-sufficient, and the permanence and stability of εὐδαιμονία is to a great degree sacrificed. We need a more comprehensive account than Aristotle appears to give even in the text that seems most promising.

As MacIntyre and others have noted, Aristotle describes two varieties of εὐδαιμονία: on the one hand, his account of the nature of humans as *rational* animals leads to a 'primary' εὐδαιμονία consisting in the ideal of contemplation; and on the other, his account of humans' nature as *political* animals produces a so-called 'secondary' εὐδαιμονία of the social and political life, characterized by 'moral' action and the exercise of the virtues in the context of one's family and community.[26]

εὐδαιμονία and the Conditions of βίος

So, how can Aristotle (or we) defend the claim that εὐδαιμονία is αὐταρκές, when it clearly depends upon external circumstances for its full expression as an ἐνέργεια?

Let us consider another limiting case Aristotle discusses, to see whether it might shed some light on this problem. Aristotle claims that εὐδαιμονία is unavailable, in principle, to certain beings—for example, non-human animals and children—because they lack the capacity πραττεῖν ἐνεργειὰς καλούς:

εἰκότως οὖν οὔτε βοῦν οὔτε ἵππον οὔτε ἄλλο τῶν ζῴων οὐδὲν εὔδαιμον λέγομεν· γὰρ αὐτῶν οἷόν τε κοινωνῆσαι τοιαύτης ἐνεργείας. διὰ ταύτην δὲ τὴν αἰτίαν οὐδὲ παῖς εὐδαίμων ἐστίν· οὔπω γὰρ πρακτικὸς τῶν τοιούτων διὰ τὴν ἡλικίαν· οἱ δὲ λεγόμενοι διὰ τὴν ἐλπίδα μακαρίζονται. δεῖ γάρ, ὥσπερ εἴπομεν, καὶ ἀρετῆς τελείας καὶ βίου τελείου.

Properly, then, we call neither an ox nor a horse nor any other one of the animals εὐδαίμων; for no such one of these participates in such activities. And for this cause neither is a child εὐδαίμων; for in no way [is he] capable of doing such [activities] on account of his age; but they call [him] blessed, saying so on account of hope. For, as we have said, [εὐδαιμονία] has need both of complete virtue and of a complete life.[27]

This capacity, then, is a precondition of εὐδαιμονία, and we can say that being a full human agent is a *sine quā nōn* for εὐδαιμονία. This might seem almost tautologous—that being a full human agent, with the capacities thereof (ἐχεῖν λογόν, for instance), is a necessary condition for εὐδαιμονία; but there is a useful parallel with the question of τὰ ἐκτός, once we remember that Aristotle's conception of a full human life, βίος, has quite specific criteria. The rational faculty is of primary importance, but not the sole criterion, for granting human status. Unlike a beast or a god, a human being is characterized by his sociality—the fact of his relations within a society and a community or πόλις. What are some of the specific features of this πολιτικεῖα? Honors or dishonors in public activity (τιμαί and ἀτιμίαι); worthy or unworthy ancestors and offspring; activity in relation to physical resources and wealth; friendships; in short, the sorts of external goods Aristotle keeps returning to. The so-called 'reliance' upon external goods that seems so dangerous to the αὐταρκεῖα criterion is, in fact, no more than a 'reliance' upon Aristotle's definition of a human being as ζῷον πολιτικόν.

How can this understanding help us to resolve the question of external goods? We can admit that the minimum standard of external goods sufficient to the achievement of εὐδαιμονία is precisely the minimum standard of a human life, βίος: food, shelter, and the rest of the things necessary for sustained physical existence, ζωή; and a family and community, which are necessary components of a particularly human life. Thus, as Aristotle puts it, προσδεῖται τούτων ὁ ἀνθρώπινος βίος, 'the human life has need of these things' (*EN* i.10, 1100b9), even though doing well or nobly does not consist in them. It is true that these minimal external elements are subject to change, and one may be deprived of them due to disaster or other misfortune. But in such a case, on Aristotle's view of what constitutes a human life, the individual is no longer leading a *life* at all.[28] The necessary conditions of a human life are thus identical with the necessary conditions of the life of the εὐδαίμων, so that any agent, living a truly human life, will necessarily already meet the threshold standards for exercising the ἐνέργεια of εὐδαιμονία, and an individual who fails to meet this threshold will thereby be incapable of achieving εὐδαιμονία.[29]

This account addresses the potential challenge an inclusivist account might face, namely, that achieving sufficient external goods to exercise the virtues, and hence attain εὐδαιμονία, might be too difficult for more than an elite few. Identifying exactly what this minimum threshold of external goods might be will be a practical inquiry of much merit, and will need to rely heavily on the scientific findings of biologists, psychologists, and sociologists.

εὐδαιμονία and θεωρία

One remaining task for this account is to explain the relation between my interpretation of εὐδαιμονία and the activity of contemplation, θεωρία. Aristotle famously identifies external goods as obstacles to the exercise of θεωρία, when he writes at *EN* x.8: τῷ δὲ θεωροῦντι οὐδενὸς τῶν τοιούτων πρός γε τὴν ἐνέργειαν χρεία, ἀλλ᾽ ὡς εἰπεῖν καὶ ἐμπόδιά ἐστι πρός γε τὴν θεωρίαν, 'the man who is contemplating the truth needs no such thing, at least with a view to the exercise of his activity; but, as one may say, they are even hindrances to his contemplation' (1178b3–5). I have made a case for identifying εὐδαιμονία *per se* as the proper subject matter for Aristotle's ethical inquiry, and μακαρία as a non-morally evaluable state of an agent's life which is characterized by both εὐδαίμων activity and a fortuitous abundance of external goods, which serves as material for the superlative exercise of the agent's εὐδαιμονία. However, it seems that this rosy picture will encounter difficulties if we admit, as Aristotle indicates we must, that external goods are positively harmful to the exercise of our highest faculty, contemplation. Can a life of εὐδαιμονία, which necessarily includes the exercise of contemplation, ever truly be benefited by the addition of abundant external goods, if these goods maim contemplation, though they may enhance virtuous activity? Are μακαρία and θεωρία, or even εὐδαιμονία and θεωρία, incompatible?

Aristotle, in talking about pleasure in the εὐδαίμων life, says in *EN* vii.13: οὐδεμία γὰρ ἐνέργεια τέλειος ἐμποδιζομένη, ἡ δ᾽ εὐδαιμονία τῶν τελείων · διὸ προσδεῖται ὁ εὐδαίμων τῶν ἐν σώματι ἀγαθῶν καὶ τῶν ἐκτὸς καὶ τῆς τύχης, ὅπως μὴ ἐμποδίζηται διὰ ταῦτα, 'no activity is complete when it is impeded, and happiness is a complete thing: this is why the εὐδαίμων needs the goods of the body and external goods, i.e. those of fortune, viz. in order that he may not be impeded in these ways' (1153b17–19). We have seen that Aristotle recognizes that external goods have the capacity to impede contemplation. Does he mean to say that we must minimize them as far as possible—as would seem to be implied by the statement that 'the man who is contemplating the truth needs *no* such thing' (emphasis mine)? Would the ideal human εὐδαίμων be an entirely self-sufficient, non-social creature, capable of constant contemplation with no need for such distractions as food, family, wealth, shelter? When I was an impoverished graduate student practicing contemplation while living on a subsistence-level wage, would my contemplation have been damaged if I had gotten a raise? This seems absurd. Yet if we look only at 1178b3–5 in isolation, we find ourselves with scarcely any way to avoid this conclusion.

We do, however, find an important insight earlier in *EN* vii.13: ἐπεὶ καὶ αὐτὴ ὑπερβάλλουσα ἐμπόδιός ἐστιν, καὶ ἴσως οὐκέτι εὐτυχίαν καλεῖν δίκαιον · πρὸς γὰρ τὴν εὐδαιμονίαν ὁ ὅρος αὐτῆς, 'even [good fortune] itself when in excess is an impediment, and perhaps should then be no longer called good fortune; for its limit is fixed by reference to happiness' (1153b22–24). Aristotle's ethical project, indeed his entire philosophical demeanor, is characterized by nothing if not an acute sensitivity to the relevance of balance, especially when it comes to matters of human conduct. We see this underlying sensibility time and again: in his methodology of 'preserving the phenomena,' in his careful consideration of alternative approaches and their insights, in his analysis of the correct configuration of a πόλις, in the centerpiece of his virtue ethics, the doctrine of the mean. It should be unsurprising that he makes a comment such as the one above; its message, that the appropriate level of good fortune is limited by reference to εὐδαιμονία, is quintessentially Aristotelian. And indeed, it gives us a useful position from which to evaluate the claim of 1178b3–5. The level of external goods appropriate to a life, or their presence or absence, is an issue determined by reference to happiness.

For example, suppose I were someone wealthy, like Mark Zuckerberg. I might feel obliged to spend all my time doing nothing but researching and supporting charitable causes, rather than studying metaphysics. Or I might have so much money that a significant part of my time and mental effort would be constantly required just to manage it. I should recognize that, in this case, what I thought was a great good, something that would enhance my opportunities for virtuous action, would be in fact detrimental to my contemplation, and that my εὐδαιμονία would be maimed. However, it is not absurd to conceive of a person who, though reasonably well-off, nevertheless is, precisely because of his situation, able to devote time to acts of munificence, loyalty, temperance, *and* contemplation. I argue that, if we take the injunction of 1153b22–24 seriously, and conceive of the role of external goods as limited by reference to εὐδαιμονία, rather than as potentially destructive of it, we can achieve a position capable of accommodating both μακαρία and θεωρία, without sacrificing one for the other.

One's Proper (ἴδια) εὐδαιμονία and Nature (φύσις)

My account rests on making a meaningful terminological distinction where Aristotle himself seems to have made none. However, it may be argued that, even if one grants the legitimacy of making such a distinction, my account fails adequately to maintain it. After all, I do not reject Aristotle's analysis of two distinct kinds of εὐδαιμονία, the contemplative and the virtuous. Further, I claim that there is a direct relationship between εὐδαιμονία and μακαρία, where the latter is an instance of the former associated with various external circumstances. However, I give only a single account of μακαρία, whereas I denote two sorts of εὐδαιμονία. Would not a complete theory include a description of μακαρία which would correspond to the different senses of εὐδαιμονία I recognize in Aristotle's theory? And if not, what sort of justification might I offer for denying the necessity of such a change?

I do, in fact, deny that making a distinction between two senses of μακαρία corresponding to the distinction between the two senses of εὐδαιμονία is a necessary step. There is not a 'primary' and a 'secondary' μακαρία, even though I admit of a 'primary' and 'secondary' εὐδαιμονία. I believe that I can justify this position in terms of the different natures of the two terms. Μακαρία is necessarily connected with external goods, according to my (and Aristotle's own) definition. However, εὐδαιμονία has no such restriction: the εὐδαίμων needs no external goods beyond those required for human life in general. When a distinction is made between contemplative and virtuous εὐδαιμονία, it is necessary to examine whether both of them permit the application of the concept of μακαρία in their respective contexts. On the one hand, virtuous εὐδαιμονία certainly has a corresponding μακαρία: the exercise of practical εὐδαιμονία admits of, and even requires, certain external goods, and it is easy to see how a notion of μακαρία is compatible with such a situation. On the other hand, it becomes much less clear that contemplative εὐδαιμονία can be made compatible with μακαρία; for contemplative εὐδαιμονία is essentially opposed to any external goods—

ἀλλ' ὡς εἰπεῖν καὶ ἐμπόδιά ἐστι πρός γε τὴν θεωρίαν, 'indeed they are, one may say, even hindrances, to his [the contemplator's] contemplation' (1178b5). The more one's external goods increase, the more they interfere with the possibility of pursuing contemplative εὐδαιμονία.

One might reply that even the contemplative εὐδαίμων requires the minimum level of external goods necessary for a human life, and so make the case that a contemplative μακαρία would describe precisely that level of external goods necessary for the leading of a life of contemplative εὐδαιμονία, but beyond which they would begin to interfere with it. However, such a move would confuse *pure* contemplative εὐδαιμονία with that achievable by human beings as composite beings. Any beings who were fully and by nature able to attain primary εὐδαιμονία would not require *any* external goods, even the minimal ones required by the best human εὐδαίμων. Contemplative εὐδαιμονία *per se* has no part in external goods at all, but only insofar as it is imperfectly approached by composite human beings. Thus, to attempt to put μακαρία on the same scale as contemplative εὐδαιμονία would be to try to apply inapplicable standards to the former; only virtuous εὐδαιμονία, by its nature concerned with external goods as they are necessary parts of a composite human life, properly corresponds to μακαρία.

What, then, is the proper way to choose between what are still two separate (and conflicting) εὐδαιμονίαι—virtuous (secondary) εὐδαιμονία and contemplative (primary) εὐδαιμονία? I am inclined to take Aristotle seriously when he says νῦν δὲ τοιοῦτόν τι ζητεῖται, 'we are now seeking such a thing [i.e. something attainable]' (1096b34).[30] Unfortunately, Aristotle himself gives us conflicting inclinations. Although he states that ὁ δὲ τοιοῦτος ἂν εἴη βίος κρείττων ἢ κατ' ἄνθρωπον, 'such a life [the complete life of perfect contemplation] would be too high for man' (1177b27), he immediately admonishes us: οὐ χρὴ δὲ κατὰ τοὺς παραινοῦντας ἀνθρώπινα φρονεῖν ἄνθρωπον ὄντα οὐδὲ θνητὰ τὸν θνητόν, ἀλλ' ἐφ' ὅσον ἐνδέχεται ἀθανατίζειν καὶ πάντα ποιεῖν πρὸς τὸ ζῆν κατὰ τὸ κράτιστον τῶν ἐν αὐτῷ, 'one must not follow those who advise him, being a man, to think of human things...but must, so far as possible...do everything in accordance with the best of the things within himself' (1177b32–34). This last passage has been interpreted as evidence that Aristotle, in the end, really considered contemplation to be intrinsically better and more choiceworthy, when at all possible, than virtuous activity. It is not my intention to dispute this claim here.

However, it seems to me that the question has been given more weight in this context than it deserves.[31] The comparison between contemplation and virtuous activity is, in Aristotle's own words, a comparison between the merely mortal and the divine. And while it is true that man has 'something divine present in him,' i.e. intellect, it is equally true that man's nature is not completely exhausted as a rational being. If we were dealing simply with a rational *being*, then we would be talking about something divine, such as a god. But since we are dealing with humans, we must remember that we are rational *animals*—that is to say, composite, embodied beings; and the fact of our corporeality is just as essential to determining our good and τέλος as is our rationality. It is critical that our analysis of Aristotle's comments on the divinity of intellect and contemplation give due consideration to this fact. As Yu has noted, the distinction between an individual who conducts his life *qua* human being and one who lives 'insofar as something divine is present in him' is a philosophically significant one, though 'not yet...fully appreciated'.[32]

We can gladly admit that a life of pure and uninterrupted contemplation is more choiceworthy *per se* than a life of virtuous activity. We can even agree (though we need not) that such a life is more choiceworthy for humans insofar as we are able to achieve it. But neither of these admissions requires that we take the further step, as the intellectualist would have us do, and claim that the contemplative life is unqualifiedly better, more appropriate (ἴδιον), or more choiceworthy for humans than the virtuous life. Although humans can, to a greater or lesser extent, approximate a life of contemplation, it is something that no human being's nature will ever allow him to achieve *in toto*. It is never appropriate for any being to neglect its ἴδιον good for the sake of pursuing one it cannot reach—as it would be inappropriate (and impossible!) for a horse to neglect its own good and τέλος *qua* horse to try to act justly, courageously or magnanimously, the hallmarks of the certainly higher, but particularly *human*, life.

In saying this, I am not 'advis[ing] us, being men, to think of human things'—at least, not in the pejorative sense Aristotle intends by this phrase. I am, however, claiming that there are real differences between the human and the divine, and that the 'human things' which are appropriate for us to strive toward are not 'merely' human, but *include* precisely that degree of divine activity which it is in our nature to achieve, and *also* that degree of social or political activity which is equally inherent in our nature. Aristotle does not base his ethics on an impossible expectation that humans should act as though we were gods. As he tells us at 1182b1–4 (emphasis mine):

> ὑπὲρ ἀγαθοῦ ἄρα, ὡς ἔοικεν, ἡμῖν λεκτέον, καὶ ὑπὲρ ἀγαθοῦ οὐ τοῦ ἁπλῶς, ἀλλὰ τοῦ ἡμῖν· οὐ γὰρ τοῦ θεῶν ἀγαθοῦ· ἀλλ' ὑπὲρ μὲν τούτου καὶ ἄλλος λόγος καὶ ἀλλοτρία ἡ σκέψις. ὑπὲρ τοῦ πολιτικοῦ ἄρα ἡμῖν λεκτέον ἀγαθοῦ.

> It is about good, then, as it seems, that we must speak, and about good not without qualification, but *relatively to ourselves. For we have not to do with the good of the gods.* To speak about that is a different matter, and the inquiry is foreign to our present purpose. It is therefore about the good of the state that we must speak.

Like Plato, Aristotle recognizes that we share a limited similarity with the divine, and so must both recognize it as divine (and hence give it an appropriately important place in our life plans) *and* determine how this component of our nature must integrate with everything else that makes us human beings.

Conclusion

Aristotle begins the *EN* by quite clearly identifying politics as the highest and most divine end of human action. Any intellectualist interpretation has what seems to me the enormous difficulty of attempting to justify an interpretation which flatly contradicts Aristotle's clearly and unequivocally stated conclusion: ἀγαπητὸν μὲν γὰρ καὶ ἐνὶ μόνῳ, κάλλιον δὲ καὶ θειότερον ἔθνει καὶ πόλεσιν. ἡ μὲν οὖν μέθοδος τούτων ἐφίεται, πολιτική τις οὖσα, 'though it is adequate [to attain the end] merely for one man, it is finer and more godlike [to attain it] for a nation or for city-states. Our inquiry, being concerned with politics, therefore aims at these'.[33]

Although the argument I have outlined in this chapter rules out the standard intellectualist position, namely that (a life of) contemplation is what Aristotle identifies as the best possible human life, preferable even to a life of virtuous activity, nevertheless we can by no means fail to provide a central place in our account for the activity of contemplation (θεωρία), that most god-like of our activities. We have said that it cannot be the *only* component of the best life, but we must certainly admit that it will remain a necessary, and in fact central, activity within the best life for human beings. A critical issue that remains open for debate, then, is how the εὐδαίμων should find the appropriate balance between his virtuous actions and his exercise of contemplation. This issue has indeed been treated extensively in the intellectualist/inclusivist debate, with scholars such as Keyt delineating various options for prioritizing virtue and contemplation within the inclusivist view.[34]

The tension between the self-sufficiency of εὐδαιμονία and its necessary reliance on at least some external goods is one that Aristotle recognized, but never fully addressed, in his account of the highest human good in the *EN*. This incompatibility, unless addressed, prevents us from understanding Aristotle's theory of εὐδαιμονία as a coherent or internally consistent account of what constitutes the human good. It also presents significant difficulties for contemporary Aristotelian commentary, as evidenced by the intense interest and ongoing debate current in philosophical treatments of the *Nicomachean Ethics*.

I offer a reinterpretation of εὐδαιμονία that eases the conflict, though not by denying the relevance or applicability of any part of Aristotle's various descriptions of εὐδαιμονία—for I believe that Aristotle was correct in recognizing both the self-sufficiency of εὐδαιμονία and its connection to external goods. Rather, I show that Aristotle's account can be resolved into a description of two distinct concepts: εὐδαιμονία *per se*, activity in accordance with complete excellence, and supplied with external goods sufficient for leading a human life; and μακαρία, which is εὐδαιμονία with the addition of good fortune in abundance. Although εὐδαιμονία requires external goods as integral to its expression as an ἐνέργεια, this reliance does not violate Aristotle's requirement of αὐταρκεῖα, since the external goods requisite for the practice of εὐδαιμονία are no more than the minimal level required to constitute a human life proper, a βίος, and so constitute no special or 'external' requirement beyond the requirement that the subject of the potentially εὐδαίμων life be a human being in the full sense of the term.

Although this interpretation has been rejected by contemporary scholars, I have shown that there is a significant philosophical tradition supporting it; that there are compelling literary and linguistic reasons to suppose it is a valid one; and that the arguments leveled against it carry weaknesses which undermine their efficacy. It is important to recognize that the εὐδαιμονία/μακαρία distinction yields a reading of Aristotle's ethical project which is internally consistent. As Cicero reminds us, nōn enim quaerō quid verum sed quid cuique dicendum sit, 'for I do not seek what [is] true, but what should be said by each one'³⁵—a necessary condition for meaningful discourse is consistency in our account.

Yet, perhaps just as importantly for the purposes of philosophical inquiry, by 'saving the phenomena' of the experience of human life, and accounting for the seemingly opposed features of self-sufficiency and the relevance of the contingent experiences of life, the thesis I defend permits us to ascribe to Aristotle a plausible belief system which offers the typical human being a reasonable chance to achieve a fulfilled life, without requiring special advantages or circumstances. Aristotle himself is committed to such an approach: as he reminds us late in Book x of the *EN*,

πίστιν μὲν οὖν καὶ τὰ τοιαῦτα ἔχει τινά, τὸ δ' ἀληθὲς ἐν τοῖς πρακτοῖς ἐκ τῶν ἔργων καὶ τοῦ βίου κρίνεται· ἐν τούτοις γὰρ τὸ κύριον. σκοπεῖν δὴ τὰ προειρημένα χρὴ ἐπὶ τὰ ἔργα καὶ τὸν βίον φέροντας, καὶ συναδόντων μὲν τοῖς ἔργοις ἀποδεκτέον, διαφωνούντων δὲ λόγους ὑποληπτέον.

Such things then have conviction; but the truth is tested in the practices from actions and life; for among these [is] the deciding factor. It is necessary then to examine the things said before, bringing them to actions and to life, and those in harmony with actions we must accept, but those disagreeing we must leave behind [as mere] theories.³⁶

Philosophy, and especially moral philosophy, is grounded in practice; and Aristotle is seeking an account of an actually livable human life. Insofar as our nature as human beings is capable, Aristotle argues cogently and enjoins us to pursue the best and divine activity of contemplation. It is a mark of Aristotle's talent as a philosopher that he does not permit the pursuit of this divine activity to distract him from investigating the totality of human life, and discovering what it means to live ethically in the world.

Notes

1 *EN* i.10, 1101a6–7.
2 The history of this debate is so wide-ranging and long-standing that no more than a sampling of the relevant literature can be presented here. Hardie's 'The Final Good in Aristotle's Ethics' *Philosophy* 40 (1965): 277–295 first distinguishes between a 'dominant' and 'inclusive' interpretation. Cooper's 'Contemplation and Happiness in Aristotle: A Reconsideration' *Synthese* 72 (1987) details his shift from intellectualism toward inclusivism. Irwin's 'Permanent Happiness: Aristotle and Solon' *Oxford Studies in Ancient Philosophy III* (Oxford, 1985) and Kenny's

'Happiness' *Proceedings of the Aristotelian Society* 66 (1965): 93–102 are excellent points of departure for embarking on any survey of this issue.

3 'final,' or 'complete,' or 'perfect'; for the most part I shall leave the term untranslated for the sake of consistency, except where a specific sense is required for the context.

4 Compare *EN* i.9, 1099b18–19: δυνατὸν γὰρ ὑπάρξαι πᾶσι τοῖς μὴ πεπηρωμένοις πρὸς ἀρετὴν διά τινος μαθήσεως καὶ ἐπιμελείας, 'for everyone not maimed as regards excellence may win it by a certain sort of study and care.' Also *Pol.* ii.2, where, in reference to Plato's Republic, Aristotle says τοῦτο μὲν γὰρ ἐνδέχεται τῷ ὅλῳ ὑπάρχειν τῶν δὲ μερῶν μηδετέρῳ, τὸ δὲ εὐδαιμονεῖν ἀδύνατον, 'it is not possible that being εὐδαίμων belongs to the whole but to none of the parts' (1264b20–22)—Aristotle apparently supposes that a εὐδαίμων city must be composed of εὐδαίμονες citizens, be they guardians or cobblers.

5 *EN* ii.4, 1105a31–b1.

6 *EN* i.10, 1100b13–19.

7 Whether εὐδαιμονία is properly an activity or rather a whole life needs to be examined. Aristotle says that ἐν ἀρχῇ γὰρ εἴρηται ὅτι ἡ εὐδαιμονία ἐνέργειά τίς ἐστιν, 'for at the beginning we said that εὐδαιμονία is a certain activity' (*EN* ix.9, 1169b28); and so elsewhere clearly and consistently through the *EN, EE,* and *MM*. Yet the lives of persons are themselves often described as εὐδαίμων; and Aristotle himself at times identifies εὐδαιμονία as a type of living, as above. Cf. 1098a6, however, where Aristotle identifies the proper definition of the rational life ([ζωή] πρακτική τις τοῦ λόγον ἔχοντος) as 'the active exercise of the rational faculty, since this seems to be the more proper sense of the term' (τὴν κατ᾽ ἐνέργειαν θετέον · κυριώτερον γὰρ αὕτη δοκεῖ λέγεσθαι). Ultimately, it seems Aristotle intends εὐδαιμονία as an ἐνέργεια, though he is sometimes not completely rigorous in his application. The importance of this identification will be addressed in section 3 below.

8 *EN* i.10, 1100b18.

9 *EN* i.8, 1099a15.

10 *MM* ii.8, 1207a18–22.

11 For Aristotle's distinction between felicitations, praise, and encomia, see *EE* ii.1, 1219b8–25. Also cf. *EN* i.12, 1101b30.

12 And the constancy of all these factors, even after his death: cf. the discussion at 1100a10 et seq.

13 Εὐδαιμονία is an activity (ἐνέργεια), not a state; and the morally relevant potentialities are the virtues (ἀρεταί), not εὐδαιμονία itself. Nonetheless, it is (I hope) indisputable that, by examining the state of the soul, we can make some meaningful progress toward distinguishing between the corresponding activities and the conditions under which they can occur. As Heinaman writes, εὐδαιμονία 'cannot exist unless the disposition for the actuality exists' (Heinaman, 34).

14 *EN* x.6, 1176a33–40.

15 Of course, it is still the case that the external goods requisite to the exercise of εὐδαιμονία are outside the agent's control, and so, to an extent, subject to chance. To what extent does this challenge the basically Socratic conception of virtue as internal? The discussion of whether external goods are instrumental for or constitutive of εὐδαιμονία has been carried on in depth by Annas and Cooper. Cf. the discussion at *EE* i.1–4, 1214a1–1215b14, particularly 1214b17: ὥστ᾽ οὐδὲ τὸ ζῆν καλῶς καὶ ὧν ἄνευ οὐ δυνατὸν ζῆν καλῶς [οὐ γὰρ ταὐτό], 'just so living well and those things without which it is impossible to live well [are not the same].'

[16] Cf. Irwin, 'Permanent Happiness: Aristotle and Solon,' 91.

[17] Heinaman 1988, 41.

[18] de Heer 1969, 102.

[19] de Heer 1969, 41–2.

[20] Also compare *Odyssey* 6.41 ff. and the *Hymn to Hermes* 249ff.

[21] *de Anima* 160.31–161.3.

[22] Stobaeus 51.12.

[23] *de Finibus* v.27.81.

[24] *EN* i.10, 1101a1–7.

[25] Cf. *MM* ii.8, 1207b16: 'happiness cannot exist apart from external goods'.

[26] I hold that the account of virtue in terms of humans' political nature is in fact the one Aristotle can credibly give as an actual normative account, and that purely contemplative εὐδαιμονία, inasmuch as it is fully achievable only by a noncomposite rational being (i.e., god), is offered as an ideal, rather than a practical goal in conflict with the εὐδαιμονία of political life. Cf. Ackrill 1974.

[27] *EN* i.9, 1099b32–1100a5.

[28] The importance of understanding the connections between Aristotle's use of βίος and ἐνέργεια and his discussion of εὐδαιμονία is highlighted by Yu ('Activity and Life in Aristotle's Theory of Εὐδαιμονία').

[29] This is consistent with Aristotle's position that neither non-human entities, such as horses or other animals, nor even human non-agents, such as children, are capable of participating in εὐδαιμονία, because they cannot participate in ἐνεργείας καλούς, as he describes at *EN* i.10, 1099b32 et seq. Just as a child lacks the very capacity for εὐδαιμονία, so too the adult human lacking a πόλις, for instance, who might otherwise be a candidate for εὐδαιμονία, fails to meet the minimum criteria for a βίος ἀνθρώπινος, and thus is also unable to act κατ' ἀρετήν.

[30] Cf. also 1102a14–15.

[31] Perhaps unsurprisingly so, since Aristotle spends so much time emphasizing the *differences* between humans and other corporeal beings, especially in the function argument at *EN* i.7 (1097b22 ff.).

[32] Yu 2001, 8.

[33] *EN* i.2, 1094b7–11.

[34] Keyt 1978, 141–43.

[35] *de Finibus* v.28.83.

[36] *EN* x.8, 1179a19–24.

Chapter 4
The Hard-Liners: The Stoics
Bite the Bullet

Χρύσιππος δὲ πάλιν ἐν τῷ Περὶ ῥητορικῆς γράφων οὕτως ῥητορεύσειν καὶ πολιτεύσεσθαι τὸν σοφὸν ὡς καὶ τοῦ πλούτου ὄντος ἀγαθοῦ καὶ τῆς δόξης καὶ τῆς ὑγιείας ὁμολογεῖ τοὺς λόγους αὐτῶν ἀνεξόδους εἶναι καὶ ἀπολιτεύτους.

Chrysippus, again, by writing in his *On rhetoric* that the wise man will make public speeches and engage in politics as if he regarded wealth and reputation and health as good, agrees that the Stoics' theories are not for public consumption and of no social relevance.

Plutarch, On Stoic self-contradictions

Introduction

Stoic philosophy has historically been evaluated as reactionary. Some scholars have analyzed its origins as a response to Epicureanism, challenging the latter's emphasis on pleasure as the good for man.[1] This interpretation takes Stoicism's founder, Zeno of Citium, to be primarily interested in discrediting hedonism as an ethical and psychological doctrine of the human good and motivation. On such an approach, Stoicism develops as what N.P. White calls a 'self-realizationist view,'[2] that is, one which locates the good life in a process of properly identifying and then fulfilling the sort of nature (φύσις) we happen to possess as the sort of beings we are. Others, like White, have taken a longer view, and focused on how Stoicism responds to its Academic forebears Plato and Aristotle. Such interpretations describe the trajectory of Stoic ethics in particular as responsive to, and critical of, a certain perceived indifference of these earlier thinkers to the connection between the foundations of their ethical doctrines and their metaphysical or cosmological conception of the universe as a whole.

The standard reasons given for framing Stoic studies comparatively are relatively pedestrian—the relative paucity of extant Stoic writing, and its transmission via eclectic compilers of philosophical ideas, like Gellius and Stobaeus, or ideological opponents like Plutarch, Cicero or Sextus Empiricus. While these grounds are far from intellectually compelling reasons to defend the value of a comparative analysis, in the context of the current project I will follow just such a comparative format, at least in the first part of the present chapter. I am less interested in with whom the Stoic philosophers actually intended to dispute[3]—an interesting historical question with significant philosophical consequences in its own right—than in finding where and how Stoic ethical thought itself grew and developed out of, and away from, the traditions of Plato and Aristotle as we have investigated them in the previous chapters. Given the guiding focus of this project as a whole, tracing the development of Socrates' humanistic ethics through the schools of his successors, particularly on the relations among human nature, happiness, and external goods, we want ultimately to shed some light on the question: did the Stoics develop an ethics that reclaimed, as they intended, philosophy's original therapeutic, humanistic, Socratic nature and goals?

In order to answer this question, however, we need first to look deeper and address the underlying question: *why* did the Stoics identify the need to reject Platonic and Aristotelian ethics in the first place? To answer this, we need to consider that the Stoics' aim was to recapture the Socratic conception of the philosophical project. 'Socratic' philosophy, however, encompasses two characteristic components (as we saw in chapter 1): first, locating virtue and happiness within the boundaries of knowledge, separating the human good from the influence of chance; and second, embracing a human-centered, rather than a divine-centered, understanding of the human good. According to the Stoics, Plato's central shortcoming was to defend the former premise at the expense of the latter; whereas Aristotle rejected the first, and though he struggled to defend a version of the second, he ultimately failed to achieve a workable and consistent synthesis. The Stoics' intent was to retain successfully the intellectualism inherent in the Socratic identity of virtue and wisdom, while keeping it grounded in, and focused upon, the lived human experience of this world. This feature of Stoic philosophy has been consistently overlooked in favor of the more obvious interpretation, the perception that the Stoics uncompromisingly dismissed as irrelevant to εὐδαιμονία the so-called external goods (not goods at all, but mere 'preferred indifferents'), *and thereupon* endorsed an ideal contemplative life as the template for the good life for humans, similar to the intellectualism of Plato. What is difficult to reconcile with this interpretation, however, is the fact that the Stoics consciously and centrally reappropriate the original Socratic goal of philosophy as the best means of living a complete human life in the world—the 'therapeutic' character of philosophy. Plato's commitment to the realm of the Forms directs his intellectualist tendencies away from the physical world and life, endorsing an abstractive, θεωρία-based ideal life. Although Aristotle is not nearly as restricted in this respect,[4] he still struggles to balance and reconcile the 'two happinesses'—that of the active life in the political, virtue-related world, and that of the abstract, contemplative life which seems the more divine.

From the Stoic standpoint, then, both Plato and Aristotle fail adequately or properly to combine Socrates' intellectualist foundation, encapsulated by his equation of ἀρετή and ἐπιστήμη, with the pragmatic application of this metaphysical fact to the experience of human life. Stoicism aimed to effect this necessary synthesis: to defend a rigorous intellectualism, but without thereby restricting ethics and its prescriptions to an abstract realm of thought or contemplation, rather keeping ἐπιστήμη attached to πρᾶξις in the context of a human life in the world.

Once we have seen the reasons behind the Stoics' responses to Plato and to Aristotle, we will have the necessary historical context to make sense of various Stoic positions specifically relevant to the analysis of external goods. This topic, we will find, is by no means philosophically exhausted or uninteresting, in spite of the standard interpretation of Stoic orthodoxy with regard to external goods, namely that they are mere 'preferred indifferents,' ἀδιάφορα προηγμένα, with precisely no relevance to, or influence on, human flourishing. Yet when Diogenes Laertius reports that 'the manner of using [indifferents] is *constitutive of* happiness or unhappiness;'[5] or when Epictetus asserts that external goods permit the exercise of προαιρήσις; or when we draw the connection between reason (λόγος), impulse (ὁρμή) and action (τὸ πράττειν); it encourages us to wonder whether the Stoic position on external goods is more subtle and sophisticated than is normally credited. I will defend a position that the Stoics could not consistently have held external goods as completely irrelevant to happiness, even though they claimed to deny them status as goods (ἀγαθά) proper, based on their metaphysical and cosmological commitments. I will also examine three problems with the standard interpretation, and see how well my view deals with these difficulties. I hope to present a conception of Stoic ethics that goes beyond its traditional interpretation as merely a different version of intellectualism, but rather as what I shall call an applied intellectualism, one whose proper sphere is necessarily that of πρᾶξις, and not θεωρία, and thus one to which external goods and their use are centrally relevant. Such a conception makes sense of the Stoics' insistence on describing their philosophical project as a 'return' to Socrates, as well as going some way toward explaining why, in particular, they believed Plato and Aristotle (and their Academic successors) went wrong, and the resulting need for a new approach. While the degree to which they successfully and consistently maintain a balance between intellectualism and humanism varies, the very fact that the Stoics acknowledged this synthesis as their goal stands in marked contrast to predominant Academic trends, as well as contemporary interpretation, and marks them as heirs indeed to the Socratic tradition.

Finding the Socratic Connection

It is fitting to begin our examination of Stoic philosophy with Socrates. After all, the Stoics themselves portrayed their school as a return to his philosophy.[6] Commentators have made much of the apparent similarities between the way the Stoics account for and describe the good human life and the description offered by Socrates. Compare the central Socratic thesis—that knowledge, full and complete, is sufficient for right action—with the basically identical, if much more developed, tenet of Stoicism that virtue is 'a certain character and power of the soul's commanding-faculty, engendered by reason, or rather, a character which is itself consistent, firm, and unchangeable reason (λόγος).'[7] Again, as we saw in chapter 1 above, Socrates considered the human condition in the world to be the proper area of inquiry for philosophy; and similarly, the Stoics exhausted philosophy in the observable world. Diogenes Laertius tells us:

τριμερῆ φασιν εἶναι τὸν κατὰ φιλοσοφίαν λόγον· εἶναι γὰρ αὐτοῦ τὸ μέν τι φυσικόν, τὸ δὲ ἠθικόν, τὸ δὲ λογικόν. οὕτω δὲ πρῶτος διεῖλε Ζήνων ὁ Κιτιεὺς ἐν τῷ Περὶ λόγου καὶ Χρύσιππος ἐν τῷ αʹ τῶν Φυσικῶν.

[The Stoics] say that philosophical discourse has three parts, one of these being physical, another ethical and another logical. This division was first made by Zeno of Citium in his book *On Discourse*, and also by Chrysippus in his *On Discourse* book 1 and in his *Physics* book 1.[8]

Aetius further fleshes out these three traditional divisions of Stoic philosophy: 'physics is practiced whenever we investigate the world and its contents, ethics is our engagement with human life, and logic our engagement with discourse, which they also call dialectic.'[9] This tripartite division, accepted by the majority of orthodox Stoics (Aristo excepted), is frequently presented in connection with various analogies—the parts of a living body, or an egg, or a fertile field, all emphasizing the organic inseparability of the parts of philosophy and their respective domains of inquiry.[10] Whether investigating substances, sages or speech-acts, philosophy for the Stoic is a practical science, just as Socrates considered it.

This harmonious convergence, however, was not the result of a smooth development over the years and schools intervening between Socrates and Zeno. Rather, the impetus that drove the Stoics to develop their own particular philosophical identity separate from their contemporaries in the Academy was their recognition that important features of Socrates' original intent had been variously lost or rejected by his successors Plato and Aristotle. Below I will examine in turn Plato's and Aristotle's respective positions on the two Socratic doctrines the Stoics considered essential, and will see how their divergence from Socrates' position informs the Stoics' response.

Refuting Plato 'Prō Formā'. The first major divergence between the Academy and the Stoa is the Stoics' metaphysical account of embodied particulars. Perhaps their greatest break with Platonism is their rejection of the existence of Forms. Not only are Forms not considered the 'truly real' objects of which the physical world is a collection of imperfect copies, they don't exist at all on the Stoic account, but are merely concepts (ἐννοήματα), figments of the soul (φαντάσματα ψυχῆς) which are linguistic fictions epistemologically useful, but not ontologically existent. Given the importance of the Forms, and the foundation they provide for Plato's story of the Good and the motivation to achieve it, the Stoic rejection of this metaphysical grounding will necessitate a quite different approach to ethics. Not only the body, but also the soul, and even the virtues (by extension as διαθεσεῖς of the soul) are considered to be physical substances according to the Stoic doctrine that 'anything that is active is a body.'[11]

The Stoic position flatly rejects the existence of Forms as ontologically prior to particulars, or, in fact, as existent at all. As Stobaeus relates:

> They say that concepts (ἐννοήματα) are neither somethings nor qualified (μήτε τινὰ...μήτε ποιά), but figments of the soul (φαντάσματα ψυχῆς) ...[t]hese, they say, are what the old philosophers called Forms (ἰδέας)....The Stoic philosophers say that there are no Forms, and that what we 'participate in' (μετέχειν) is the concepts.[12]

The general principle on which this doctrine stands is a thoroughly materialist conception of ontology.[13] Cicero tell us, 'Zeno also differed from [the Platonists] in thinking that it was totally impossible that something incorporeal...should be the agent of anything, and that only a body was capable of acting or of being acted upon (τὸ ποιοῦν καὶ τὸ πάσχον).'[14] The capacity to act or be acted upon is characteristic of existents in general;[15] and so to deny this capacity to incorporeal entities is sufficient to deny them existence. As a result of this material particularism, Stoics account for universals and generals as, in specific instances of thought, ἔννοιαι, or 'conceptions'; and in general (that is, as the 'objects' of such thoughts), ἐννοήματα, 'concepts' (Diogenes Laertius 7.60–1).[16] Thus, Stoic ontology centrally claims that μόνα εἶναι λέγοι, only particulars exist.[17]

This 'demotion' should not at all be taken as indicating that the Stoics did not consider universals of critical importance, nor that complex and challenging questions do not exist concerning them. Indeed, the so-called 'natural' concepts, which arise 'naturally' and 'undesignedly,' are said by some Stoics even to *constitute* λόγος (Aetius 4.11.4, SVF 2.83), inviting inquiry into the relations between the human mind and the inherent intelligibility of the κόσμος, a central Stoic tenet. Concepts are as central to Stoic epistemology, and their doctrines of correspondence truth, sense perception, and the reliability of judgments, as ever they were to Plato. But their value, significant as it is, is strictly epistemological, not metaphysical. And it is precisely this difference which will lead, as we shall see, to a rather distinct departure from Plato in spite of their many *prima facie* similarities of outlook and doctrine.

Aristotle and the Identity of Virtue and Wisdom. Whereas Plato rejects Socrates' second doctrine, that the perceptible world is the proper domain of philosophical inquiry in its highest sense, Aristotle argues against his first claim, the identity of virtue and wisdom. Aristotle's main argument runs thus: if, as Socrates claims, all virtues are forms of wisdom, the next step of one's investigation should be to try to discover specifically what wisdom means, since it can be used either 'truly' (ἀλεθῶς) or 'to err' (ἀμαρτανεῖν). For example, if a chef intentionally burns a meal, he is (mis)using his wisdom in the second way, that is, as a sort of ignorance. If justice is a form of wisdom, as Socrates claims, and wisdom can be used either correctly or incorrectly, it follows that someone who had the wisdom of justice could 'use' it incorrectly, i.e. as its opposite, injustice; and so one might come to be unjust on account of justice—an evident absurdity, according to Aristotle. This *reductio* leads Aristotle to the conclusion that specific virtues cannot be forms of knowledge, because an agent cannot be ignorant out of knowledge, ἀπὸ ἐπιστήμη (*EE* 1246a31–b2); and hence, in general, virtue cannot be wisdom.[18]

On its own merits, Aristotle's argument seems conclusive in rejecting the Socratic identification of virtue with wisdom. But it fails to clarify what Socrates meant by 'knowledge' (ἐπιστήμη) or 'wisdom' (σοφία) when he argues that knowledge is what guarantees that an agent will make correct use of goods. Socrates seems committed to defending the thesis that wisdom (σοφία) *never* errs (*Euthydemus* 280a7–8), and so he may not have accepted even the *possibility* of misusing σοφία. Aristotle's example of misusing knowledge, someone who knows grammar but intentionally errs in its application, refers to the sort of knowledge Socrates attributes to craftsmen, a sort he explicitly claims to lack (*Apology* 22d3–4). But this is not the kind of knowledge Socrates calls 'knowledge of what is good and bad.' Nor can the knowledge craftsmen have be that which prevents the agent from confusing an apparent good with a real good. It is simply a practical knowledge that, for Socrates, goes no way toward guaranteeing happiness to the one possessing it. Socrates says that by acting according to knowledge we will do well and be happy; but this kind of knowledge is not the sort of knowledge craftsmen have. Rather, the knowledge that makes the agent happy is knowledge of what is good or bad;[19] and this sort of knowledge is incapable of being misused. Socrates considered the only bad action to be being deprived of knowledge;[20] but being deprived of knowledge is not the result of a deliberate misuse of knowledge, as Aristotle assumed, but rather from a lack of knowledge, i.e. from ignorance, a different and opposing cognitive state. Socrates observes that it may happen that a particular action might actually turn out to be bad or harmful to the agent (*Gorgias* 468d5–6), and since no one pursues what is harmful to himself, it follows that the agent has not performed his action wanting it; the agent did not know that what he thought was beneficial for him was actually harmful.[21] The wrongdoer's choice in such a case is based on ignorance, and his wrong choice results from his wrong epistemic state—opinion (δόξα)—since no one willingly and knowingly performs an act harmful to himself.[22] This passage illustrates that an agent having a doxastic belief as his characteristic epistemic state can be wrong with regard to what he thinks is good. What the Socratic passages usually suggest is the stronger claim that someone having δόξα as his characteristic cognitive state *always* fails. On the Socratic position, then, the cognitive state of the agent is crucial for the correct assessment of what the good is, and for the quality of the particular actions he can perform.

The Stoic articulation of the virtues as forms of wisdom rests in part on how they conceive of the soul and its faculties. For the Stoics, the soul is a single substance (the so-called 'unitary' view attributed first to Chrysippus), characterized centrally by its commanding-faculty, or ἡγεμονικόν, which finds expression through various faculties and dispositions. With this background, when Sextus Empiricus reports the Stoic definition of virtue as πως ἔχον ἡγεμονικὸν καθεστηκυῖα, a 'disposition of the commanding-faculty,'[23] and Aetius says that οἱ Στωικοί φασιν εἶναι τῆς ψυχῆς ἀνώτατον μέρος τὸ ἡγεμονικόν...καὶ τοῦτο λογισμὸν καλοῦσιν, 'the Stoics say that the commanding-faculty is the soul's highest part...they also call it the reasoning faculty,'[24] we can see the Socratic doctrine cast in specifically Stoic terms.

Aristotle and the Socratic Paradox. While the so-called 'Socratic paradox' that virtue (ἀρετή) is knowledge (ἐπιστήμη) constitutes one of the few positive doctrines of the mostly aporetic Socrates (cf. chapter 1 above), its consequences made it inadmissible within Aristotle's philosophical framework.[25] Aristotle's consideration of ἀκρασία as a live ethical problem (*EN* vii), as well as his detailed analysis of the particular virtues in Books iii–v of the *EN*, illustrate his distance from the Socratic position. Further, Aristotle argues implicitly against the 'extreme intellectualism' of Socrates at *Meta.* 1046b7–9 and *Phys.* 251a32, where he argues that ἐπιστήμη, insofar as it is a sort of λόγος, can embody both a given characteristic and its privation; and hence, one could err intentionally even with knowledge—a direct rejection of Socrates' thesis. By contrast, as we have seen, the Stoics revive and consistently embrace the strong Socratic intellectualist identification of ἀρετή and ἐπιστήμη.

Aristotle does grant Socrates the claim that if one truly knows, he cannot err: 'the position that Socrates sought to establish actually seems to result' (*EN* vii.3 1147b14). But we must bear in mind that this cession comes in the context of a much more fine-grained distinction of knowledge, and of action theory, than Socrates provided. Aristotle is willing to grant the Socratic thesis in ideal cases of so-called 'true' knowledge—when the individual possesses knowledge, correctly identifies its relevance to the particular circumstances of action, formulates the proper practical syllogism, and is not physically prohibited from acting according to his reason. In such cases, right and virtuous action will always and necessarily flow from knowledge. However, Aristotle's goal is to provide an explanation for the non-ideal, but more interesting, cases we actually observe, when an individual who seems to have knowledge somehow fails to act virtuously. To explain such cases, Aristotle relies on several distinctions which the Socratic account lacks. First, 'it *will* make a difference whether, when a man does what he should not, he has the knowledge but is not exercising it, or *is* exercising it.'[26] The man who merely possesses, but does not exercise, knowledge is still said to 'know'; and while the former case does not seem problematic, the latter does. Second, Aristotle recognizes the distinction between knowledge expressed as universal and particular propositions, and further universals predicable of the agent versus those predicable of the object (1147a1–9). Each of these distinctions in the 'manners of knowing' (1147a8) reduces the scope of the problem, explaining the perceived conflict between knowledge and willing action toward what is not good as one of several 'mismatches' between knowledge and action. In the end, there is no contradiction or paradox, and the purported counterexamples to the Socratic thesis are explicable in terms of a series of equivocations of terminology. However, in following this route, Aristotle does not solve the Socratic paradox in such a way that he can accept Socrates' thesis as a meaningful part of his ethics; rather, he 'explains away' the problem, leaving Socrates' intellectualist thesis as trivially true, but irrelevant and inapplicable to the substantive issues Aristotle goes on to address.

Aristotle on Reason and Virtue. A second reason the Stoics differ from Aristotle with respect to the second Socratic thesis is evident in their respective analyses of the relation between the virtues, αἱ ἀρεταί, and reason, λόγος. At first glance, it seems that Aristotle and the Stoics might be in accordance with each other in defining ἡ ἀρετή. Aristotle calls it a state of the soul (*EN* ii.5 1106a11); it 'both brings into good condition the thing of which it is the excellence and makes the work of that thing be done well' (1106a15–17); it is the 'mean not in the object but relative to us' (1106b5); and it is of course determined in reference to reason, being 'more exact and better than any art' (1106b15). His most complete definition is given at 1106b36–1107a2: ἔστιν ἄρα ἡ ἀρετὴ ἕξις προαιρετική, ἐν μεσότητι οὖσα τῇ πρὸς ἡμᾶς, ὡρισμένῃ λόγῳ καὶ ὡς ἂν ὁ φρόνιμος ὁρίσειεν, 'excellence, then, is a state concerned with choice, lying in a mean relative to us, this being determined by reason and in the way in which the man of practical wisdom would determine it.'

The Stoic definition of ἀρετή sounds quite similar. The virtues are those dispositions, διαθεσεῖς, of the commanding-faculty, τὸ ἡγεμονικόν, which are 'in accordance with right reason,' κατὰ λόγον. ἀρετή is 'a consistent character, choiceworthy for its own sake and not from fear or hope or anything external' (*LS* 61A, *DL* 7.89). It is, most fundamentally, 'living in agreement [with nature].' Plutarch offers the following comprehensive definition, which he says is commonly agreed upon by the majority of Stoics despite their specific doctrinal disputes: 'all these men agree in taking virtue to be a certain character and power of the soul's commanding-faculty, engendered by reason, or rather, a character which is itself consistent, firm, and unchangeable reason.'[27]

Aristotle's and the Stoics' accounts seem to agree, at least, that ἀρετή is a 'state' of the soul (either ἕξις or διαθέσις) in some way determined by, or in accordance with, λόγος. However, the Stoic account does not include any explicit reference to 'the mean relative to us,' ἡ μεσότης ἡ πρὸς ἡμᾶς. If we want to find some such characteristic of Stoic ἀρετή, we must look for it obliquely.[28] Still more substantive, though, is the divergence between the two accounts on the question of the virtues' specific relation to λόγος. For while Aristotle admits that ἀρετή is *determined by* reason, ὡρισμένῃ λόγῳ (1107a1), is *in accordance with* right reason, κατὰ τὸν ὀρθὸν λόγον (1144b26), and is the state which *implies* the presence of right reason, ἡ μετὰ τοῦ ὀρθοῦ λόγου ἕχις (1144b27), he nevertheless quite explicitly maintains a clear distinction between his account and Socrates': Σωκράτης μὲν οὖν λόγους τὰς ἀρετὰς ᾦετο εἶναι (ἐπιστήμασς γὰρ εἶναι πάσας), ἡμεῖς δὲ μετὰ λόγου, 'Socrates, then, thought the excellences were forms of reason (for he thought they were, all of them, forms of knowledge), while we think they *involve* reason' (1144b28–30). In rejecting Socrates, Aristotle directly opposes the Stoic definition, λόγον οὖσαν αὐτὴν ὁμολογούμενον καὶ βέβαιον καὶ ἀμετάπτωτον, 'a character which *is itself* consistent, firm, and unchangeable reason.'

This crucial difference in understanding virtue is but one manifestation of a characteristic, and systematic, difference between the Aristotelian and Stoic systems. Aristotle is content to allow virtue a somewhat flexible range, such that there can be moral virtues and intellectual virtues, each having a different fundamental mode of expression. But since, for the Stoics, all human experience is equally expressive of the universal λόγος, and since the ἡγεμονικόν is a unitary faculty of the soul, the Stoics have no need for ἀρετή to be *anything but* λόγος itself.

Stoic Theory: A Primer

Now that we have seen the Stoic position on Socrates' two original doctrines—what, for the sake of brevity, I will call the intellectualist and the humanist doctrines—and their reasons for reacting against Plato and Aristotle, the task remains to investigate how the Stoics developed these theses in ways innovative and specific to themselves. Of particular relevance to the current project will be to trace how these two metaphysical doctrines inform Stoic ethics in ways relevant to understanding clearly how the Stoics conceived of the relation between the good and τὰ ἐκτός, or in the preferred Stoic terminology, τὰ ἀδιάφορα προηγμένα.

The Stoic commitment to the humanist principle—that the perceptible realm constitutes reality and the proper locus of philosophical research—grows into a fully-developed conception of the good whose features, I will argue, are explicable in terms of the relation of 'blending,' or κρᾶσις δι' ὅλου, between the two fundamental metaphysical principles. We shall see the general Stoic approval of the intellectualist position manifest in their ethical doctrines in their discussion of the preferred indifferent. In both cases, the particularly Stoic appropriation and interpretation of the Socratic thesis culminates in an ethical thesis which will be of crucial significance to our eventual evaluation of their position on external goods.

κρᾶσις δι᾽ ὁλοῦ *and the Stoic Go(o)d.* A natural consequence or application of their physical particularism is the Stoics' characterization of the relation between soul and body, and particularly, between the world-soul and its 'body,' that is, the physical universe. While for Plato and Aristotle the First Cause or Prime Mover 'had been conceived in a two-fold fashion as a) outside the world on which it acted, and b) as non-corporeal or spiritual in nature,'[29] for the Stoics the world-soul, insofar as it is identified with the λόγος which is one of the two ἀρχαί of physical existence, is, we might say, immanent in the corporeal world.[30] Not only might we say this, but the Stoics themselves repeatedly make this explicit claim. They support it with cosmological arguments, as Diogenes Laertius does:

> [the Stoics] use κόσμος in three ways: of god himself, the peculiarly qualified individual consisting of all substance, who is indestructible and ingenerable...they also describe the world-order [κόσμος] as 'world'; and thirdly, what is composed out of both (*DL* 7.137, *SVF* 2.526)

Cicero provides arguments from analogy with living beings:

> For every nature which is not isolated and simple but conjoined and composite must have within itself some commanding-faculty [*principatum*, Cicero's translation of ἡγεμονικόν]...So it must be the case that the element which contains the commanding-faculty of the whole of nature is the best of all things...Therefore the world must be god, and all the power of the world must be sustained by a divine element (Cicero, *On the nature of the gods* 2.28–30)

Other Stoics support their claim by considering the nature of matter itself, in terms reminiscent of Aristotle's form-matter distinction:

> Zeno says that this very substance [*essentia*] is finite and that it is the one common substrate [*substantia*] of everything which exists...[A]s is the case with the innumerable different shapes of wax as well, so he thinks there will be no form or shape or any quality at all intrinsic to matter...yet it is always united and inseparably connected with some quality or other...[I]t does not   lack

breath and vitality from eternity, to set it in motion rationally (Calcidius 292, *SVF* 1.88)

On first glance, this doctrine of the immanence of god in the physical world might seem nearly identical to the immanence of Plato's world-soul through the 'receptacle' in the *Timaeus* (52a-d). However, the crucial difference rests in Plato's commitment to the two realms of reality, the unchanging and intelligible realm of Forms and the changing and perceptible reality of everyday existence. Since things in the perceptible realm necessarily have causes for their coming into existence (*Tim.* 28a4–c3), and the observable κόσμος is καλλιστόν (*Tim.* 29a5), the only possible cause (αἴτιον) of the world is something from the realm of the perfect Forms. But, as we saw above, Stoic ontology reserved no place for the Forms, and so the similarities with Plato's cosmology are, at best, superficial. Where the order and beauty of the universe for Plato are a mere copy of the true order and beauty in the realm of the Forms, the Stoic account avoids this devaluing of the world's κόσμος and identifies it itself with true order through the immanence of λόγος.

The Stoics talk about the immanence of soul in body generally, and of the world-soul in particular, in terms of a specific type of mixture, κρᾶσις δι' ὅλου, or 'blending.'[31] Given the Stoics' adherence to the principle that causal efficacy is reserved solely for corporeal objects, taken together with their consideration of god or λόγος as the 'vital force' or principle of change, movement, and instantiation of qualities in corporeal objects, such an account is necessary to explain how two corporeal substances—one vital, one inert—are so integrally combined.

The most complete extant description of the Stoic account of κρᾶσις δι' ὅλου is in Alexander's *On mixture*, though the idea appears earlier (as attested in Diogenes Laertius 7.151, Plutarch *On common conceptions* 1078b-e, Stobaeus 1.155). Here Alexander recounts Chrysippus's theory of κρᾶσις as one of three types of mixture. The first type occurs by juxtaposing two substances, 'while they each preserve their own substance and quality at their surface contact in such a juxtaposition as occurs, one may say, with beans and grains of wheat when they are placed side by side' (216.14–218.6, *SVF* 2.473). A second type of mixture entails the complete fusion of its elements, but also thereby the destruction of those elements and their respective properties, resulting in a new substance, as happens in, for example, a chemical reaction. Neither of these two types of mixture, however, suffices to account for the character of the relation of the 'breath,' or active principle, with the entirety of the corporeal world, a relation Chrysippus describes this way: 'the whole of substance is unified by a breath [πνεῦμα] which pervades [διήκων] it all, and by which the universe is sustained [συνέχεται] and made interactive with itself [σύμπαθές ἐστιν αὐτῷ]' (*SVF* 2.473). This peculiar type of mixture occurs 'when certain substances and their qualities are mutually coextended through and through [ἀντιπαρεκτεινομένοι ἀλλήλαις], with the original substances and their qualities being preserved in such a mixture' (*SVF* 2.473).

Unlike Plato, who conceived of the craftsman Demiurge, in the proem of the *Timaeus*,[32] as pre-existing, having rationally constructed the world using the Forms as models (*Tim.* 29b1: 'it follows by unquestionable necessity that this world is an image of something'); and unlike Aristotle's prime mover, whose existence is immobile (*Phys.* viii.6 258b12), eternal (*Phys.* viii.6 258b11), self-contained (*Phys.* viii.6 259b15), simple, without parts or magnitude (*Phys.* viii.10 266a10–11), separate from the world (*Meta.* xii.9 1074b15–1075a10, *Movement of animals* 3 699a12–15); the Stoic god—itself a corporeal substance, active, rational, and orderly—is not only *in* the world, but *of* it in the most real sense. It itself constitutes τὸ ὅλον. Plato's quintessential description of the good is exemplified in the *Phaedo*:

> Then he will do this most perfectly [i.e. grasp true reality] who approaches the object with thought alone, without associating any sight with his thought, or dragging in any sense perception with his reasoning, but who, using pure thought alone, tries to track down each reality pure and by itself, freeing himself as far as possible from eyes and ears, and in a word, from the whole body, because the body confuses the soul and does not allow it to acquire truth and wisdom whenever it is associated with it.[33]

The philosopher's soul progresses to the rim of heaven, separate from all traditions or concrete ways of life 'whole and unblemished...in the pure light.' Looking with the pure vision of reason, the soul understands truth purely and *per se*:

> It has a view of Justice as it is; it has a view of Self-control; it has a view of Knowledge—not the knowledge that is close to change, that becomes different as it knows the different things which we consider real down here. No, it is the knowledge of what really is what it is.[34]

Aristotle's position on the separation of the world and its good is similar:

We must consider also in which of two ways the nature of the universe contains the good or the highest good, whether as something separate and by itself, or as the order of the parts. Probably in both ways, as an army does. For the good is found both in the order and in the leader, *and more in the latter*; for he does not depend on the order but it depends on him.[35]

The Stoic position on the nature of the good, by contrast, is summed up thus:

The god of the Stoics, inasmuch as he is a body, sometimes has the whole substance as his commanding-faculty [ἡγεμονικόν]; this is whenever the conflagration is in being; at other times, when world-order [διακόσμησις] exists, he comes to be in a part of substance [οὐσία].[36]

and

Our school holds that what is good is a body because what is good acts, and whatever acts is a body. What is good benefits (*prodest*); but in order to benefit, something must act; if it acts, it is a body. They say that wisdom is a good. It follows that they must be speaking of it too as corporeal....There is no good except where there is a place for reason....That is finally perfect which is perfect in accordance with universal nature, and universal nature is rational.[37]

God, and the good, are located precisely in the λόγος which pervades τὸ πᾶν as the second genus, τὸ ποῖον. As Long and Sedley write, 'As a character of the commanding-faculty, which itself consists of breath, virtue, and thus the prime instance of the good, is corporeal' (*LS* v.1 377).

The Good, the Bad, and the (Preferred) Indifferent. Given the Stoic commitments outlined above—philosophy's role as therapeutic for the lived human existence, and the denial of a standard for the good located in the realm of the intelligible, but rather locating it in the instantiation of the physical universe—someone unfamiliar with Stoic doctrine might find it tempting to suppose that they would be likely to assign value to the external goods. After all, prosperity, health, and honor, unlike the goods of the soul, have the physical world as their essential context; so perhaps, our Stoic ingénue might posit, insofar as they contribute to the individual's good *qua* embodied, Stoic doctrine might allow them a place—albeit perhaps only a minor place—among the things considered to be goods.

Even a cursory familiarity with the Stoic position, however, quashes such a hope. From Zeno and Chrysippus onward, the unanimity of the Stoic rejection of externals as goods is consistent. The core analysis of τὰ ἐκτός is given in Diogenes Laertius:

> [The Stoics] say that some existing things are good, others are bad, and others are neither of these....Everything which neither does benefit nor harms is neither of these: for instance life, health, pleasure, beauty, strength, wealth, reputation, noble birth, and their opposites, death, disease, pain, ugliness, weakness, poverty, low repute, ignoble birth and the like...For these things are not good but indifferents of the species 'preferred' [ἀδιάφορα...προηγμένα].[38]

To support this claim, the Stoics need no more complicated theoretical analysis than the traditional identification of the good with benefit, combined with a notion of firmness (τὸ βέβαιον) or 'fixity' (ἡ πῆξις):

> For just as heating, not chilling is the peculiar characteristic [ἴδιον] of what is hot, so too benefiting, not harming, is the peculiar characteristic of what is good. But wealth and health no more benefit than they harm. Therefore wealth and health are not something good.[39]

Goods, on this argument, have the 'peculiar characteristic' (what is proper or essential to their very nature) of benefiting (τὸ ὠφελεῖν) the individual who possesses them; and further, οὐδέν ἄλλο, 'not otherwise,' that is, goods are reliable and consistent in producing *nothing but* benefit. It is the fact that health, wealth, and such things are capable of both benefiting *and* harming that disqualifies them from the class of goods. Diogenes describes that which is essentially and peculiarly characteristic of any good thing, namely, what is elsewhere in the Stoic literature called 'firmness' or 'fixity' (βεβαιοτής): it is not simply that one can be or is occasionally benefited by some state of affairs—if it were, the class of goods would be enormous, and would indeed include such external contingencies as health, property, social standing, and the like; but rather, the good is always and only beneficial, and nothing that is not always and only beneficial is good. Consistency is key for happiness itself: 'happiness consists in virtue, since virtue is a soul which has been fashioned to achieve consistency [ὁμολογίαν] in the whole of life' (*LS* 61A).[40] By contrast, the preferred indifferent lacks any essential connection with benefit and, by extension, the good. Many preferred indifferents are 'in accordance with nature' (κατὰ φύσιν, *LS* 58C), meaning that they are things that a well-formed and well-functioning being will naturally strive for, on the Stoic conception of οἰκείωσις (*LS* 57A).[41]

This account must be supplemented with some further explanation of what specifically the Stoics considered 'benefiting' to entail. On this point, we find very little significant disputation or doctrinal variation among the Stoics; the core explanation of benefit is always given in terms of harmony or accordance with nature and right reason: 'some proper functions are perfect, and...these are also called right actions' (Stobaeus 2.86.4); 'since reason, by way of a more perfect management, has been bestowed on rational beings, to live correctly in accordance with reason comes to be natural for them' (Diogenes Laertius 7.86). A complete understanding of the Stoics' conception of the connection between φύσις and λόγος must include a familiarity with their naturalistic presuppositions about the origin of ethical value. By observing the natural processes and behaviors of plants, non-human animals and infants, Stoics perceived that living things seem intrinsically to possess the impulse to preserve themselves and their particular constitution. From this basis, they conclude that nature, since it is responsible for the impulses of living things, must itself be operating according to the principles of rationality which we recognize as characterizing the natural development of organisms. This picture of a rationally active nature or universe is what lies behind the Stoic association of nature, reason, and the foundation of ethical action.

Since we have now established what the Stoics mean by the good (that which always and only benefits) and by benefit (that which is in accordance with nature and reason), it still remains to be determined what sorts of things meet their criteria to be considered good. We have already seen that many items which are commonly believed to be goods are, on these criteria, not really goods at all: 'life, health, pleasure, beauty, strength, wealth, reputation, noble birth...are not good but indifferents of the species "preferred"' (Diogenes Laertius 7.102). The things that appear to (and sometimes do in fact) benefit us, and thereby seem worthy to be considered goods, fail to qualify as truly good precisely because each of them is capable of producing *both* benefit *and* harm—thus falling short of the οὐδὲν ἄλλο standard which essentially characterizes the good. Even though possessing great wealth, for example, does sometimes benefit one, it is easy to conceive of—or even point to historical examples of—wealth resulting in harm to its possessor. This variability or lack of βεβαιοτής is characteristic of all these so-called external goods; and in fact it can be extended to *any* condition or state of affairs subject to definite description.

Let me attempt to clarify what I mean by this variability. Suppose we decide that some item on the list of external goods is, in fact, truly a good, whose possession results always and only in benefit to ourselves and, in general, the state of the world is better when we possess it. Even further, suppose that, all things being equal, we are correct, and anyone who possesses this external good is indeed always and only benefited by it, and the world at large is also so benefited. But imagine now that we fall into the power of a corrupt tyrant; and that this tyrant decides to effect great evils upon the world by conscripting into his army all persons with this external good. (We are assuming that he does in fact have the power to do as he intends.) Surely in such a case, it would be better overall if there were no, or at least few, people capable of conscription into the tyrant's army, i.e., people who possess this external good. This thought experiment is proposed by Aristo of Chios as reported by Sextus Empiricus in *Against the professors* 11.64–7. The Stoics, then, were particularly sensitive to the impact contingent circumstance has upon ethical action; in fact, this forms the basis of the well-known Stoic distinction between value and indifference.

We see the roots of the Stoic position in Plato's *Euthydemus*, where Socrates says:

> So, to sum up, Clinias, I said, it seems likely that with respect to all the things we called good in the beginning, the correct account is not that in themselves they are good by nature, but rather as follows: if ignorance controls them, they are greater evils than their opposites, to the extent that they are more capable of complying with a bad master; but if good sense and wisdom are in control, they are greater goods. In themselves, however, neither sort is of any value.[42]

This summary comes at the end of Socrates' 'unprofessional and ridiculous' demonstration intended to convince young Clinias, son of Axiochus, to devote himself to wisdom and virtue. Beginning with the question of how to do well (εὐ πραττεῖν), Socrates and Clinias enumerate the standard list of external goods—health, wealth, noble birth, power, honor, etc.; they then come to the position above, that the value of τὰ ἐκτός derives from their *use* by wisdom, and is not intrinsic, but instrumental.

This position does not seem particularly troublesome: no one, I think, would hesitate to admit that most things that benefit us are subject to this sort of role reversal, given the appropriate circumstances. However, upon a little consideration, we are likely to respond that, even so, there are in fact *some* things that are good in themselves, always and only beneficial: things such as honesty, justice, benevolence, courage, good faith. And indeed, the Stoics did not wish to deny the possibility of the good *simpliciter* by excluding *external* goods from consideration. They, too, held that certain things were in fact properly called good: namely, the virtues. Diogenes Laertius writes, 'The virtues—prudence, justice, courage, moderation and the rest—are good' (7.101). Stobaeus weighs in: 'The activities which accord with virtue are right actions, such as acting prudently, and justly' (2.86.4). Diogenes Laertius adds the following: '[S]ome proper functions are always proper while others are not. It is always a proper function (καθῆκον) to live virtuously' (7.109). The virtues are those dispositions of the ἡγεμονικόν which are in accordance with right reason (κατὰ λόγον); as such, they are by definition always and only beneficial, since reason is the very standard by which benefit is determined. Hence, the virtues are necessarily good, so too their practice; and the Stoics have as a result a greatly reduced, but absolutely dependable, class of items they can confidently describe as true goods, and hence true components of the happy human life, a life lived κατὰ λόγον, as well as κατὰ φύσιν: the life of the sage, whose happiness is imperturbable because it depends on nothing subject to chance.

Applied Intellectualism

We have seen, then, the following components of Stoic theory: their support of the Socratic identity of virtue and wisdom; the doctrine of the so-called 'preferred indifferent,' which follows from the first; their material particularism; and their consequent doctrine of κρᾶσις δι' ὅλου, locating the ultimate good within the physical world as a principle of order, κοσμία or λόγος.

Given the importance of the Forms, and the foundation they provide for Plato's story of the Good and the motivation to achieve it, the Stoic rejection of this metaphysical grounding will necessitate a quite different approach to ethics. They reject entirely the possibility of immaterial entities, such as νοῦς or ψυχή, endorsing rather a complete (if not reductionist) materialism. Not only the body, but also the soul, and even the virtues (by extension as διαθεσεῖς of the soul) are considered to be physical substances according to the Stoic doctrine that 'anything that is active is a body' (Cicero, *Academica* 1.39, *SVF* 1.90). The Stoics define ἀρετή as 'choiceworthy for its own sake,' and not for the sake of anything external (*LS* 61A, *DL* 7.89)—this is representative of their intellectualist excision of the good from externals. However, as we have seen, where Plato goes wrong is to make the further claim that therefore ἀρετή is *instantiated* as separate from externals.

The Stoics recognize that this step is unwarranted, and expressly avoid the error in their descriptions of virtue and the life of the sage. Even while they firmly defend the sufficiency of knowledge for virtue (and hence happiness: *LS* 61A), insofar as the achievement of virtue is precisely the achievement of the realization of the good as accordance with λόγος, order, and/or κοσμία, the consequences of this realization are quite noticeably different from the typical intellectualist position. While Plato would claim that a sage will of course act morally virtuously in the world, but this fact is merely an artefact of the imperfection of the physical world—essentially and ideally, action in the world is unnecessary—the Stoic position on the metaphysical inseparability of body and soul leads to a different conclusion, namely, that the physical κόσμος is the natural, and only, sphere or range of expression of ἐπιστήμη. As Long and Sedley have articulated it, 'central to Stoic ethics is the claim that virtue is an utterly self-sufficient art of living.'[43]

The traditional Stoic account of the development of moral virtue is as follows. φύσις is such a thing that, when something is brought into being, it 'naturally' pursues actions that tend to self-sustaining and - preservation; these ends are the most general and basic expressions of benefit and 'good.' This is what the Stoics call οἰκειῶσις. When an organism acts 'in accordance with' nature and pursues these things (for example, food or shelter) it pursues *sumenda,* and these acts are *officia* or καθήκοντα. This is equivalent to instinct, or impulse. When a person becomes aware that an act benefits him, and then chooses to perform that act *for this reason*, this represents a step up from the basic tendency of all organisms naturally to pursue those things that benefit it. When a person realizes that the value of an act consists in its very reason-directedness, rather than in its instrumental value as a *sumendum,* this is the highest development of ethical awareness, and this person's acts are no longer καθήκοντα, but are κατορθώματα. And as we have seen, the pursuit of things in accordance with our nature is constitutive of happiness, the highest end (Stobaeus 2.77.16 [*SVF* 3.16], Diogenes Laertius 7.87, Epictetus *Discourses* 1.6.22).

The Stoics' metaphysical background rests largely on their determinism to support their thesis that external goods are irrelevant to ethics. The only thing actually within our control is our will, and whether or not to make it accord with the world. Of course, to rest solely on this would be something of a failure to address the issue, a variation of the general problem of causal determinism within ethics. The Stoics, at the very least, advocate acting *as though* our will had causal efficacy; and their Socratic framework and goals are precisely the idea that philosophy is therapeutic, not only individually, but socially, and that the things toward which we are naturally inclined (the preferred indifferents) tend in general to express the λόγος of the world—and this is not simply to be left to the inevitable mechanistic development of causal chains, but become κατορθώματα precisely because they are *acts* which *instantiate* the λόγος shared between the individual human will and the world commanding-function, ἡγεμονικός (a sophisticated occasionalism, perhaps?). κοσμία is relational; and the ψυχή (both world and individual) is 'universally commingled,' κρᾶσις δι' ὅλου, with the physical self.

The attentive reader will already have noticed an unresolved tension lurking in the interstices of this fusion of Socratic themes. This tension manifests itself when we examine particular applications of Stoic doctrine, as recommendations for acting. The Stoics have a commitment, on the one hand, to locating the final good *within* the world; on the other, to denying that anything external to the will is a moral good, or is at all relevant to happiness. In this section, we will identify three specific cases which present problems for Stoicism precisely because of this fundamental tension: the Stoic position on 'rational suicide,' the possibility of virtue failing to produce benefit, and the question of whether or not happiness requires or entails consistency over time. In each of these cases, there is a deep challenge to the consistency of the theoretic underpinnings of the Stoic project when applied in the sphere of action. I will demonstrate first, the nature of the challenge; next, that a traditional reading of Stoicism fails to resolve the challenge in a satisfactory way; that there exists within the Stoic framework the means for resolving these tensions to produce an internally consistent theory; and that these means lie in a more nuanced reading of the doctrine of preferred indifferents and their relation to happiness.

Case Study #1: ὠφελεῖα, κοσμία, and the Sage's Suicide. However
much the Stoics liked to claim that the sage's happiness is *so* untouched
by externals that even the sufferings of Priam would not affect his
happiness (*SVF* 3.585), this claim sounds a not quite resonant note with
another quintessentially Stoic doctrine: under certain circumstances, the
sage will choose suicide. Cicero reports Cato's words on the reasons a
Stoic sage would choose to end his life:

> When a man has a preponderance of things in accordance with nature, it is his
> proper function to remain alive; when he has or foresees a preponderance of
> their opposites, it is his proper function to depart from life. This clearly shows
> that it is sometimes a proper function...for the wise man to depart from life. (*LS*
> 66G)

The criteria for suicide are the lack of *quae secundum naturam sunt*,
Cicero's translation of τὰ κατὰ φύσιν. When the circumstances of the
sage's life have reached a point at which he no longer has sufficient
resources or opportunities available to him to act virtuously—to select
things in accordance with nature and to reject their opposites (*LS* 59A,
64A)—it becomes not only permissible, but his proper function
(*officium*, καθῆκον) to depart from life (*dē vitā excedere*). Now, if no
external goods ever could or did touch the sage's happiness; and if said
happiness consists exclusively in the κοσμία or *concordia* of his will and
soul with the world; and if happiness is indeed 'the end, for the sake of
which everything is done' (*LS* 63.A.1) what possible justification could
there be to prompt such an action?

Evaluating the situation simply in terms of the good *qua* benefit
(ὠφέλεια), there is an easy answer: in a situation where no good or
benefit results to anyone, it could indeed be better to remove oneself
from the situation entirely; by extension, if the situation encompasses
one's whole (foreseeable) life, suicide can indeed be reasonable. But this
analysis presupposes not only that external circumstances affect
happiness, but that they do to such an extent that, were the sage to
continue living rather than committing a 'rational' suicide, his happiness
would be compromised. (For, if his happiness could have continued
undiminished, why ever would the sage commit suicide?) Of course, one
might argue that, in such a case, the sage is simply acting 'as if' his life
circumstances mattered to him (cf. the introductory quote at the head of
this chapter). But if his actions 'as if' take the Stoic as far as suicide—
especially since the Stoic worldview rejects the notion of an eternal

soul—how much can one honestly differentiate between the Stoic sage acting 'as if' he values his life circumstances and his *actually* valuing them?

This is, to say the least, puzzling. The Stoics claim that happiness (the highest end) is constituted by the pursuit of the things in accordance with nature (one's own nature *and* cosmic nature, since the former is but a portion of the latter); and that, when someone comes to lack external goods to such an extent that he can no longer pursue these things and act virtuously, it becomes his proper function to die 'although he is happy.' Presumably this means that the sage's happiness would be compromised should he fail to depart from life when it was appropriate to do so; and so he is faced with the choice of living unhappily, or not living at all.[44] What results when the sage commits an appropriate suicide? Certainly he has not sustained his happiness after the fact; the most that can be said is that his choice (προαίρησις) was part of his happiness, and he sustained his happiness as long as he was alive, but his happiness was coterminal with his life, and ended precisely when the latter did. External goods are at least necessary preconditions for εὖ ζῆν, if the sage is compelled to give up life entirely—even when it is a life with full happiness—rather than live in their absence. While τὰ ἐκτός are still not ἀγαθά proper, neither can they be considered indifferent to happiness, not even 'preferred' indifferents. In fact, this seems rather closer to an Aristotelian conception of the relation of external goods to the preconditions for living a human life than to the traditional interpretation of Stoicism. The advantage of the present interpretation is that it gives the Stoic sage a defensible reason to explain his choice to commit a 'proper' suicide, one which makes this choice consistent with his position on the value of externals. Whereas suicide based on the lack of completely valueless items is an absurd doctrine for the Stoics to defend, suicide based on the lack of necessary preconditions for leading a good life is a rather plausible and consistent doctrine.

One might respond further, however, that, after all, the happiness of the Stoic sage lies in the concordance of his will with the universal λόγος, not in any particular or personal achievement or state of his own. If the κόσμος entails that I, in my particularity, should lead a life under circumstances that preclude my individual flourishing, Stoic doctrine indicates, says the objector, that, paradoxically, my happiness lies in realizing and accepting that I cannot achieve happiness.

Frankly, I cannot conceive that this position is coherent. Such a move would require Stoicism to advocate a eudaimonic hierarchy under which the individual's happiness is a goal secondary to the happiness of the κόσμος. Setting aside the fact that there is no hint of such a ranking in the Stoic literature, it seems rather clear that the κοσμία of the world cannot be a goal for an individual to strive for. For one thing, the world is *already* in a state of κοσμία, independent of any individual's actions; for another, to subordinate the individual's happiness to the universal order is to misunderstand the nature of Stoic happiness. Happiness for the sage is in a sense two-fold in nature; it is first the instantiation of the universal order, and second, the cognitive and assenting recognition of, and participation in, this order. To remove the particular individual from this conception would be to eviscerate it, and render it essentially useless for producing psychological motivation for individuals. Rather than distorting our understanding of such a fundamental concept, it seems more suitable, and justifiable, to maintain the evident and plausible importance of individual flourishing for the sage's happiness. And, as is argued above, the way to do this is to allow a place for external goods in the happiness of the sage.

Case Study #2: When Virtue Fails to Benefit. We saw above that the Stoics use the notion of consistent benefit as their criterion for identifying the good. We may find this definition appealing and plausible. Unfortunately, we cannot accept it unqualifiedly. For it has a serious vulnerability, one which the Stoics recognized as sufficient grounds to disqualify a whole class of initially plausible candidates for the good. Recall Aristo's thought experiment of the evil tyrant. Now, however, instead of the possession of some external good such as health or strength, suppose that the monarch's criterion of conscription is possession of some one or another of the Stoic *virtues*—prudence, wisdom, etc.[45] How will this affect our understanding of the virtues, and of their status as true goods according to the criterion of consistent benefit? For it is apparent that, in at least one situation—under the rule of the evil tyrant—it is possible that possession of a virtue brings about positive harm, something a true good cannot do on the Stoic account. It seems, then, that even the practice of the *virtues* is susceptible to moral inversion, given appropriate circumstances.

The Stoics' assertion that everything is material, including the mind and its virtues, means that they cannot, as does Plato or Aristotle, stipulate a difference in *kind* between preferred indifferents and goods, but only a difference in *degree*—specifically that the latter always benefit, whereas the former are variable. However, this thought experiment demonstrates that this criterion fails as the standard to sort the indifferents from the goods, since the virtues too, in at least one case, produce results identical to indifferents such as wealth or health.

How might the Stoics respond? In one of two ways: by rejecting benefit, and choosing something else, as the essential criterion of the good; or by backing away from the requirement of complete consistency. The first maneuver would be too radical a rejection of a conceptual connection common to ancient thought, and especially integral to Socrates' concept of the good (see chapter 1); besides, absent something like Plato's Forms, there is no other viable candidate to take the place of benefit as a plausible essential or characteristic feature of the good.

What would be involved in the second option, that is, softening the requirement of complete consistency? For one thing, it accords better with the metaphysical characteristics of Stoic doctrine. Indifferents and virtues alike are material substances, and so insofar as they operate alike in the physical κόσμος, they are both just as unlikely to achieve a perfect correspondence in their results. While complete consistency is intelligible, Stoicism is committed to locating the good in the perceptible order of the world, a realm in which such consistency is approachable rather than attainable.

There is a second advantage of retaining the connection between goods and benefit while jettisoning a complete consistency. We can acknowledge that indifferents do, at least sometimes, actually produce benefit, a position that seems not only plausible, but in line with the orthodox Stoic view that 'the manner of using [indifferents] is constitutive of happiness or unhappiness (τῆς ποιᾶς αὐτῶν [ἀδιαφόρων] χρήσεως εὐδαιμονικῆς οὔσης ἢ κακοδαιμονικῆς)' (Diogenes Laertius 7.104–5, *SVF* 3.119).[46] This admission is also made sensible by referring to another of the Stoics' common descriptions of preferred indifferents, namely, 'things in accordance with nature' (τὰ κατὰ φύσιν) (Stobaeus 2.79.18; 2.83.10; Sextus Empiricus *Against the Professors* 11.65; Epictetus *Discourses* 2.6.9, *SVF* 3.191). We have seen (above) that the basic Stoic definition of ὠφέλεια is in terms of action κατὰ φύσιν, according to nature; and so to admit that preferred indifferents do, in fact, make some difference to the sage's happiness follows naturally from the Stoics' own conception of benefit.

Case Study #3: Duration of Time and Rational Consistency. Stobaeus reports Chrysippus as follows:

> The man who progresses to the furthest point performs all proper functions without exception and omits none. Yet his life...is not yet happy, but happiness supervenes on it when these intermediate actions acquire the additional properties of firmness and tenor and their own particular fixity.[47]

But here lies a puzzle. Apparently a man can progress 'to the furthest point' and not yet be happy; this statement seems to entail that performing all the appropriate proper functions—even all the appropriate *perfect* proper functions—is not a sufficient condition for happiness. One's actions in life must acquire this 'firmness' or 'fixity,' which then results in happiness supervening on the life in question. However, if we compare this with another account of the Stoic position on the nature of goods, we observe a serious conflict:

> [The Stoics say a] good is not increased by the addition of time, but even if someone becomes prudent only for a moment, in respect of happiness he will in no way fall short of someone who employs virtue for ever and lives his life blissfully in virtue.[48]

Granted, Plutarch is not a sympathetic commentator, and it would be seriously naïve for us to take his presentation of Stoic doctrines at face value. Nevertheless, it does not seem a gross misrepresentation of the Stoics to ascribe to them the belief that the goodness of a thing is not affected by its duration—especially in the broader context of their conception of the good as essentially identical with right reason, which, if anything, is quintessentially not time relative. Yet the Stoics maintained that, once an individual achieves that 'consistent, firm and unchangeable' character that is virtue, the harmony of one's soul with the rational, natural order of the world then *compels* the sage's actions, and *a fortiori* his assent to the correct φαινόμενα. And so we are left with this question: how could the man who is momentarily prudent, described in Plutarch's account as happy, acquire the 'firmness' or 'fixity' identified as the necessary condition for happiness in Stobaeus' account?

This internal difficulty in Stoic ethics points to a fundamental uncertainty about the appropriate way to evaluate the impact of temporal contingency upon the achievement of happiness. As such, it rests on a problematic and inconsistent understanding of the nature of the good, especially as it relates to or is instantiated in actual observable practice in the world. As in the previous case, we found that, no matter what initial description, or what account, of the good the Stoics give, it is vulnerable in practice to moral inversion, rendering even such paradigmatic goods as the virtues not intrinsically, but only contextually, good; in the present case, the Stoic position regarding what is sufficient to constitute a happy life is unclear, and the problem again arises from a lack of clarity concerning the nature of the good—here, whether an isolated act can bestow happiness, or only a sustained, consistent disposition. And if the latter, what are the criteria for it? My answers to these problems will rely upon an analysis of the notion of consistency, and what sense we can make of this idea.

The issue of consistency lies at the heart of all of these difficulties. In the case of the moral inversion of the virtues, the Stoic position assumes that the virtuous person's consistency in action, evaluated according to the standard of rationality, can be exactly defined by referring to the results of such action—namely, always and only benefiting. However, the given thought experiment shows that we cannot rely upon *any* external results or circumstances to define universally what rational consistency means. Thus, the Stoics are left with a notion of rational consistency that is self-defining. In the case of determining happiness, we want to include consistency as a criterion for happiness, yet it seems counterintuitive to ascribe moral significance to matters of time duration, especially since, as outlined above, we have no satisfactory conception of consistency with which to start.

How might the Stoics go about achieving a satisfactory description of rational consistency? This is a difficult task; it is essentially the same challenge as faces any virtue ethics, namely, how to give a description of what is virtuous when the only relevant criterion is that which we are trying to define. This is what has led contemporary critics of virtue ethics to challenge it: the fact that virtue is not expressible in a rule or generalizable standard, but is essentially context dependent.

One possible way for the Stoics to respond to this challenge would be to follow defenders of Aristotelian virtue ethics and say that, although many, perhaps most, virtuous actions or dispositions we hold are relative to our environment, culture, and personal habituation and history, nevertheless there are certain virtues which hold regardless of these factors, simply in virtue of being the proper functions of human beings *qua* human beings, and so applicable regardless of particular circumstance. Unfortunately, such a move will not suffice to extricate a Stoic defender from the above problems, regardless of its efficacy for Aristotelian virtue ethics, because it merely brings him back to the original Stoic position—that there are perfect proper functions for *all* human beings, and that they are so because they accord with a rational nature. We must find another way out.

The Stoic might instead respond to the problem at hand by claiming that there is an epistemological gap, even for the sage, that accounts for puzzles such as the moral inversion attending the virtues in the evil monarch thought experiment. If there is some fundamental feature either of the world, or of the nature of goodness or benefit, or of the human mind, which necessarily precludes a complete grasp of any given morally relevant case, then this might account for our inability to resolve the apparent conflict we perceive. But such a presupposition goes contrary to the basic Stoic understanding of nature as a fully rational, and hence explicable, entity; and to the belief that the ideal life of the sage, though difficult to achieve, is not unattainable. Accepting the premise that it is in principle impossible for a human being to always and fully grasp the entirety of the ethical sphere, or that nature is mysterious in a way inaccessible to the precepts of rational investigation, would be antithetical to the entire Stoic project.

The third alternative is, I think, the most likely, although perhaps also the most likely to be resisted. The basic problem we face arises when we attempt to give external parameters by which to measure or gauge the good. Certainly, this is a worthy, even essential, endeavor for conducting our lives, and coming up with such standards is indeed one of the major responsibilities of any ethics. However, as Aristotle recognized, even sciences deal with what is 'for the most part,' and the experience of the lived human life provides ample evidence that a responsible ethics will also admit of counterexamples, borderline cases, and ambiguity. The search for external definitions or guidelines for the good is an important pragmatic tool; but it should not be mistaken for capturing the complete essence of what is good, a task for which language is fundamentally inadequate. No matter what explanation or description one offers to account for the nature of the good, the recipient of the explanation or description must already be such as to grasp the relevance of the explanation given. Aristotle recognized this; but it is also analogous to reason in general. There is nothing in a description or explanation of rational argumentation that compels *any* given person to accept its validity; rather, one must previously be disposed to accepting reasons *as* compelling. In just this way, one's inner acceptance of the rational good as a worthy standard for action can be *described* by, but can never be *compelled* by, *any* explanation *at all*. Yet compulsion, or at least motivation, is what we are looking for when we ask an ethics to account for the good. It is due, I think, to the fact that a certain sort of explanation-giving is extremely philosophically productive in certain areas of inquiry that we are inclined to try applying this same method, or these same standards, to projects to which they are less suited. We need to be more circumspect in determining whether our usual methods of inquiry are appropriate to the issues we face; we will find ourselves better prepared to find satisfactory, sensible, and consistent answers to these inquiries.

However, this does not leave us (or the Stoics) gesturing vaguely at an ineffable notion of the good. We have seen that the Stoics have many precise descriptions of it. The good is corporeal (Seneca *Epistulae* 117.2); it is ὠγέλεια ἢ οὐχ ἔτερον ὠφελείας, 'benefit or not other than benefit' (Sextus Empiricus *Against the professors* 11.22, *SVF* 3.75); it is 'living in agreement with nature,' which is 'in accordance with the nature of oneself and that of the whole, engaging in no activity wont to be forbidden by the universal law, which is the right reason pervading everything' (Diogenes Laertius 7.87–89), and this description—'living in agreement'—is attributed to Stoic thought from Zeno onward (Stobaeus 2.75.11).

So far, the picture seems unproblematic. However, when the Stoics try to specify what they mean by consistency, they tend to equivocate between two distinct notions. On the one hand, consistency is understood as the perfect, universal reason, λόγος; and as such is the internal coherence, expressed in such principles as that of non-contradiction, of reason generally conceived. In cosmological application, consistency becomes the thesis that this logical coherence underlies and informs all of existence, τὸ πᾶν. This notion of consistency is one of the core doctrines of the Stoic web of belief, and is argued and defended as the basis of many, if not most, of their other physical, logical, and ethical doctrines.

On the other hand, the notion of consistency on which turns the relation of happiness to fixity is not this quality of inherent consistency, but is rather a sort of reliability; that is, the contingent determination of whether the proper functions one performs continue predictably over time. This is the same notion of consistency on the basis of which the Stoics argue against considering τὰ ἐκτός goods proper, as I have argued above.

On what grounds, or for what reasons, do the Stoics appropriate this conception of consistency? Perhaps the clearest statement of the Stoic motivation is given by Cicero:

> In my opinion, virtuous men are also supremely happy (*beatissimī*). For if a man is confident of the goods that he has, what does he lack for living happily? Or how can someone who lacks confidence (*diffidit*) be happy? Yet a man who adopts the threefold division of goods [virtue, bodily goods, and material goods] inevitably lacks confidence. For how will he be able to be confident of bodily strength or secure fortune? Yet no one can be happy without a good which is secure, stable and lasting (*stabilī et fixō et permanente*)...The man who would fear losing any of these things cannot be happy. We want the happy man to be safe, impregnable, fenced and fortified, so that he is not just largely unafraid, but completely (*nōn ut parvō metū praeditus sit, sed ut nullō*).[49]

Unfortunately, this statement does not provide any supporting argumentation, but merely appeals to an intuition that true happiness requires an absolute guarantee. But do the Stoics *need* this guarantee? Not at all; as we see in Plutarch, there is already a countervailing current in Stoic thought recognizing the irrelevance of duration to happiness. And so, given that the arguments for the distinction between goods and preferred indifferents rest on this same desire for an absolute guarantee, it becomes much less clear that there is any compelling basis for denying the relevance of external goods to happiness.

Conclusion

Of the schools of ancient Greek philosophy, the Stoics are perhaps the least amenable to any reconciliation between the happy human life and external goods. And yet, in spite of their adherence to a strict doctrinal division separating the wheat of the virtues from the chaff of indifferents, Stoicism at its root cannot entirely turn away from the world to a perfect and ideal realm. Committed to a self-consciously Socratic way of philosophizing, Stoics admit and embrace the perceptible world as the focus of philosophy—what is real, what is true, and what is good is precisely to be found within the scope of the observable world and our dealings with it, rather than abstracted away. The Stoic commitment to Socrates' philosophical realism fundamentally orients their project toward accepting the relevance of real states of affairs and events, especially for ethics. It is when Stoicism turns to the second Socratic precept, an intellectualist attitude toward the identity of virtue and wisdom, and formulates upon it the doctrine of the preferred indifferent, that the underlying tension comes to light. Yet even so, a Stoic like Epictetus can say ἐπὶ γῆς γὰρ ὄντας καὶ σώματι συνδεδεμένους τοιούτῳ καὶ κοινωνοῖς τοιούτοις πῶς οἷόν τ' ἦν εἰς ταῦτα ὑπὸ τῶν ἐκτὸς μὴ ἐμποδίζεσθαι; 'for we are on the earth and bound by an earthly body and earthly partners. How then could we fail to be hampered by externals with regard to these things?' (*LS* 62K). The irreducible impact external circumstances have on the happiness even of the sage is found time and again within Stoicism. Insofar as the Stoics take Socrates' two doctrines as the aim of their entire philosophical system, Stoicism cannot avoid admitting preferred indifferents as meaningful contributors to the good life. Section 4.3 above contains the center of my argument that the Stoics are necessarily committed to recognizing preferred indifferents as goods, based on their underlying metaphysics. The fundamental distinction between the good and goods is not, as for Plato, a difference of kind. The good is the λόγος or κοσμία, which is the ordering *of the world*. And the goods proper, i.e. the virtues, are those characters of our commanding-faculty which benefit us through particularly instantiating this λόγος. My claim is that, since the Stoics admit that preferred indifferents are the same basic type of thing, i.e. material bodies, as the virutes, and indeed the good itself; and that preferred indifferents do in fact sometimes benefit us; therefore there is *prima facie* reason to suppose that preferred indifferents matter for the good life, albeit much less so than the virtues. Beyond this *prima facie* plausibility, however, the sections above present the case that certain Stoic positions are rendered inconsistent if one assumes that preferred indifferents are in fact indifferent to the sage's flourishing, but these same positions become reasonable if one admits preferred indifferents a place as contributors to happiness.

Inwood provides a concluding comment on Stoicism as a eudaimonic ethics:

> The *telos* of life, happiness, then, is not what we consciously aim at, but something built into our nature as human beings. Our nature defines what it means for us to be happy and perfect in our kind, and in this respect Stoic ethics

is as 'naturalistic' as Aristotle's—or indeed any ethics that employs a version of the function argument to ground human happiness in human nature.[50]

What do the Stoics themselves say about our human nature? Nemesius tells us:

> [According to Chrysippus] Every generated being has something given to it by fate: water has cooling as its gift, and each kind of plant has bearing a certain fruit; stones and fire have downward and upward movement respectively; so too animals, as their gift, have assent and impulse [συγκατατίθεσθαι καὶ ὁρμᾶν].[51]

As animals, our natural 'gift,' that which intrinsically characterizes us as the sort of being we are, is the capacity to assent, the soul's faculty to 'use impressions' (Epictetus 62.K.3), that is, to commit oneself to the value of 'the state of affairs which forms the content of an impression' (LS 1, 322); and impulse, ὁρμή, the soul's capacity to move or stretch toward its proper object. Although we share both of these faculties with non-human animals, our particularly human faculties are of course informed by reason; in the case of impulse, the Stoics refer to 'rational impulse,' λογική ὁρμή. Stobaeus writes 'One would correctly define rational impulse by saying that it is a movement of thought toward something in the sphere of action.'[52] The telling phrase in this description, however is 'in the sphere of action,' ἐν τῷ πράττειν. Our natural faculty is directed at, and exercised in, action.

Notes

1. As, for instance, Pohlenz, *Die Stoa* (Göttingen 1970–72).
2. White 1979, 147.
3. For an excellent article on this kind of discussion, see N.P. White, 'The Basis of Stoic Ethics,' *Harvard Studies in Classical Philology* 83 (1979).
4. See Nussbaum, 'Therapeutic Arguments: Epicurus and Aristotle,' in M. Schofield and G. Striker, eds., *The Norms of Nature* (Cambridge: Cambridge University Press, 1986).
5. Diogenes Laertius 7.104, *SVF* 3.119, emphasis mine.
6. At least, as they had access to Socratic doctrines as mediated through the Cynics; compare e.g. the anecdote in Diogenes Laertius' *Lives* recounting Zeno's introduction to the figure of Socrates.
7. Plutarch, *On moral virtue* 441d.
8. Diogenes Laertius 7.39.1.
9. Aetius 1, Preface 2 *SVF* 2.35.
10. Similarly, the branches of philosophy are referred to as ἀχώριστά ἀλλήλων in Sextus Empiricus *Against the professors* 7.19.

11 Cicero, *Academica* 1.39, *SVF* 1.90.

12 *SVF* 1.65.

13 With the exceptions of the 'sayables' (λεκτά), void, place, and time. The Stoics recognize these four entities as non-corporeal, but necessary, entities for understanding the universe. However, they presumably cannot interact with bodies, since only corporeal bodies can interact, leaving us with an incomplete understanding of how the Stoics themselves dealt with this puzzle. Unfortunately, according to Long and Sedley, 'no satisfactory discussion of the problem has survived' (*LS* 1987 v1, 165).

14 Cicero, *Academica* 1.39, *SVF* 1.90.

15 Not only was this accepted within the Stoic school, but was a well-established principle in the Platonic and Aristotelian traditions as well. Cf. e.g. Plato, *Sophist* 247d8–e4; Aristotle, *Topics* vi.9 139a4–8, vii.7 146a21–32.

16 Simplicius (*On Aristotle's Categories* 105.8–16, *SVF* 2.278) has preserved the so-called 'Not-someone' (οὔτις) paradox, an interesting account of the Stoic response to the potential problems associated with Platonic hypostatization of universals.

17 Syrianus, *On Aristotle's Metaphysics* 104.21, *SVF* 2.361. As is typical for a metaphysical system that denies the existence of anything that is not a body, Stoic metaphysics had to develop alternative ways to account for commonplace experience of things like qualities (τὰ ποῖα), species or types (πως ἔχων), and relations between bodies (πρός τί πως ἔχων), which seem non-corporeal *per se*. Although an investigation into the Stoics' schema of four genera, originated by Chrysippus, is beyond the scope of this chapter, some familiarity with it, and especially with the latter two genera, is extremely helpful for defending the plausibility of Stoic particularism. For a comprehensive treatment of this topic in the ancient literature, see Plutarch *On common conceptions* 1077c–1084a, Simplicius *On Aristotle's Categories* 66–67, 166.15–29, 217–18. For contemporary interpretation, see the venerable Long and Sedley 1987 v.1, 163–66, 172–79.

18 Aristotle's criticism derives from his view that wisdom is a sort of λόγος, and the same λόγος can exhibit a thing and its privation (*Metaphysics* 1046b7–9). Someone with knowledge (ὁ ἐπιστήμων) can make a mistake willingly (ἁμαρτάνει ἑκών: *Physics* 251a32–33).

19 Plato, *Charmides* 173d–e, 174b–c.

20 Plato *Protagoras* 345b5; *Euthydemus* 281e, 292b.

21 see also *Meno* 77b–78b.

22 Kahn calls this the 'prudential paradox' (see his 1996: 92, n. 40, and Plato, *Apology*, 25c5–d3).

23 Sextus Empiricus *Against the professors* 11.24, SVF 3.75.

24 Aetius 4.21.1, 53H, SVF 2.836.

25 *EN* vi.13 1144b25–30.

26 *EN* vii.3 1146b33–4.

27 Plutarch, *On Moral Virtue* 440E.8.

28 As, perhaps, in Plutarch's reference to Zeno's qualification of the scope of application of each virtue (*On Stoic self-contradictions* 1034c).

29 Duncan 1952, 129.

30 There are important similarities between the cosmology of Plato, especially in the *Timaeus*, and that of the Stoics, not least of which is that, in both, cosmology serves as the foundation for an ethical superstructure, specifically by identifying the possibility for εὐδαιμονία as bringing one's individual soul into alignment with the divine reason

or cosmic order, and by identifying god with the active, organizing principle of the cosmos, the λόγος which for both Plato and the Stoics (though in significantly different capacities, as we shall see below) describes the goal of human beings *qua* rational. For one of the few comprehensive treatments of the historical and philosophical connections between Platonic and Stoic physics, see H.J. Krämer (1971), *Platonismus und hellenistische Philosophie* (Berlin: Walther de Gruyter) 108–131.

[31] For the background of the distinction between types of mixture, see Aristotle *On generation and corruption* i.10, 328a24–28. Sandbach (1985) argues against any Aristotelian influence on Stoic doctrine here; however see Long and Sedley (1987, ii.288) for an opposing interpretation.

[32] Or in the *Laws* 903b4–d3 (*pace* Solmsen, 'Plato's Theology' 156: 'The passage which we are discussing is the prototype of Stoic theology. It may also be its fountainhead'). This Platonic 'providentialism' may have given rise to one feature of Stoic theology, but it is at most a starting-point from which the Stoics advanced in a direction not anticipated or accepted by Plato.

[33] Plato, *Phaedo* 66a.

[34] Plato, *Phaedrus* 247d.

[35] Aristotle, *Meta.* xii.10 1075a11–15, emphasis mine.

[36] Origen, *Cels.* 4.14 [*SVF* 2.1052].

[37] Seneca, *Epistulae* 117.2, 124.14.

[38] Diogenes Laertius 7.101–2.

[39] Diogenes Laertius 7.103.

[40] Fixity will be examined further in section 4.3 below.

[41] It is worth observing that οἰκείωσις is itself a manifestation of the cosmic order or λόγος; and so there does seem to be *some* necessary connection to be made between the natural order and its particular instantiations (i.e. τὰ κατὰ φύσιν) and the order or harmony constitutive of happiness, κατὰ λόγον.

[42] Plato, *Euthydemus* 281d.

[43] Long and Sedley 1988 v.1, 383.

[44] I do not say that the choice is between becoming unhappy or remaining happy, because, after all, happiness is consistently parsed as εὖ ζῆν; to expand its definition to include εὖ θανεῖν would be a significant departure from tradition, and a move that, while worthwhile, would constitute a separate project.

[45] I assume that the tyrant can and does reliably identify virtuous sages, even though he himself is not one. Although this assumption, that a person not himself virtuous can reliably identify those who are, is not beyond challenge, I am accepting it for the sake of the present argument.

[46] It is true that εὐδαιμονικός can mean not only 'constitutive of' happiness but also merely 'conducive to' it (cf. Xenophon *Memorabilia* 4.2.34 and Plato *Phaedrus* 253c for the former, Aristotle *EN* 1176b16 for the latter meaning). In either case, however, the χρῆσις ἀδιαφόρων is acknowledged to have *some* bearing upon the sage's happiness—a crucial admission, given the emphasis usually placed on the character of indifferents as 'things which contribute *neither* to happiness *nor* to unhappiness (τὰ μήτε πρὸς εὐδαιμονίαν μήτε πρὸς κακοδαιμονίαν συνεργοῦντα)' (58.B, DL 7.104–5.1, SVF 3.119, emphases mine).

[47] Stobaeus 5.906, 18–907, 5; *SVF* 3.510.

[48] Plutarch, *On common conceptions* 1061f.

[49] Cicero, *Disputationes Tusculanae* 5.40–41.

[50] Inwood 1999, 555.
[51] 53.O, Nemesius 291.1–6, SVF 2.991.
[52] Stobaeus 2.87.6, SVF 3.169, 53.Q.

Chapter 5
Applied Intellectualism: The Eudaimonist Synthesis

[W]ithout basic linguistic knowledge a philosopher is often led astray, perhaps in the same way as a philologist is handicapped by lack of sufficient training in philosophy.

K. F. Leidecker, 'Concepts by Intuition and the Nature of Sanskrit Philosophical Terminology'

One popular way to describe what philosophy does is to say that it deals with the 'eternal questions.' One need only take a look at logical positivism or Cartesian dualism, however, to realize that some questions are more 'eternal' than others, particularly in metaphysics and epistemology; as our knowledge of the sciences underlying the physical universe and our mental lives grows, the questions we ask necessarily become refined, or even change to different questions altogether. Not many of us ask questions any more about the quintessence, occasionalism, or monads.

When we look at the central question of the ancient Greek philosophers, however—namely, what is the best possible human life?—we find that this issue is as fully live today as ever it was in the Academy. We human beings have not stopped desiring to live lives characterized by satisfaction, completeness, a sense of purpose, close relations with other people, growth, honor, and material prosperity. Nor have we definitively answered the questions associated with the pursuit of this desire. We struggle to identify authentic happiness, recognizing that we are sometimes, perhaps often, mistaken in this identification. It is not clear what relation the happy life has to our human natures: whether it is something achieved through struggle, in spite of innate imperfections; whether self-interest plays the central determining role; whether it is something outside our control, or mostly dependent on our state of mind or perspective. We see people born with every advantage who report a subjective sense of dissatisfaction in spite of it all, and yet again, we see individuals who seem at peace and content in the face of extreme deprivation. On the other hand, we also know seemingly virtuous people who struggle daily to 'do their duty,' while achieving no personal satisfaction, and libertines who cheerfully ignore egregious suffering in pursuit of their own material prosperity, and never give it a second thought.

This book has taken as its topic of inquiry the connection between the possession and use of external goods and leading a happy human life. There is a central tension evident here between two equally intuitive, yet conflicting, positions. On one hand, health or wealth, or prosperity generally, are generally accepted as parts of an authentically, and fully, happy life. The person who flourishes does so not merely in virtue of a narrowly applied set of behaviors or states, but rather precisely insofar as, in a wide range of areas of living and conduct—the intellectual, the moral, the physical, the social, the technical, the spiritual—he exhibits an overarching, all-encompassing state of excellence that transcends any one of these individually. On the other hand, we just as surely accept the premise that achieving happiness is within the control of the individual human agent. It would be incomprehensible (ἄτοπος, as Aristotle might say) for the world to be such that the best kind of life for us should be, in principle or in practice, inaccessible to our human efforts, or that we should be held morally responsible for accomplishments or failings which result from circumstances beyond our control.

I have approached this general topic with a two-part hypothesis. First, an historical thesis: four major schools of thought in ancient Greek philosophy—those of Socrates, Plato, Aristotle, and the Stoics—have a philosophically significant area of convergence among their respective treatments of εὐδαιμονία and external goods. Underlying their apparent conflicts and differences, I believe it is possible to discern a common set of assumptions involving completeness—τελειοτής—and sufficiency—τὸ ἱκανόν.

Socrates is known for maintaining the thesis that true happiness cannot be damaged by mere external circumstances, no matter how extreme. From this starting point, it is attractive to attribute to him the further position that external circumstances play no part in true happiness, especially when he says things like 'my belief is that to have no wants is divine; to have as few as possible comes next to the divine; and as that which is divine is supreme, so that which approaches nearest to its nature is nearest to the supreme.' Yet I think this would be a mistake. After all, moderation, not deprivation, is the keyword we find so often in his discussions, and Socrates himself never endorses nor practices detachment from the enjoyment of the goods of fortune when they are appropriate. The right use and enjoyment of external goods is crucial to the practice of moderation and to happiness: what people usually call 'goods'—including moral virtues, such as justice, temperance, and courage—count as goods if and only if practical wisdom and wisdom proper rule over them (*Euthydemus* 281a8–e1). Given that Socrates' aim is to search out the sorts of things that truly count in living a specifically *human* life, I have examined the evidence to support the idea that Socrates recognized a suitable place for the goods of chance in his conception of the happy life, rather than attempting to exclude them. This evidence is found in two specific areas of Socratic thought—first, in Socrates' well-known claim that virtue and wisdom are the same; second, in what might be called his 'humanistic' conception of philosophy. In the first case, we find that the interentailment of virtue and wisdom is inadequate to support a strong intellectualist interpretation of Socrates' ethical project; instead, external goods sufficient for their proper use constitute the practice of εὐδαιμονία. In the second, analysis indicates that Socrates considers completeness and self-sufficiency traits of a divine, and not human, life and experience. The good ἴδιον to a divine nature is characterized by these two, whereas that which is proper to human nature has a rather different flavor, resting instead on considerations of ὠφελία, or benefit.

Plato's *Philebus* is one place where we find some interesting insights into Plato's understanding of the role of external goods in happiness. The good 'is necessarily bound to be perfect (τελείος)' (*Philebus* 20d1) and is *sufficient* (ἵκανος): in setting up a fair comparison between the life of pleasure and the life of reason, Plato's Socrates reminds us that 'if either of the two is the good, then it must have no need of anything in addition. But if one or the other should turn out to be lacking anything, then this can definitely no longer be the real good we are looking for' (*Philebus* 20e5–6). Yet the interesting feature of this dialogue is that Plato characterizes the best human life as a 'mixture' or 'combination' of reason and pleasure. Just as one living the life of pure, unadulterated pleasure 'would thus not live a human life but the life of a mollusk' (21c), neither does the life of pure reason qualify as the good life, 'since otherwise it would be sufficient, perfect, and worthy of choice for any of the plants and animals that can sustain [it], throughout their lifetime' (22b). The exact character of this 'mixture' is investigated in some depth as the dialogue progresses; however, the salient point to note initially here is the definite non-intellectualist consequences of Plato's position. It is frequently emphasized that Plato, following Socrates, identifies virtue and the good with knowledge; it is not as frequently noted that he does not thereby mean to devalue applied knowledge or science. When discussing the method of mixing knowledge and pleasure together in the well-balanced life, Socrates asks Protarchus which sciences should be included in the mix—the purest and truest only, or some of the others as well:

> **Soc.** [O]ne kind [of science] deals with a subject matter that comes to be and perishes (τὰ γιγνόμενα καὶ ἀπολλύμενα), the other is concerned with what is free of that, the eternal and self-same (ὡσαύτως ὄντα ἀεί). Since we made truth our criterion, the latter kind appeared to be the truer one....If we took from each sort the segments that possess most truth and mixed them together, would this mixture provide us with the most desirable life (τὸν ἀγαπητότατον βίον), or would we also need less-true ones? **Prot.** We should do it this way, it seems to me. **Soc.** Suppose, then, there is a person who understands what justice itself is and...all the rest of what there is....Will he be sufficiently versed in science if he knows the definition of the circle and of the divine sphere itself but cannot recognize the human sphere? **Prot.** We would find ourselves in a rather ridiculous (γελοίαν) position if we were confined entirely to those divine kinds of knowledge (ἐν ταῖς θείαις...ἐπιστήμαις), Socrates! **Soc.** But how about music: Ought we also to mix in the kind of which we said a little earlier that it is full of lucky hits and imitation (στοχάσεώς τε καὶ μιμήσεως) but lacks purity (καθαρότητος ἐνδεῖν)? **Prot.** It seems necessary to me, if in fact our life is supposed to be at least some sort of *life* (εἴπερ γε ἡμῶν ὁ βίος ἔσται καὶ ὁπωσοῦν ποτε βίος).[1]

The answer agreed upon by Socrates and Protarchus is the broader alternative: the best human life needs even the applied sciences, those fields of knowledge whose objects are the imperfect, impermanent products of generation, and even the sorts of pursuits that involve chance, if our life is to be a meaningful lived experience.

In spite of the strong arguments made by the intellectualist tradition, I am inclined to take Aristotle seriously when he says νῦν δὲ τοιοῦτόν τι ζητεῖται, 'we are now seeking such a thing [i.e. something attainable]' (1096b34) in our search for happiness. It is true that Aristotle himself gives conflicting signals: although he states that 'such a life [the complete life of perfect contemplation] would be too high for man' (1177b27), he immediately admonishes us: 'one must not follow those who advise him, being a man, to think of human things...but must, so far as possible,...do everything in accordance with the best of the things within himself' (1177b32–34). This last passage has been interpreted as evidence that Aristotle, in the end, really considered contemplation to be intrinsically better and more choiceworthy, when at all possible, than virtuous activity. However, it seems to me that we should put this issue in its appropriate context. The comparison between contemplation and virtuous activity is, in Aristotle's own words, a comparison between the merely mortal and the divine. And while it is true that man has 'something divine present in him,' i.e. his intellect, it is equally true that man's nature is not completely exhausted as a rational being. If we were dealing simply with a rational *being*, then we would be talking about something divine, such as god. But since we are dealing with humans, we must remember that we are rational *animals*—that is to say, composite, embodied beings; and the fact of our corporeality is just as essential to determining our good and τέλος as is our rationality. It is critical that our analysis of Aristotle's comments on the divinity of intellect and contemplation give due consideration to this fact.

We can gladly admit that a life of pure and uninterrupted contemplation is more choiceworthy *per se* than a life of virtuous activity. We can even agree (though we need not) that such a life is more choiceworthy *for humans*—insofar as we are able to achieve it. But neither of these admissions requires that we take the further step, as the intellectualist would have us do, and claim that the contemplative life is unqualifiedly better, more appropriate (ἴδιον), or more choiceworthy for humans than the virtuous life. Although humans can, to a greater or lesser extent, approximate a life of contemplation, it is something that no human being's nature will ever allow him to achieve. It is never appropriate for some being to neglect its ἴδιον good for the sake of pursuing one it cannot reach—as it would be inappropriate (and impossible!) for a horse to neglect its own good and τέλος *qua* horse to try to act justly, courageously or magnanimously.

In saying this, I am not 'advis[ing] us, being men, to think of human things'—at least, not in the pejorative sense Aristotle seems to have intended by this phrase. I am, however, claiming that there are real differences between the human and the divine, and that the 'human things' which are appropriate for us to strive toward are not 'merely' human, but *include* precisely that degree of divine activity which it is in our nature to achieve, and *also* that degree of social or political activity which is equally inherent in our nature. Aristotle does not base his ethics

158

on an impossible expectation that humans should act as though we were gods. As he tells us at 1182b1–4 (emphases mine):

> It is about good, then, as it seems, that we must speak, and about good not without qualification, but *relatively to ourselves*. For *we have not to do with the good of the gods*. To speak about that is a different matter, and the inquiry is foreign to our present purpose. It is therefore about the good of the state that we must speak.

Rather, he recognizes that we share a limited similarity with the divine, and so must both recognize it as divine (and hence give it an appropriately important place in our life plans) and determine how this component of our nature must integrate with everything else that makes us human beings.

For the Stoics, what sorts of things meet the criterion of being good, that is, as they define it, being always and only beneficial? Diogenes Laertius explains why certain items commonly held to be goods, such as wealth or bodily health, do not in fact qualify as good:

> For just as heating, not chilling, is the peculiar characteristic of what is hot, so too benefiting, not harming, is the peculiar characteristic of what is good....Furthermore they say: that which can be used well and badly is not something good. (Diogenes Laertius 7.103)

The Stoic concept of 'fixity' entails that the good is always and only beneficial, and nothing that is not always and only beneficial is good. On this account, of course, most things are not really goods at all: 'life, health, pleasure, beauty, strength, wealth, reputation, noble birth...are not good but indifferents of the species "preferred"' (Diogenes Laertius 7.102). Things that appear to (and sometimes do in fact) benefit us, and thereby seem worthy to be considered goods, fail to qualify as truly good precisely because each of them is capable of producing *both* benefit *and* harm—thus falling short of the 'always and only' standard which essentially characterizes the good.

The Stoics begin with a definition of the good as that whose peculiar property is that it is always beneficial. Their position is a fascinating study in the growth and development of philosophical thought over time, given their self-conscious rejection of their immediate predecessors in the traditions of Plato and Aristotle, and their avowed re-appropriation of Socrates. Whereas they considered Platonism to have veered too far from Socrates' human concerns, characterizing the aims of philosophy rather as divine and essentially 'otherworldly,' with the theory of Forms being the prime example of this trend; and Aristotle's work was insufficient inasmuch as he rejected the Socratic thesis that virtue is wisdom; the Stoics' intent is to synthesize coherently these two trends, resulting in what I call an 'applied intellectualism.' This approach permits the Stoics to adhere to the strict Socratic intellectualist thesis, evidenced most strongly in their doctrine of preferred indifferents, a doctrine which, at first glance, seems the very antithesis of any tendency to incorporate external goods into a complete account of human flourishing. However, we find that the Stoics' metaphysical commitments are relevant to their notion of the good; specifically, their doctrine of physical particularism has the consequence that any description of the good itself must be as a physical body. As a result, even in this philosophical school seemingly most completely and fundamentally opposed to accepting external goods as at all worthy of moral consideration, there is a necessary connection between external goods and human happiness.

Beyond resolving an intriguing puzzle of interest to historians of philosophy, however, what is the need for such a unified account of external goods? My second thesis is evaluative: that there is relevance and value to investigating and approaching a resolution of the ancient debate on external goods, not only for historical purposes, but for the living project of ethics as prescriptive for our lives. [2]

Contemporary ethics is the philosophic discipline concerned with both describing and prescribing human actions and modes of living, offering rational and pragmatic guidance for our interactions with each other on a daily basis. In this context, should the ethicist concerned with relevantly engaging the lives of students, economists, doctors, soldiers and CEOs care about the ancients' thoughts on chance, virtue, and flourishing? Yes, for several important and related reasons.

One of the most urgent issues facing contemporary ethics is that facing philosophy generally: discovering and describing its role and relevance in our contemporary world of science, cultures, and value systems of all kinds vying for attention in the 'marketplace of ideas.' As philosophers, we find traditional assumptions and expectations insufficient to validate our projects; long-established pillars of the philosophical community and investigation are found to be presumptions grounded, at least in practice, in specific cultural and historical factors, few of which can make legitimate claims on our assent absent rigorous supporting research in the wide—and ever-widening—world of knowledge beyond the Western analytic tradition. Especially in ethics, the branch of philosophy most particularly committed to bridging the gap between theory and practice, the conscientious philosopher can no longer—if indeed (s)he ever could—rest content with the presumption that the complexities of human interactions, on the local and global scales, are usefully explicable by a theory that takes into account only those factors within the conscious control of individual human agents. Discoveries in the sciences compel us to acknowledge many factors which we have barely begun to recognize, let alone control, yet which are undeniably causally efficient in the most immediate and fundamental aspects of our lives: psychology, with its discoveries about how pre-conscious, unconscious, and non-rational factors influence decision-making and character in even the most reflective and critical agents; economics, where we see potent forces impacting the availability of the basic prerequisites for human biological existence for huge segments of the world's population—abstract market pressures traceable to no conscious agent, but rather explicable via mathematical models that represent the ebb and flow of currency and commodities; sociology, investigating the very real ways in which social groups—religious communities, governments, corporations—must be acknowledged as on par with human individuals in terms of agency, and whose actions, motivations, and intentions are often irreducible to those of their component persons; neuroscience, demonstrating the irreducible and fundamental causal links between our subjective mental experiences and the biological and chemical processes that constitute them.

We may well be disinclined to admit that this messy and complex picture truly represents our proper field of study. Yet it would surely be disingenuous to avoid confronting these difficulties by clinging to the claim that what is outside our control is thereby removed from the realm of our ethical responsibility. Given such a world as ours, with a multitude of enormously efficacious impersonal forces of our own making, and given the great capacity for harm we have built up through our impersonal systems of abstract agency, to endorse any abdication of personal responsibility would represent, at the least, the antithesis of the ethical project, at worst an enormous crime. Besides, we must take care not to construct a false dilemma: the addition of so many factors influencing our lives has by no means verified the determinist thesis. We still enjoy an incredible range in which to exercise our individual free will, and consciously make choices for certain reasons, with certain intentions, driven by certain motivations, in spite of certain consequences; and these decisions, influenced though they are by such a host of external circumstances, are still our own moral choices. They remain properly evaluable as such, and the ethical project is still the best way we have to provide the rational human agent with reliable guidance to live justly and fairly.

We can now see how these considerations motivate the present project of interpreting the connections between external prosperity, virtue, knowledge, and εὐδαιμονία. The ancients generally accept the claim that, on the one hand, εὐδαιμονία is something within our power to achieve, regardless of our circumstances. On the other hand, they also recognize that certain common external goods—physical health, education, social standing—are frequently present or absent due to circumstances that are *a fortiori* beyond our control. If we consider it necessary to avoid the charge of elitism, any acceptable eudaimonistic theory must find a way to allow more than the privileged few to attain εὐδαιμονία, since few individuals, if any, are completely furnished with all requisite external goods. Still, such a project must carefully balance the influences of chance events with the roles of virtuous character and knowledge (both dependent upon education) in achieving εὐδαιμονία. There is an evident and useful parallel between the problem framed by the ancient eudaimonists—explaining the influence of chance and the role of moral education in achieving happiness—and that facing contemporary ethicists—exploring the extent of the influence of uncontrolled factors over our moral decision-making, as compared with the exercise of our rational, morally informed free will. I am inclined to press the strong claim that these are in fact the same issue, simply dressed in different terminology; but one need not go so far to recognize the value of exploring this connection. The parallel structure of the two issues provides a legitimate basis for investigating the history and consequences of the one, with the hope of discovering insights relevantly applicable to the other. Having discovered a coherent basis for the ancients' way of dealing with chance, virtue, and happiness, we can reasonably hope to continue to find interesting and useful things to say about their relationships in the context of contemporary approaches to these issues.

162

Notes

1   Plato, *Philebus* 62ba4–5.
2   I am certainly not the first to operate under this presumption. The tradition of explicitly mining the ancients' thoughts, and specifically their eudaimonism, for relevant insights into contemporary ethics is long and well-founded. For a representative sample, cf. H. Sturt 1903, 'Happiness,' *International Journal of Ethics* 13.2, pp. 207–221; J. Moffitt Jr. 1938, 'The Pursuit of Human Happiness,' *Ethics* 49.1, pp. 1–17; D.A. Lloyd Thomas 1968, 'Happiness,' *The Philosophical Quarterly* 18.71, pp. 97–113; J. Kekes 1982, 'Happiness,' *Mind* 91.363, pp. 358–376; G. Harman 1983, 'Human Flourishing, Ethics, and Liberty,' *Philosophy and Public Affairs* 12.4, pp. 307–322.

Bibliography

Primary Texts

Armstrong, G.C. (tr.) (1988). *Aristotle: Magna Moralia* (Cambridge: Harvard University Press Loeb Classical Library).

Arnim, J. (ed.) (1905). *Stoicorum Veterum Fragmenta.* 4 vols. (Leipzig: B.G. Teubner).

Barnes, J. (ed.) (1984). *The Complete Works of Aristotle: The Revised Oxford Translation.* 2 vols. (Princeton: Princeton University Press).

Bernardakis, G.N. (ed.) (1889). *Plutarchus Moralia*, 7 vols. (Leipzig: B.G. Teubner).

Bruns, I. (ed.) (1887). *Alexandri aphrodisiensis praeter commentaria scripta minora*, vol. 2. (Berlin: G. Reimer).

Calder, W.M. et al. (eds.) (2002). *The Unknown Socrates: Translations, with Introduction and Notes, of Four Important Documents in the Late Antique Reception of Socrates the Athenian* (Wauconda IL: Bolchazy Carducci Publishers).

Cooper, J.M. (ed.) (1997). *Plato: Complete Works* (Cambridge: Hackett Publishing Company).

Dover, K.J. (ed.) (1968). *Aristophanes' Clouds* (Oxford: Clarendon Press).

Fotinis, A. (tr.) (1979). *The De Anima of Alexander of Aphrodisias: A Translation and Commentary* (Washington DC: University Press of America).

Freese, J.H. (tr.) (1990). *Aristotle: The Art of Rhetoric* (Cambridge: Harvard University Press Loeb Classical Library).

Hett, W.S. (tr.) (1995). *Aristotle's On the Soul* (Cambridge: Harvard University Press Loeb Classical Library).

Hicks, R.D. (ed.) (1925). *Diogenes Laertius: Lives of Eminent Philosophers*, 2 vols. (Cambridge: Harvard University Press Loeb Classical Library).

Hude, C. (ed.) (1908). *Herodoti Historiae*, vol. 1. (Oxford: Clarendon Press).

Leutsch, E.L. and F.G. Schneidewin (eds.) (1839). *Paroemiographi Graeci* (Göttingen).

Long, A.A., and D.N. Sedley (eds.) (1987). *The Hellenistic Philosophers.* 2 vols. (Cambridge: Cambridge University Press).

Marchant, E.C. and O.J. Todd (trs.) (2002). *Xenophon: Memorabilia, Oeconomicus, Symposium, Apology* (Cambridge: Harvard University Press Loeb Classical Library).

Rackham, H. (tr.) (1931). *Cicero: De finibus bonorum et malorum* (New York: G. P. Putnam's Sons).

—— (tr.) (1988). *Aristotle: Eudemian Ethics* (Cambridge: Harvard University Press Loeb Classical Library).

—— (tr.) (1999). *Aristotle: Nicomachean Ethics* (Cambridge: Harvard University Press Loeb Classical Library).

Tredennick, H. (tr.) (1996). *Aristotle: Metaphysics: Books I-IX* (Cambridge: Harvard University Press Loeb Classical Library).

Wachsmuth, C. (ed.) (1884). *Ionnis Stobaei Anthologii*, 5 vols. (Berlin: Weidman).

Wright, M.R. (ed.) (1991). *Cicero: On Stoic Good and Evil* (Warminster: Aris & Phillips Ltd).

Secondary Sources

Ackrill, J.L. (1974). 'Aristotle on *Eudaimonia*,' *Proceedings of the British Academy* 60, 339–359.

Adam, A.M. (1918). 'Socrates, "*Quantum Mutatus ab Illo*",' *The Classical Quarterly* 12.3/4, 121–139.

Adkins, A.W.H. (1963). 'Friendship and Self-Sufficiency in Homer and Aristotle,' *The Classical Quarterly* 13, 30–45.

—— (1978). '*Theōria* versus *Praxis* in the *Nicomachean Ethics* and the *Republic*,' *Classical Philology* 73, 297–313.

Algra, K., J. Barnes, J. Mansfeld, and M. Schofield (eds.) (1999). *The Cambridge History of Hellenistic Philosophy* (Cambridge: Cambridge University Press).

Annas, J. (ed.) (1985). *Oxford Studies in Ancient Philosophy*, vol. 3 (Oxford: Clarendon Press).

—— (1990). 'The Hellenistic version of Aristotle's *Ethics*,' *The Monist* 73, 80–96.

—— (1993). *The Morality of Happiness* (Oxford: Oxford University Press).

—— (1995). 'Reply to Cooper,' *Philosophy and Phenomenological Research* 55, 599–610.

Avnon, D. (1995). '"Know Thyself": Socratic Companionship and Platonic Community,' *Political Theory* 23.2, 304–329.

Badhwar, N.K. (1996). 'The Limited Unity of Virtue,' *Nous* 30.3, 306–329.

Bakewell, C.M. (1909). 'The Unique Case of Socrates,' *International Journal of Ethics* 20.1, 10–28.

Bambrough, R. (1960). 'Socratic Paradox,' *The Philosophical Quarterly* 10.41, 289–300.

Barney, R. (2003). 'A Puzzle in Stoic Ethics,' *Oxford Studies in Ancient Philosophy* 24, 303–340.

Baron, J.R. (1975). 'On Separating the Socratic from the Platonic in Phaedo 118,' *Classical Philology* 70.4, 268–9.

Belfiore, E. (1980). 'Elenchus, Epode, and Magic: Socrates as Silenus,' *Phoenix* 34.2, 128–137.

Bosanquet, B. (1905). 'Xenophon's Memorabilia of Socrates,' *International Journal of Ethics* 15.4, 432–443.

Bostock, D. (2000). *Aristotle's Ethics* (Oxford: Oxford University Press).

Brandwood, L. (1990). *The Chronology of Plato's Dialogues* (Cambridge: Cambridge University Press).

——— (1976). *A Word Index to Plato* (Leeds: W.S. Maney & Son).

Brickhouse, T.C. and N.D. Smith (1983). 'The Origin of Socrates' Mission,' *Journal of the History of Ideas* 44.4, 657–666.

——— (2000). *The Philosophy of Socrates* (Boulder CO: Westview Press).

Brown, S.H. (1933). 'Socratic Method and Aristotle's Definition of the Good,' *International Journal of Ethics* 43.3, 329–338.

Bubner, R. (1973). 'Action and Reason,' *Ethics* 83.3, 224–236.

Burkert, W. (1985). *Greek Religion* (Cambridge: Harvard University Press).

Caston, V. and D.W. Graham (eds.) (2002). *Presocratic philosophy: essays in honour of Alexander Mourelatos* (Burlington VT: Ashgate).

Christian, L.G. (1972). 'The Figure of Socrates in Erasmus' Works,' *Sixteenth Century Journal* 3.2, 1–10.

Clark, S. (1972). 'The Use of "Man's Function" in Aristotle,' *Ethics* 82.4, 269–283.

Clay, D. (2000). *Platonic Questions: Dialogues With The Silent Philosopher* (University Park: Pennsylvania State University Press).

Cooper, J.M. (1975). *Reason and Human Good in Aristotle* (Cambridge: Harvard University Press).

166

—— (1977). 'Plato's Theory of Human Good in the *Philebus*,' *Philosophical Review* 86.

—— (1985). 'Aristotle on the Goods of Fortune,' *Philosophical Review* 94, 173–96.

—— (1987). 'Contemplation and Happiness in Aristotle: A Reconsideration,' *Synthese* 72.

—— (1995). 'Eudaimonism and the Appeal to Nature,' *Philosophy and Phenomenological Research* 55, 587–98.

—— (1996). 'Eudaimonism, the Appeal to Nature, and "Moral Duty" in Stoicism,' in Engstrom and Whiting (1996), 261–84.

Crooks, J. (1998). 'Socrates' Last Words: Another Look at an Ancient Riddle,' *The Classical Quarterly* 48.1, 117–125.

Csikszentmihalyi, M. (1990). *Flow: The Psychology of Optimal Experience* (New York: Harper & Row).

—— (2001). *Good Work: When Excellence and Ethics Meet* (New York: Basic Books).

Curzer, H.J. (1990). 'Criteria for Happiness in Nicomachean Ethics 17 and X 6–8,' *The Classical Quarterly* 40.2, 421–432.

Dahl, N.O. (1991). 'Plato's Defense of Justice,' *Philosophy and Phenomenological Research* 51.4, 809–834.

Dean-Jones, L. (1995). 'Menexenus—Son of Socrates,' *The Classical Quarterly* 45.1, 51–57.

Depew, D.J. (ed.) (1980). *The Greeks and the Good Life* (Indianapolis: Hackett Publishing Company).

Detel, W., A. Becker and P. Scholz (2003). *Ideal and Culture of Knowledge in Plato* (Stuttgart: Franz Steiner Verlag).

Devereux, D. (1981). 'Aristotle on the Essence of Happiness,' in O'Meara, D.J. (ed.) (1981). *Studies in Aristotle* (Washington).

Dodds, E.R. (1951). *The Greeks and the Irrational* (Berkeley: University of California Press).

Doris, J.M. (1998). 'Persons, Situations, and Virtue Ethics,' *Nous* 32.4, 504–530.

Dubs, H.H. (1927). 'The Socratic Problem,' *The Philosophical Review* 36.4, 287–306.

Duff, A. (1976). 'Must A Good Man Be Invulnerable?,' *Ethics* 86.4, 294–311.

Duncan, A.R.C. (1952). 'The Stoic View of Life,' *Phoenix* 6.4, 123–138.

Edmonds, R.G. III (2000). 'Socrates the Beautiful: Role Reversal and Midwifery in Plato's Symposium,' *Transactions of the American Philological Association (1974–)* 130, 261–285.

Engstrom, S., and J. Whiting (eds.) (1996). *Rethinking Duty and Happiness: Aristotle, the Stoics, and Kant* (Cambridge: Cambridge University Press).

Ferejohn, M.T. (1984). 'Socratic Virtue as the Parts of Itself,' *Philosophy and Phenomenological Research* 44.3, 377–388.

Ferguson, A.S. (1913). 'The Impiety of Socrates,' *The Classical Quarterly* 7.3, 157–175.

Ferrari, G. (1987). *Listening to the Cicadas: A Study of Plato's Phaedrus* (Cambridge: Cambridge University Press).

Field, G.C. (1913). *Socrates and Plato* (Oxford: Parker and Co.).

——— (1924). 'Socrates and Plato in Post-Aristotelian Tradition—I,' *The Classical Quarterly* 18.3/4, 127–136.

——— (1925). 'Socrates and Plato in Post-Aristotelian Tradition—II,' *The Classical Quarterly* 19.1, 1–13.

Fine, G. (ed.) (2000). *Plato* (Oxford: Oxford University Press).

Fortenbaugh, W.W. (ed.) (1983). *On Stoic and Peripatetic Ethics. The Work of Arius Didymus* (New Brunswick and London: Rutgers University Press).

Frede, D. (1990). 'Fatalism and Future Truth,' *Proceedings of the Boston Area Colloquium in Ancient Philosophy* 6, 195–227.

——— (1999). 'On the Stoic Conception of the Good,' in K. Ierodiakonou (ed.) (1999). *Topics in Stoic Philosophy* (Oxford: Oxford University Press).

Gewirth, A. (1991). 'Can Any Final Ends Be Rational?,' *Ethics* 102.1, 66–95.

Goldin, O. (2002). 'To Tell the Truth: *Dissoi Logoi* 4 and Aristotle's Response,' in Caston and Graham (2002).

Gonzalez, F.J. (2000). 'Socrates on Loving One's Own: A Traditional Conception of Filia Radically Transformed,' *Classical Philology* 95.4, 379–398.

Gooch, P.W. (1983). 'Aristotle and the Happy Dead,' *Classical Philology* 78, 112–16.

——— (1985). 'Socrates: Devious or Divine?,' *Greece & Rome* 2nd ser. 32.1, 32–41.

——— (1987). 'Socratic Irony and Aristotle's "Eiron": Some Puzzles,' *Phoenix* 41.2, 95–104.

Gordon, R.M. (1964). 'Socratic Definitions and "Moral Neutrality",' *The Journal of Philosophy* 61.15, 433–450.

Gosling, J. (1987). 'Stoics and *akrasia*,' *Apeiron* 20, 179–82.

Gould, J.B. (1974). 'The Stoic Conception of Fate,' *Journal of the History of Ideas* 35.1, 17–32.

Gray, V.J. (1989). 'Xenophon's Defence of Socrates: The Rhetorical Background to the Socratic Problem,' *The Classical Quarterly* 39.1, 136–140.

Hackforth, R. (1958). *Plato's Examination of Pleasure: A Translation of the Philebus with Introduction and Commentary* (Cambridge: Cambridge University Press).

Hardie, W.F.R. (1965). 'The Final Good in Aristotle's Ethics,' *Philosophy* 40, 277–95.

——— (1968). *Aristotle's Ethical Theory* (Oxford: Clarendon Press).

Harman, G. (1983). 'Human Flourishing, Ethics, and Liberty,' *Philosophy and Public Affairs* 12.4, 307–322.

de Heer, C. (1969). *Makar, Eudaimōn, Olbios, Eutuchēs* (Amsterdam: Adolf M. Hakkert).

Heinaman, R. (1988). '*Eudaimonia* and Self-Sufficiency in the *Nicomachean Ethics*,' *Phronesis* 33, 31–53.

——— (1993). 'Rationality, Eudaimonia and Kakodaimonia in Aristotle,' *Phronesis* 38, 31–56.

Hobbes, A. (2000). *Plato and the Hero: Courage, Manliness and the Impersonal Good* (Cambridge: Cambridge University Press).

Ierodiakonou, K. (ed.) (1999). *Topics in Stoic Philosophy* (Oxford: Oxford University Press).

Inwood, B., and P. Donini (1999). 'Stoic ethics,' in Algra et al. (1999), 675–738.

Irwin, T.H. (1985). 'Permanent Happiness: Aristotle and Solon,' *Oxford Studies in Ancient Philosophy*, 89–124.

——— (1986). 'Stoic and Aristotelian conceptions of happiness,' in Schofield and Striker (1986), 205–44.

——— (1991). 'Aristippus Against Happiness,' *The Monist*, 55–82.

——— (1991b). 'The Structure of Aristotelian Happiness,' *Ethics* 101, 382–91.

——— (1995). *Plato's Ethics* (Oxford: Oxford University Press).

—— (1996). 'Kant's criticisms of eudaemonism,' in Engstrom and Whiting (1996), 63–101.

Joyce, R. (1995). 'Early Stoicism and Akrasia,' *Phronesis* 40, 315–35.

Kahn, C.H. (1973). *The Verb Be in Ancient Greek* (Dordrecht: D. Reidel).

—— (1981). 'Did Plato Write Socratic Dialogues?,' *The Classical Quarterly* 31.2, 305–320.

Kekes, J. (1982). 'Happiness,' *Mind* 91.363, 358–376.

Kenny, A. (1965). 'Happiness,' *Proceedings of the Aristotelian Society* 66, 93–102.

—— (1978). *The Aristotelian Ethics* (Oxford: Clarendon Press).

—— (1992). *Aristotle on the Perfect Life* (Oxford: Clarendon Press).

Kerferd, G.B. (1947). 'The Doctrine of Thrasymachus in Plato's *Republic*', *Durham University Journal* 9, pp. 19–27.

Keyt, D. (1978). 'Intellectualism in Aristotle,' *Paideia*, Special Aristotle Issue, 138–57.

Klein, S. (1989). 'Platonic Virtue Theory and Business Ethics,' *Business & Professional Ethics Journal* 8.4, pp. 59–82.

—— (2000). *Endoxic Method and Ethical Inquiry* (New York: Peter Lang Publishing).

Krämer, H.J. (1971). *Platonismus und hellenistische Philosophie* (Berlin: Walther de Gruyter).

Kraut, R. (1973). 'Egoism, Love, and Political Office in Plato,' *The Philosophical Review* 82, 330–44.

—— (1979a). 'The Peculiar Function of Human Beings,' *Canadian Journal of Philosophy* 9, 467–78.

—— (1979b). 'Two Conceptions of Happiness,' *The Philosophical Review* 88.2, 167–197.

—— (1989). *Aristotle on the Human Good* (Princeton: Princeton University Press).

Lawrence, G. (1993). 'Aristotle and the Ideal Life,' *The Philosophical Review* 102.1, 1–34.

Levi, A.W. (1956). 'The Idea of Socrates: The Philosophic Hero in the Nineteenth Century,' *Journal of the History of Ideas* 17.1, 89–108.

Lloyd Thomas, D.A. (1968). 'Happiness,' *The Philosophical Quarterly* 18.71, 97–113.

Lodge, R.C. (1923). 'Soul, Body, Wealth, in Plato. (I),' *The Philosophical Review* 32.5, pp. 470–490.

170

——— (1924). 'Soul, Body, Wealth, in Plato. (II),' *The Philosophical Review* 33.1, pp. 470–490.

Long, A.A. (1968). 'Aristotle's Legacy to Stoic Ethics,' *Bulletin of the Institute of Classical Studies* 15, 72–85.

——— (1970/71). 'The logical basis of Stoic ethics,' *Proceedings of the Aristotelian Society* 71, 85–104. Repr. in Long (1996), 134–155.

——— (1989). 'Stoic eudaimonism,' *Proceedings of the Boston Colloquium in Ancient Philosophy* 4, 77–101. Repr. in Long (1996), 179–201.

——— (1996). *Stoic Studies* (Cambridge: Cambridge University Press).

——— (1971). 'Freedom and Determinism in the Stoic Theory of Human Action,' in Long, A.A. (ed.) (1971). *Problems in Stoicism* (London: Athlone Press).

——— (1988). 'Socrates in Hellenistic Philosophy,' *The Classical Quarterly* 38.1, 150–171.

McDonald, M. (1978). *Terms for Happiness in Euripides* (Göttingen).

McDowell, J. (1980). 'The Role of *Eudaimonia* in Aristotle's Ethics,' in Rorty, A.O. (ed.). *Essays on Aristotle's Ethics* (Berkeley).

Moffitt, Jr., J. (1938). 'The Pursuit of Human Happiness,' *Ethics* 49.1, 1–17.

Moline, J. (1983). 'Contemplation and the Human Good,' *Nous* 17.1, 37–53.

Moore, J.S. (1935). 'A Suggestion Regarding Plato and Socrates,' *Mind* 44.173, 68–69.

Morgan, M.L. (1990). *Platonic Piety: Philosophy and Ritual in Fourth Century Athens* (New Haven: Yale University Press).

Mueller, G. (1933). 'Another Approach to Socrates,' *International Journal of Ethics* 43.4, 429–439.

Nichols, M.P. (1984). 'The Republic's Two Alternatives: Philosopher-Kings and Socrates,' *Political Theory* 12.2, 252–274.

Nussbaum, M.C. (1985). 'Therapeutic Arguments: Epicurus and Aristotle,' in Schofield, M., and G. Striker (eds.) (1986). *The Norms of Nature: Studies in Hellenistic Ethics* (Cambridge: Cambridge University Press).

——— (1986). *The Fragility of Goodness* (New York: Press Syndicate of the University of Cambridge).

——— (1995). 'Aristotle on Human Nature and the Foundations of Ethics,' in Altham, J.E.J. (ed.) *World, Mind, and Ethics* (Cambridge: Cambridge University Press).

O'Meara, D.J. (ed.) (1981). *Studies in Aristotle* (Washington).

Parker, C.P. (1916). 'The Historical Socrates in the Light of Professor Burnet's Hypothesis,' *Harvard Studies in Classical Philology* 27, 67–75.

Preus, A. and G.L. Kustas (eds.) (2001). *Essays in Ancient Greek Philosophy* (Albany: State University of New York Press).

Price, A.W. (1980). 'Aristotle's Ethical Holism,' *Mind* 89, 341.

Pritzl, K. (1983). 'Aristotle and Happiness After Death,' *Classical Philology* 78, 101–11.

Purinton, J. (1998). 'Aristotle's Definition of Happiness (*NE* 1.7, 1098a16–18),' *Oxford Studies in Ancient Philosophy*: 259–97.

Reesor, M.E. (1983). 'The Stoic Idion and Prodicus' Near-Synonyms,' *The American Journal of Philology* 104.2, 124–133.

Reeve, C.D.C. (1992). *Practices of Reason* (Oxford: Oxford University Press).

Robinson, T. (2001). 'The *Dissoi Logoi* and Early Greek Skepticism,' in Preus and Kustas (2001).

Roche, T.M. (1988). '*Ergon* and Εὐδαιμονία in *Nicomachean Ethics* I: Reconsidering the Intellectualist Interpretation,' *Journal of History of Philosophy* 26, 175–94.

Rogers, A.K. (1925a). 'A Note on Socrates and Aristotle,' *Mind* 34.136, 471–475.

———(1925b). 'The Ethics of Socrates,' *The Philosophical Review* 34.2, 117–143.

Rorty, A.O. (1978). 'The Place of Contemplation in Aristotle's Nicomachean Ethics,' *Mind* 87.347, 343–358.

———(ed.) (1980). *Essays on Aristotle's Ethics* (Berkeley).

Sandbach, F.H. (1940). 'Plutarch on the Stoics,' *The Classical Quarterly* 34.1/2, 20–25.

———(1985). *Aristotle and the Stoics* (Cambridge: Cambridge Philological Society).

Schankula, H.A.S. (1971). 'Plato and Aristotle: εὐδαιμονία, hexis, or energeia?,' *Classical Philology* 66.4, 244–246.

Schofield, M. (1991). *The Stoic Idea of the City* (Cambridge: Cambridge University Press), Repr. (1999) with new epilogue.

——— and G. Striker (eds.) (1986). *The Norms of Nature: Studies in Hellenistic Ethics* (Cambridge: Cambridge University Press).

Scholz, P. (2003). 'Philosophy Before Plato: On the Social and Political Conditions of the Composition of the *Dissoi Logoi*,' in Detel, Becker and Scholz (eds.) (2003).

Shea, J. (1988). 'The Commensurability of Theorizing and Moral Action in the Nicomachean Ethics,' *Philosophy and Phenomenological Research* 48.4, 753–755.

Sherman, N. (1987). 'Aristotle on Friendship and the Shared Life,' *Philosophy and Phenomenological Research* 47.4, 589–613.

Solmsen, F. (1942). *Plato's Theology* (Ithaca: Cornell University Press).

Stewart, J.A. (1917). 'Socrates and Plato,' *Mind* 26.104, 393–406.

Stocker, M. (1981). 'Value and Purposes: The Limits of Teleology and the Ends of Friendship,' *The Journal of Philosophy* 78.12, 747–765.

Striker, G. (1991). 'Following nature: a study in Stoic ethics,' *Oxford Studies in Ancient Philosophy* 9, 1–73. Repr. in Striker (1996), 221–80.

––––– (ed.) (1996). *Essays on Hellenistic epistemology and ethics* (Cambridge: Cambridge University Press).

Sturt, H. (1903). 'Happiness,' *International Journal of Ethics* 13.2, 207–221.

Sullivan, R.J. (1977). 'Some Suggestions for Interpreting *Eth. Nic.* 10.7–9,' *The Southern Journal of Philosophy* 15, 129–38.

Tarrant, D. (1932). 'The Tradition of Socrates,' *Greece & Rome* 1.3, 151–157.

––––– (1938). 'The Pseudo-Platonic Socrates,' *The Classical Quarterly* 32.3/4, 167–173.

Taylor, A.E. (1911). *Varia Socratica* (St. Andrews).

Taylor, C.C.W. (ed.) (1994). *Oxford Studies in Ancient Philosophy* XII (Oxford: Clarendon Press).

Thayer, H.S. (1964). 'Plato: The Theory and Language of Function,' *The Philosophical Quarterly* 14.57, 303–318.

Thornton, M.T. (1982). 'Aristotelian Practical Reason,' *Mind* 91.361, 57–76.

Vander Waerdt, P.A. (ed.) (1994). *The Socratic Movement* (Ithaca: Cornell University Press).

Vasiliou, I. (1996). 'The Role of Good Upbringing in Aristotle's Ethics,' *Philosophy and Phenomenological Research* 56.4, 771–797.

Verrall, A.W. (1895). *Euripides, The Rationalist: A Study In The History Of Arts And Religion* (Cambridge: Cambridge University Press).

Vlastos, G. (ed.) (1971). *Plato: A Collection of Critical Essays*, 2 vols. (Garden City: Doubleday).

—— (1973). *Platonic Studies* (Princeton: Princeton University Press).

—— (1981). 'Happiness and Virtue in Socrates' Moral Theory,' *Proceedings of the Cambridge Philosophical Society* 30, 181–312.

—— (1991). *Socrates: Ironist and Moral Philosopher* (Ithaca NY: Cornell University Press).

Wedin, M.V. (1981). 'Aristotle on the Good for Man,' *Mind* 90.358, 243–262.

White, M.J. (1980). 'Aristotle's Temporal Interpretation of Necessary Coming-to-Be and Stoic Determinism,' *Phoenix* 34.3, 208–218.

White, N.P. (1979). 'The Basis of Stoic Ethics,' *Harvard Studies in Classical Philology* 83, 143–178.

—— (1995). 'Conflicting Parts of Happiness in Aristotle's Ethics,' *Ethics* 105.2, 258–283.

Whiting, J. (1986). 'Human Nature and Intellectualism in Aristotle,' *Archiv für Geschichte der Philosophie* 68, 70–95.

Wilkes, K.V. (1978). 'The Good Man and the Good for Man in Aristotle's Ethics,' *Mind* 87.348, 553–571.

Williams, B. (1962). 'Aristotle on the Good: A Formal Sketch,' *The Philosophical Quarterly* 12.49, 289–296.

Young, C.M. (1994). 'Plato and Computer Dating,' in Taylor, C.C.W. (ed.) (1994). *Oxford Studies in Ancient Philosophy* XII (Oxford: Clarendon Press).

Yu, J. (2001). 'Aristotle on *Eudaimonia*: After Plato's *Republic*,' *History of Philosophy Quarterly* 18 (2), 115–138.

—— (2003). 'Will Aristotle Count Socrates Happy?,' in ——and J. Gracia (eds.) (2003). *Rationality and Happiness: from the Ancients to the Early Medievals* (Rochester: University of Rochester Press), 51–73.

—— and J. Gracia (eds.) (2003). *Rationality and Happiness: from the Ancients to the Early Medievals* (Rochester: University of Rochester Press).

Zeller, E. (1881). *A History Of Greek Philosophy From The Earliest Period To The Time Of Socrates* (London: Longmans, Green, and Co.).

Index

activity, 9, 21, 63, 70, 77, 84, 85, 88, 89,
  91, 95, 96, 97, 103, 106, 107, 110,
  111, 112, 113, 114, 115, 145, 157
Anaxagoras, 33, 35, 36
Aristophanes, 18, 21, 48, 163
Aristotle, vii, 1, 2, 9, 12, 14, 25, 31, 37,
  40, 48, 49, 50, 70, 72, 74, 85, 87, 88,
  89, 90, 91, 92, 93, 94, 95, 96, 97, 98,
  102, 103, 104, 105, 106, 107, 108,
  109, 110, 111, 112, 113, 114, 115,
  116, 117, 118, 119, 121, 123, 124,
  125, 126, 127, 128, 130, 140, 144,
  148, 149, 150, 154, 156, 157, 158,
  163, 164, 165, 166, 167, 168, 169,
  170, 171, 172, 173
balance, 18, 53, 70, 73, 108, 113, 119,
  120, 161
benefit, 4, 7, 11, 12, 13, 18, 30, 31, 32,
  33, 34, 37, 44, 45, 72, 80, 92, 131,
  132, 133, 134, 136, 137, 138, 140,
  141, 144, 145, 147, 155, 158
blending, 127, 129
chance, 1, 5, 8, 9, 15, 28, 83, 84, 88, 90,
  92, 93, 94, 98, 100, 102, 114, 115,
  118, 135, 155, 156, 159, 161
Charmides, 3, 23, 27, 42, 49, 149
circumstance, 10, 13, 32, 43, 75, 90, 91,
  97, 98, 102, 134, 144
commanding-faculty, 11, 120, 124, 126,
  128, 131, 147
completeness, 1, 91, 153, 154, 155
composite, 41, 53, 73, 78, 83, 110, 111,
  128, 157
contemplation, 55, 66, 74, 77, 87, 105,
  107, 108, 110, 111, 112, 114, 119,
  156, 157
Croesus, 1
Cyrenaic, 17
Diogenes Laertius, 11, 12, 13, 20, 40,
  48, 119, 120, 122, 128, 129, 132,
  133, 135, 137, 141, 145, 148, 150,
  158, 163
divine, 4, 5, 8, 24, 28, 32, 33, 34, 35, 36,
  41, 47, 52, 54, 55, 56, 58, 66, 67, 68,

69, 71, 73, 74, 75, 77, 82, 96, 100,
  101, 102, 111, 112, 114, 118, 128,
  150, 154, 156, 157, 158, 159
elenchus, 37
embodied, 39, 41, 65, 75, 76, 78, 111,
  121, 131, 157
Euthydemus, 3, 24, 27, 29, 41, 43, 44,
  46, 49, 50, 123, 134, 149, 150, 155
excellence, 1, 9, 63, 88, 89, 90, 91, 92,
  96, 99, 100, 113, 115, 126, 154
external goods, 1, 2, 5, 9, 10, 13, 15, 18,
  21, 24, 26, 28, 31, 41, 42, 44, 46, 47,
  50, 51, 52, 65, 69, 83, 87, 88, 89, 90,
  91, 92, 94, 95, 97, 102, 103, 104,
  106, 107, 108, 109, 110, 113, 115,
  116, 118, 119, 128, 131, 134, 135,
  137, 138, 139, 140, 146, 154, 155,
  159, 161, *See* ἐκτός
fixity, 11, 132, 142, 146, 158
flourishing. *See* εὐδαιμονία
focal meaning, 3
Forms, vii, 6, 37, 51, 58, 66, 69, 73, 77,
  78, 79, 85, 119, 121, 122, 129, 130,
  135, 141, 159
fortune, 3, 5, 36, 41, 44, 45, 47, 92, 93,
  94, 100, 107, 108, 113, 146, 155
goods, 2, 3, 4, 5, 9, 10, 11, 12, 14, 15, 18,
  23, 24, 28, 30, 31, 41, 42, 44, 45, 46,
  47, 49, 50, 52, 60, 67, 69, 72, 78, 79,
  83, 86, 87, 88, 89, 90, 91, 92, 94, 95,
  97, 102, 103, 104, 106, 107, 109,
  110, 113, 115, 118, 119, 123, 131,
  132, 133, 134, 135, 139, 140, 141,
  142, 143, 146, 147, 155, 158, 159,
  161
happiness, 1, 3, 4, 5, 12, 13, 14, 15, 18,
  23, 25, 26, 27, 28, 29, 32, 33, 39, 40,
  41, 42, 45, 46, 47, 49, 52, 53, 54, 57,
  58, 65, 69, 73, 74, 75, 78, 84, 87, 90,
  91, 96, 98, 99, 101, 103, 104, 107,
  108, 116, 118, 119, 123, 132, 135,
  136, 137, 138, 139, 140, 141, 142,
  143, 146, 147, 148, 150, 153, 154,

155, 156, 159, 161, 168, *See*
εὐδαιμονία
Herodotus, 1, 15
human life, 1, 5, 6, 8, 10, 14, 28, 33, 35,
   41, 48, 52, 54, 56, 57, 58, 65, 69, 77,
   78, 80, 82, 83, 86, 88, 90, 92, 93, 94,
   95, 97, 98, 106, 109, 110, 112, 113,
   114, 119, 120, 121, 135, 139, 144,
   146, 153, 154, 155, 156
ignorance, 45, 57, 123, 124, 134
inclusivism, 2, 50, 114
instrumental, 27, 28, 66, 115, 134, 136
Instrumental Principle, 27
intellectualism, 2, 37, 50, 53, 114, 118,
   119, 120, 125, 159
interentailment, 25, 155
justice, 3, 4, 8, 18, 20, 31, 38, 40, 51, 52,
   53, 54, 56, 58, 59, 60, 61, 62, 63, 65,
   66, 69, 73, 75, 76, 78, 82, 84, 85, 86,
   123, 135, 155, 156
knowledge, 1, 2, 3, 5, 7, 8, 11, 15, 18, 21,
   32, 35, 37, 40, 42, 44, 45, 46, 47, 50,
   57, 71, 76, 79, 80, 81, 82, 83, 84, 94,
   118, 120, 123, 124, 125, 127, 130,
   136, 149, 153, 156, 160, 161
Meno, 3, 24, 25, 37, 41, 44, 46, 47, 49,
   149
middle period, 36, 56
mixed, 8, 52, 70, 78, 82, 83, 86, 156
natural philosophy, 4, 18, 33, 35
order, 4, 10, 23, 31, 52, 59, 60, 62, 63,
   70, 71, 72, 76, 93, 97, 107, 118, 128,
   129, 131, 135, 136, 140, 141, 142,
   150
pain, 31, 70, 132
Philebus, 3, 6, 7, 8, 51, 63, 69, 70, 71, 78,
   79, 80, 81, 82, 83, 86, 155, 162, 166,
   168
Plato, vii, 1, 2, 3, 4, 5, 6, 8, 11, 14, 15, 17,
   18, 19, 20, 21, 22, 23, 24, 29, 35, 36,
   37, 47, 48, 49, 50, 51, 52, 53, 54, 55,
   56, 58, 59, 60, 61, 63, 64, 65, 66, 67,
   69, 70, 71, 72, 73, 74, 75, 76, 77, 78,
   79, 80, 82, 83, 84, 85, 86, 112, 115,
   117, 118, 119,121, 122, 123, 127,
   128, 129, 130, 134, 135, 136, 140,
   141, 147, 149, 150, 154, 155, 158,
   162, 163, 165, 166, 167, 168, 169,
   170, 171, 172, 173
pleasure, 6, 7, 8, 9, 13, 69, 70, 71, 72,
   79, 80, 81, 82, 84, 85, 92, 107, 117,
   132, 133, 155, 158

Plotinus, 74
Plutarch, 11, 117, 118, 126, 129, 142,
   146, 148, 149, 151, 171
practical wisdom, 3
preferred indifferents, 14, 118, 119,
   132, 137, 141, 146, 147, 159
proper function, 52, 76, 77, 85, 135,
   138, 139
proprium, 25, 52
Republic, 3, 21, 31, 49, 51, 53, 54, 56,
   58, 59, 60, 61, 63, 64, 65, 66, 70, 71,
   75, 77, 78, 79, 81, 83, 84, 85, 86, 115,
   164, 169, 170, 173
self-sufficiency, 10, 34, 71, 90, 91, 92,
   97, 104, 113, 114, 155
Skeptic, 17
Socrates, vii, 1, 2, 3, 4, 5, 6, 7, 8, 11, 15,
   17, 18, 19, 20, 21, 22, 23, 24, 25, 26,
   27, 28, 29, 30, 31, 32, 33, 34, 35, 36,
   37, 38, 39, 40, 41, 42, 43, 44, 45, 46,
   47, 48, 49, 50, 51, 53, 56, 57, 58, 59,
   60, 61, 62, 63, 67, 71, 76, 80, 81, 82,
   83, 84, 85, 118, 119, 120, 121, 123,
   124, 125, 127, 134, 141, 147, 148,
   154, 155, 156, 158, 163, 164, 165,
   166, 167, 168, 169, 170, 171, 172,
   173
Socratic, 1, 3, 4, 5, 6, 11, 14, 17, 18, 19,
   20, 21, 22, 23, 24, 25, 27, 31, 32, 33,
   34, 35, 36, 37, 40, 42, 43, 44, 48, 49,
   53, 80, 115, 118, 120, 121, 123, 124,
   125, 126, 128, 135, 137, 147, 148,
   155, 159, 164, 165, 166, 167, 168,
   169, 172
Solon, 1, 114, 116, 168
soul, 4, 7, 9, 11, 38, 39, 42, 52, 53, 54,
   55, 59, 61, 62, 63, 64, 65, 66, 67, 68,
   69, 70, 71, 72, 73, 74, 75, 76, 77, 78,
   79, 80, 83, 84, 85, 86, 91, 94, 96, 97,
   115, 120, 121, 122, 124, 126, 127,
   128, 129, 130, 131, 132, 135, 136,
   138, 139, 142, 148, 150
Sovereignty Thesis, 28
Stobaeus, 12, 86, 116, 118, 122, 129,
   133, 135, 137, 141, 142, 145, 148,
   151
Stoic, 2, 11, 12, 14, 17, 31, 48, 86, 117,
   118, 119, 120, 121, 122, 124, 126,
   127, 128, 129, 130, 131, 132, 133,
   134, 135, 136, 137, 138, 139, 140,
   141, 142, 143, 144, 145, 146, 147,

148, 149, 150, 158, 164, 165, 166,
167, 168, 170, 171, 172, 173
Sufficiency Thesis, 26, 42
suicide, 137, 138, 139
teleology, 40
Theaetetus, 3, 36, 51, 52, 56, 58, 67, 73,
75
tripartite, 52, 61, 67, 69, 83, 121
virtue, 1, 2, 3, 5, 8, 9, 11, 14, 23, 25, 26,
27, 28, 29, 37, 39, 40, 42, 47, 49, 54,
56, 59, 70, 74, 78, 82, 84, 88, 91, 93,
95, 96, 97, 98, 102, 103, 104, 105,
108, 113, 115, 116, 118, 120, 123,
124, 126, 127, 131, 132, 134, 135,
136, 137, 140, 142, 143, 146, 147,
148, 149, 154, 155, 156, 159, 161
well-being. *See* εὐδαιμονία
well-doing, 3, 41
wisdom, 3, 4, 25, 32, 35, 37, 40, 41, 42,
43, 44, 45, 47, 58, 59, 68, 71, 73, 76,
86, 118, 123, 124, 126, 130, 131,
134, 135, 140, 147, 149, 155, 159
Xenophon, 4, 17, 18, 19, 20, 21, 24, 33,
34, 35, 37, 38, 48, 50, 150, 164, 165,
168
ἀγαθά, 24, 28, 30, 41, 44, 45, 46, 50, 53,
119, 139
ἀγαθόν, 11, 23, 24, 28, 29, 30, 31, 36,
45, 81
ἀδιάφορα προγημένα, 127
ἀρετή, 24, 25, 26, 27, 28, 39, 44, 49, 78,
99, 101, 102, 119, 124, 126, 127,
136
ἀρμονία, 54, 59, 63, 65, 66, 67, 69, 79,
83, 85
αὐτὰ καθ' αὑτά, 46, 47
αὐτάρκης, 91
βεβαιοτής, 132, 133
βίος, 8, 82, 90, 91, 105, 106, 110, 113,
116, 156
δαιμόνια, 4, 5, 33, 36, 40
δαιμόνιον, 20, 33
δικαιοσύνη, 38, 49, 51, 53, 54, 55, 59,
60, 61, 63, 65, 66, 67, 73, 75, 78, 83,
84, 85
ἐκτός, 41, 43, 44, 46, 50, 90, 106, 127,
132, 134, 139, 146
ἐννοήματα, 121, 122
ἐνέργεια, 89, 90, 91, 95, 105, 106, 107,
113, 115, 116

ἐπιθυμητικόν, 52, 65, 67, 77, 78, 79
ἐπιστήμη, 25, 44, 45, 119, 123, 124, 136
ἔργον, 63, 77
εὐδαιμονία, 1, 2, 9, 14, 15, 18, 21, 24,
25, 26, 27, 28, 29, 30, 32, 34, 38, 39,
40, 41, 42, 43, 44, 45, 46, 48, 49, 50,
51, 52, 53, 54, 55, 65, 66, 67, 69, 73,
75, 76, 77, 78, 79, 83, 84, 85, 87, 88,
89, 90, 91, 92, 93, 94, 95, 96, 97, 98,
99, 100, 101, 102, 103, 104, 105,
106, 107, 108, 109, 110, 113, 115,
116, 118, 150, 154, 155, 161, 171
εὐπραγία, 3, 41
εὐτυχία, 3, 41, 44, 92
ἡγεμονικόν, 124, 126, 127, 128, 131,
135
θεῖα, 33, 34, 68
θεωρία, 66, 67, 77, 107, 109, 112, 119,
120
θυμοειδές, 52, 65, 67, 77, 78, 79
ἴδιον, 11, 25, 34, 39, 72, 77, 78, 111,
132, 157
κρᾶσις δι' ὅλου, 86, 127, 129, 135, 137
κόσμος, 62, 63, 73, 74, 75, 122, 128,
129, 139, 140, 141
λόγος, 45, 73, 75, 87, 112, 119, 120,
122, 125, 126, 127, 128, 129, 131,
133, 135, 136, 137, 139, 145, 147,
149, 150
λογιστικόν, 52, 65, 67, 71, 72, 74, 77,
78, 79, 86
μακαρία, 90, 93, 94, 95, 98, 99, 100,
101, 102, 104, 107, 109, 110, 113
οἰκείωσις, 133, 136, 150
ὁμοίωσις θεῷ, 36, 51, 52, 54, 55, 56, 57,
58, 67, 73, 74, 75
πρᾶξις, 46, 60, 65, 66, 119, 120
σοφία, 3, 37, 44, 45, 46, 58, 59, 123
ταύτόν, 24, 25, 26, 49, 53
τεχνή, 14, 15
τέλος, 9, 14, 29, 60, 68, 73, 91, 111, 157
τἀνθρώπινα, 4, 36
τάξις, 62, 63, 85
φρονῆσις, 3
φύσις, 30, 60, 77, 79, 83, 109, 117, 133,
136
ὠφέλεια, 24, 30, 31, 33, 34, 35, 138,
141

STUDIES IN THEORETICAL AND APPLIED ETHICS ⟩

Sherwin Klein, *General Editor*

This series invites book manuscripts and proposals in English on either theoretical or applied ethics. Books submitted on traditional moral philosophers or on one or more ethical problems they have considered are welcome. However, authors should demonstrate strong connections between historical and contemporary philosophical concerns in ethics. Preference will be given to works that deal with perennial philosophical issues in ethics in an original, clear, and scholarly manner rather than manuscripts which have historical significance alone. Books that approach applied ethics, for example, business and biomedical ethics, from a philosophical perspective are also welcome. Manuscripts should display expertise in both philosophy and the areas illuminated by the philosophical insights.

Please send manuscripts and proposals with author's vitae to

Sherwin Klein
Petrocelli College of Continuing Studies
Fairleigh Dickinson University
150 Kotte Place
Hackensack, NJ 07601

To order other books in this series, please contact our Customer Service Department:

(800) 770-LANG (within the U.S.)
(212) 647-7706 (outside the U.S.)
(212) 647-7707 FAX

Or browse online by series:

www.peterlang.com